SPEAKING OUT

SPEAKING OUT

Writings on Sex, Law, Politics, and Society
1954–1995

ANTONY GREY

CASSELL

For a catalogue of related titles in our
Sexual Politics/Global Issues list
please write to us at the address below

Cassell
Wellington House
125 Strand
London
WC2R 0BB

PO Box 605
Herndon
VA 20172

First published 1997

British Library Cataloguing-in-Publication Data
A catalogue record for this book is available from the British Library.

ISBN: 0–304–33340–9 (hardback)
       0–304–33344–1 (paperback)

Front cover photograph © Paul Mattsson

Designed and typeset by Ben Cracknell Studios
Printed and bound in Great Britain by Biddles Ltd, Guildford and King's Lynn

FOR

ERIC THOMPSON

WITH LOVE AND GRATITUDE

Contents

Acknowledgements

I am grateful to Steve Cook for commissioning this book, and I appreciate the careful attention which his colleagues at Cassell have given to preparing its publication.

Most of the material included has previously been published elsewhere. I am indebted to the following for their courtesy in agreeing to its inclusion here:

Stainer & Bell Ltd and Galliard Ltd for permission to reprint 'Homosexual Law Reform' from *The Tactics of Pressure*, ed. Brian Frost, 1975, pp. 38–56.

The University of Leeds for permission to reprint extracts from Occasional Paper No. 6 of the Centre for Social Work and Applied Studies.

Academic Press Limited London for permission to reprint 'Pornography and Free Speech' from *The Influence of Pornography on Behaviour*, ed. Maurice Yaffé and Edward C. Nelson, 1982, pp. 47–64.

The editors of the following newspapers and journals for permission to reproduce articles which first appeared in their columns: *The Ethical Record, Faith and Freedom, Free Life, The Freethinker, Forum, The Independent, New Humanist, New Statesman and Society, Open Mind, The Scotsman, Wolverhampton Chronicle, Wolverhampton Express and Star.*

Preface

It was not merely by accident that I became Secretary of the Homosexual Law Reform Society. Ever since I realized as a teenager that I was attracted emotionally and physically towards members of my own sex, while the most I could offer to or accept from women was unerotic friendship, my life's ambition was to do something tangible to remove the fearfulness and the stigma which blighted the lives of men like myself.

Coming, as I did, from a respectable, middle-class, professional family, I did not have the option in those days (the 1940s and 1950s) of 'coming out'; nor did I feel free to lead an actively gay sex life. In fact – incredible as today's young lesbians and gay men may think it – I had little sexual experience (apart from schoolboy fumblings) until I was getting on for 30.

It was not until the Wolfenden Report was published in 1957, with its call for a change in the law providing a chink of light in the all-pervasive gloom, that I contacted the newly formed Homosexual Law Reform Society and began to meet other gay men who, like myself, were willing to risk their personal safety in order to campaign for change.

I have described the early days of the Homosexual Law Reform Society, and its almost incredible good fortune first in surviving, and then in achieving its main aim, in *Quest for Justice* (Sinclair-Stevenson, 1992). While I came to play a key role in the Society's campaign, I could not have done so without the dedication of its founders – notably Tony Dyson (still a valued friend after forty years) – and all the helpers (mostly unpaid) who gave their unstinting support during our ten-year campaign. Looking back, I would do the same again: but preferably without a lot of the hassle which I experienced – sometimes from unexpected quarters.

Although our quest for justice for gay men and women has made remarkable progress, I would be the first to recognize that we are still far from achieving the goal of a sexually equal society – still less a sexually sane one. Homophobia is still rampant in many quarters where I once hoped it would have died out by now; and far too many of the daft old myths about homosexual people as 'unnatural', 'a danger to children', etc. are still alive and resurface almost daily: a huge task of public education remains. But – notwithstanding the hammer blow of AIDS – we should take heart from what has been achieved in the second half of the twentieth century.

When I was a wartime schoolboy, same-sex sex was only mentioned, if at all, in horrified whispers as a foul and degenerate perversion. Today, there are thousands of women and men – and teenagers, too – who are standing up every day to proclaim that Gay is Good and Gay is Proud. I am privileged to have played my part in that transformation.

During forty years' campaigning for gay rights, I have had several hundred articles and letters published. What follows is a selection of those which seem worth preserving for the historical record. I know that some of these pieces – especially the earlier ones – may strike 1990s gay activists as very tame and even timid. I can only ask my readers to use their historical imagination, and to step backward into what was, when I was growing up, an 'age of the dinosaurs' for those of us who love other people of our own sex.

PART ONE

REFORMING THE LAW

Letter to *The Sunday Times*,
2 April 1954

In a forthright leading article ('Law and Hypocrisy', 28 March 1954), The Sunday Times *became the first national newspaper to broach the subject of homosexuality, roundly criticizing the existing law and calling for its review. This article produced a flood of correspondence, some of which was subsequently reprinted as a pamphlet. My letter (although sent anonymously from the depths of the closet) was the first personal campaigning action I ever took; and even though it was not printed, the act of writing and sending it was a liberating experience – a significant point in my life story. Some of the sentiments are expressed in terms which now seem over-solemn and even mealy-mouthed, and I no longer agree with all that I said then (especially the priggish condemnation of promiscuity) – but much of it still makes sense to me now.*

Your admirable and forthright leading article emboldens me to offer deeply felt thanks for the ray of hope which your sane approach to the grievous problems of homosexuality offers to the abnormal. Recent months have seen a public ventilation of the subject which would have been unthinkable even a year ago. This is all to the good; for although one cannot but be dismayed at some of the deep-rooted prejudices and misconceptions which have been expressed, it does at last seem possible that a sustained and purposeful campaign by the many authoritative voices (not the least of which, Sir, is yours) who believe that the present state of the law is not only unjust but is productive of some distinctly harmful social consequences, may result in legislation within a measurable time.

I write this letter, not to make once again any of the valid objections to the present state of the law which have been cogently canvassed in your recent pamphlet . . . but to ask you to assist in educating public opinion to look above and beyond the immediate legal issues to the deeper problems posed by the fact of homosexuality.

As you rightly say, it is a social problem; it is also an individual problem, and there is perhaps no such person as 'the typical homosexual'. Newspaper accounts and the proceedings of the criminal courts must together give many ordinary people the idea that all male homosexuals are by definition habitually promiscuous, addicted to constant vice and liable to indecently assault any other male, given the slightest opportunity.

Yet there must be very many like myself – perhaps even a majority – who, without ever having been approached by another, have known themselves to be irrevocably 'queer' from early adolescence; have for one reason or another – idealism, inhibitions or timidity – denied themselves any physical relationships; and who reach their later twenties or thirties with the energy-consuming stresses imposed by their unsatisfied emotional needs and the constant mental dilemma of their general situation heightened every year. Even if not technically criminals, like our practising brothers, we are oppressed perhaps even more keenly than they by our consciousness of the injustice of the law against the private acts of consenting adult inverts.

But there would be little improvement, even if the law were altered, if we were only transferred from the lawyer's frying pan into the psychiatrist's fire. The present lamentable tendency of criminologists to attribute crimes of whatever variety to mental illness is leading both law and psychology sadly astray. If certain forms of behaviour are antisocial they must be prevented by the law; and though the mental abnormality of the offender may be an explanation of his behaviour, it is not an excuse. The homosexual wishes the law to redefine more justly what are in fact antisocial activities on his part; he should not rush to surrender all personal responsibility for his character by accepting the hypothesis that he is mentally ill. Abnormal, yes, and in a small minority; subject to certain inherent disadvantages which call for understanding rather than for pity from his fellow men and women; neurotic only insofar as that understanding is lacking.

We shall not get any nearer to such necessary understanding by holding that, even if all those of homosexual temperament should not be in prison, they should all be on psychoanalysts' couches twice a week. In the first case . . . there would not be nearly enough prisons; in the second, there would not be nearly enough couches. And the differing opinions of the medical profession on homosexuality, on its origins and on its 'cure', are extremely disconcerting to those who might seek for guidance if they felt convinced that it existed. In fact, they get the collective impression that most so-called 'mental experts' are no better at running other people's lives than the average person is at running his own. . . .

There is a third alternative, which offers far more hope to the homosexual, and, I believe, to society. It is for us all to work for the integration of the homosexual individual into society, rather than for his degradation or transformation. For, like the poor, some homosexuality will always be with us. Even granting for the sake of argument – though I am far from convinced – that the whole cause of this phenomenon lies in the parental relationships of the earliest years, it will be long before we breed a race of potential parents enlightened enough to be 100 per cent successful in giving every child the right start necessary for a normal life. . . .

A most deplorable aspect of homosexuality, from any point of view, is the promiscuity which characterizes the behaviour of so many . . . and justifies the strictures of viciousness which are so commonly brought against them. The most urgent aim of those who are enlightened enough to seek the integration of the invert into society must be to heighten his sense of moral responsibility and self-respect, which can only be done by creating a moral climate throughout society as a whole such that the mere fact of his inversion will no longer cause him to be regarded as a pariah. It is perhaps asking a great deal to seek recognition of the fact that the nature of his love is no more 'unnatural' to the invert than normal heterosexual attraction is to the heterosexual person – but I believe that nothing less than some degree of social acceptance of this fact, with a concomitant encouragement of the ideal of constancy and disapprobation of promiscuity, can effect an amelioration of the homosexual problem.

One recognizes, of course, that no homosexual relationships can ever be 'moral' in the sense that marriage is the only truly moral sexual relationship; but by frowning less heavily upon the invert's attempt to obtain a permanent connection based upon affection than upon promiscuous behaviour akin to prostitution, society would be pointing a way to the solution of the invert's personal problems, and thus helping to lessen his incidence as a social problem. It is not really surprising that those who, when they discover that they have the misfortune to be abnormal, discover also that the very thought of love on their part is tainted with criminality, are likely to throw moral restraint aside more readily than do the general run of people – or that this trait is liable to spread beyond the sexual sphere of character. By denying the invert any claim to morality or respectability, society thus conferred upon him the gift of moral irresponsibility.

Development of moral stature, of any kind of responsibility, can only take place in conditions of freedom; our own political history since 1688 provides abundant illustration of this truth. By acknowledging that a man who remains a homosexual can aspire to and attain a certain moral integrity without demanding of him an involuntary celibacy, society would take the essential step towards solving some of these anxious problems, and could enforce far more effectively the protection of youth. . . .

It is regrettable that I am unable to offer any proofs of my own integrity other than the views which I have . . . expressed. I cannot expect you to publish a long and unsigned letter, but I trust that you will make any use of it which you think proper in your efforts to shed light on the homosexual problem and to promote social health.

Yours faithfully,

HOMOSEXUAL

Law and Morality

In the spring of 1961 the first issue of the Albany Trust's journal, Man and Society, *appeared.* Man and Society *was published by the Trust at irregular intervals during the next thirteen years, and I contributed articles or reviews to almost every issue. In issue No. 1 I joined in what became known as the 'Devlin Debate'. This was a philosophical discussion concerning the proper limits of the criminal law in relation to morality, sparked off by Lord Justice (later Lord) Devlin's famous assertion, in his Maccabean Lecture* The Enforcement of Morals, *that the public's 'intolerance, indignation and disgust' had an essential role to play in framing the law. As Lord Devlin wrote his lecture partly in rebuttal of the Wolfenden Report, I was especially pleased when, a few years later, he accepted the Homosexual Law Reform Society's invitation to be one of the signatories to a letter published in* The Times *supporting the Wolfenden proposals on homosexuality.*

People are accustomed to believe, and have been
encouraged in the belief by some who aspire to the
character of philosophers, that their feelings on the
regulation of human conduct are better than
reasons, and render reasons unnecessary.

John Stuart Mill, *On Liberty*, 1859

In the Wolfenden Report,[1] the proper limits of the criminal law in relation to homosexuality and prostitution are defined in accordance with the formula that, in the field of sexual behaviour, the law has three legitimate functions: 'to preserve public order and decency, to protect the citizen from what is offensive and injurious, and to provide sufficient safeguards against exploitation and corruption of others'.

Beyond this, 'it is not, in our view, the function of the law [the committee said] to intervene in the private lives of citizens, or to seek to enforce any particular pattern of behaviour'. They justified their recommendation that homosexual acts between consenting adults in private should no longer be a criminal offence by the 'decisive' importance of allowing individual freedom of choice and action in matters of private morality:

> Unless a deliberate attempt is to be made by society, acting through the agency of the law, to equate the sphere of crime with that of sin, there must remain a realm of private morality and immorality which is, in brief and crude terms, not the law's business.

This assertion, and the conclusions derived from it, are subjected to critical and powerful scrutiny in Lord Justice Devlin's British Academy Maccabean Lecture on *The Enforcement of Morals*.[2] Whilst admitting that the line which the law draws between sin and crime is in many places illogical, Sir Patrick Devlin strongly denies that the criminal law's sole legitimate purpose is the protection of the individual, stigmatizing the Wolfenden Report's 'search for some single principle to explain the division between crime and sin' as an error of jurisprudence. In his view, the law has a higher and more positive purpose – the protection of society, which term denotes 'the institutions and community of ideas, political and moral, without which people cannot live together'. And he strongly disapproves of any suggestion that the State, as society's representative, can afford a tolerant attitude of *laissez-faire* towards its citizens' private lives. 'Society', he says, 'cannot ignore the morality of the individual any more than it can his loyalty; it flourishes on both and without either it dies.'

Such a doctrine has far-reaching implications: the more so as Lord Justice Devlin infers that the concept of morality is meaningless apart from religion, and seems to think that if the religious sanction of the criminal law is undermined, more rational tests are relatively worthless. He does indeed affect, since Christian teaching is no longer universally accepted, to discern broader criteria by which society may rightfully pass judgement on matters of morals, and maintains that there is such a thing as a 'public morality' – citing the Wolfenden Committee's own emphasis upon the need to protect the young from 'corruption' as tacit recognition of this fact:

> If men and women try to create a society in which there is no fundamental agreement about good and evil they will fail. . . . For society . . . is held by the invisible bonds of common thought. . . . A common morality is part of the bondage. The bondage is part of the price of society; and mankind, which needs society, must pay its price.

This entails recognition of society's indubitable right 'to use the law to preserve morality in the same way as it uses it to safeguard anything else essential to its existence'.

It follows that the limitations postulated by the Wolfenden Committee to the law's proper intervention in affairs of private morality are 'wrong in principle'; and in Lord Justice Devlin's eyes they are unworkable in practice too – because *all* sexual immorality involves the exploitation of human weakness. He therefore denies any *theoretical* limits to the power of the State to legislate against immorality, maintaining that 'the suppression of vice is as much the law's business as the suppression of subversive activities'.

But even Lord Justice Devlin has to concede that there must be some *practical* limits to the law's incursion into realms of private behaviour. And here his argument stands revealed at its weakest. For having spurned a boundary drawn upon rational principles, and having reluctantly granted that in these days religious dogma is not likely to command unquestioned acceptance, he offers for our guidance nothing better than society's collective 'intolerance, indignation and disgust': these, he tells us, are the forces behind the moral law, and the final arbiters which we should allow to deprive the individual of his freedom of choice.

After so much high-sounding talk about society's moral nature, it is disconcerting to find so careful an intellect in the vanguard of a headlong retreat from reason. Sir Patrick Devlin's forensic skill and compelling language predispose his readers to give the greatest possible weight to the case which he makes; the inadequacy of his conclusion is all the more glaring. True, he presents this unholy trio of 'intolerance, indignation and disgust' in the best light he can – as 'the power of common sense'. He prays in aid that ubiquitous mainstay of London Transport and the English judicial system, 'the man on the Clapham omnibus', who, multiplied twelvefold and required to give a unanimous verdict, is, it seems, always the best judge not only of guilt but of morality – not only of crime but of sin. And *The Enforcement of Morals* sometimes gives the impression that, in its learned author's estimation, 'sins' are nothing more nor less than activities which twelve right-thinking English jurymen would feel bound to condemn.

Lord Justice Devlin's Maccabean Lecture, for all its distinction, is curious in that it seeks to rehabilitate in juristic terms a metaphysical conception of the State as the embodiment of moral attributes transcending individual rights, and yet ultimately rests these lofty claims upon nothing higher than the majority's instinctive revulsion – the morality of prejudice. Possibly this is because his desire to link the law's claims more firmly once again to religious principle stops Sir Patrick Devlin from giving its full weight to the idea of a humanly inspired, avowedly rational moral code. No doubt centuries of religious toleration have resulted in a degree of tolerance – and indifference as well – in society towards the views and behaviour of others which many sincere people – both Christian and non-Christian – find deeply repugnant. Yet in seeking a theoretical justification for curbing private freedom along the lines which he has done, Lord Justice Devlin has surely fallen into errors of principle ultimately more destructive and objectionable than the irregular sexual indulgences which he reprobates; and the practical outcome of his doctrines, if they were ever rigorously enforced, would surely be the effective end of those democratic rights of free thought, speech, and action which most people in this country take too much for granted.

A completely satisfactory principle for limiting State interference with the lives of individual citizens may never be evolved. Sir Patrick Devlin leans towards that 'organic' theory of society which, from Plato through Rousseau and Hegel, has elevated the claims of the State into a moral absolute. Such doctrines are really only pseudo-moralistic because they reduce, in the last analysis, to the claims of Power. Power, it is true, exists in variegated forms which are usually far more subtle than mere naked force. Burke's emphasis on tradition and prejudice as valuable elements in the life of society find strong echoes in the conservative minds of every age, as in the words of Sir Patrick Devlin.

These thoughts have a respectable ancestry. But so do those which reflect an attempt to apply more rational standards to the organization of society and to the devising of just laws; and this other stream of thought – that of pragmatic reform – is surely of more significance, both philosophically and politically, in the evolution of English life. Lord Justice Devlin cannot have forgotten that Jeremy Bentham was one of the precursors of scientific jurisprudence, nor that his famous principle of Utility – 'the greatest happiness of the greatest number' – was primarily devised as an instrument for measuring justice and promoting law reform, and only incidentally came to be regarded as an economic doctrine. Nor that Utilitarianism produced one of the greatest of all English individualist philosophers – John Stuart Mill.

Mill's attempt at a completely logical formulation of a limit to State and legal intervention into private life was no more successful than that of other thinkers; the inherent contradictions in his distinction between 'self-regarding' actions and those affecting others have been frequently demonstrated. But his passionate assertion in the essay *On Liberty* (1859) of the paramount importance of extending the boundaries of an individual's freedom to think and act as he chooses to the maximum extent remains at the heart of our social aspirations today just as much as when he wrote it, over one hundred years ago. His belief that 'the only freedom which deserves the name is that of pursuing our own good in our own way'; that 'each is the proper guardian of his own health, whether bodily or mental or spiritual'; and that 'mankind are greater gainers by suffering each other to live as seems good to themselves than by compelling each to live as seems good to the rest', leads naturally to his dislike of public opinion – which 'means, at the best, some people's opinion of what is good or bad for other people' – being given the force of law:

> There are many who consider as an injury to themselves any conduct which they have a distaste for, and resent it as an outrage to their feelings . . . this standard of judgment, thinly disguised, is held up to mankind as the dictate of religion and philosophy by nine-tenths of all moralists and speculative writers. These teach that things are right because they are right; because we feel them to be so. They tell us to search in our own minds and hearts for laws binding on ourselves and on all others.

The reader of Lord Justice Devlin's Maccabean Lecture may well echo Mill's reflection that 'to extend the bounds of what may be called moral police, until it encroaches upon the most unquestionably legitimate liberty of the individual, is one of the most universal of all human propensities'. There may be little more irrefutable logic in Mill's essay than in Sir Patrick's lecture; but the words of the former still make the most effective rejoinder to the latter: a man's own good, either physical or moral, is not a sufficient warrant for interfering with his liberty of action:

> He cannot rightfully be compelled to do or forbear because it will be better for him to do so, because it will make him happier, because, in the opinion of others, to do so would be wise or even right. . . . Over himself, over his own body and mind, the individual is sovereign.

To Mill and all those who, like him, believe profoundly that coercion and virtue go ill together, there can be no meaningful morality without liberty; freedom means freedom to choose; and the risk that not everyone will choose rightly must be borne by any democratic society which seeks to strengthen the true moral worth of its citizens as free men and women.

This is the liberal's classic reply – and his only possible reply – to all who seek to bind mankind in excessive tutelage. To those who hold with Sir Patrick Devlin that a common morality is society's spiritual cement, and that legal enforcement of it is justified by the lessons of history which show that 'the loosening of moral bonds is often the first stage of disintegration', the liberal will retort that all influences making for change and progress are inherently disruptive, and that to make conservation the prime aim of State activity is to condemn oneself to stagnation and impotence. To advance at all, mankind must take risks; and the enhancement of freedom doubtless entails greater risks to the conventionally minded than does its suppression. But it also holds out the best hopes of survival.

To a free man in a free society Lord Justice Devlin's position is not really tenable. Admittedly he concedes that the individual 'cannot be expected to surrender to the judgment of society the whole conduct of his life'; that a balance must be struck; and that most people would agree that this should entail 'toleration of the maximum individual freedom that is consistent with the integrity of society', together with respect for privacy 'as far as possible'. But since the decision to punish is the prerogative of 'intolerance, indignation and disgust', and the law is to be entitled to suppress anything that 'every right-minded person is presumed to consider immoral', there is not much gain in these concessions – they seem unlikely to extend very far in borderline cases, which are the ones that matter; tolerance is in little danger of being carried to excess by 'right-minded' people!

Lord Justice Devlin does not hesitate to admit, in a significant passage, the untidy state of the law where it affects sexual behaviour:

> The line that divides the criminal law from the moral is not determinable by the application of any clear-cut principle. It is like

a line that divides land and sea, a coastline of irregularities and indentations. There are gaps and promontories, such as adultery and fornication, which the law has for centuries left substantially untouched. Adultery of the sort that breaks up marriage seems to me to be just as harmful to the social fabric as homosexuality or bigamy. The only ground for putting it outside the criminal law is that a law which made it a crime would be too difficult to enforce; it is too generally regarded as a human weakness not suitably punished by imprisonment. All that the law can do with fornication is to act against its worst manifestations; there is a general abhorrence of the commercialization of vice, and that sentiment gives strength to the law against brothels and immoral earnings. There is no logic to be found in this. The boundary between the criminal law and the moral law is fixed by balancing in the case of each particular crime the pros and cons of legal enforcement in accordance with the sort of considerations I have been outlining. The fact that adultery, fornication and lesbianism are untouched by the criminal law does not prove that homosexuality ought not to be touched.

Indeed, he goes on to say that if, looking at it 'calmly and dispassionately', homosexuality is regarded as a vice so abominable that its mere presence is an offence, 'I do not see how society can be denied the right to eradicate it'.

The Times, commenting on this lecture in one of its more esoteric moods, found 'a moving and welcome humility in the conceptions that society should not be asked to give its reasons for what, in its heart, it feels intolerable; and that the hearts of Judges, however necessarily complex and subtle their judgments, must remain simple and straight'. This is indeed obscurantist nonsense of a pernicious nature. Justice must above all else be rational if it is to command loyalty. To base a system of jurisprudence upon 'intolerance, indignation and disgust' (however 'calm and dispassionate' – if such a contradictory state of mind were feasible) is utterly repugnant to Christian theology and a debasement of the Church's conception of the Moral Law, in which reason has its proper – and exalted – place.

To elevate instinct into society's lawgiver can lead only – and by a swift road – to total despotism. Lord Justice Devlin cursorily dismisses the central question of political obligation by observing: 'a rebel may be rational in thinking that he is right but he is irrational if he thinks that society can leave him free to rebel'. This may be correct from a legalistic standpoint; but it is too shallow and specious to be the last word on life's practical problems in all their manifold aspects.

Whether deliberately or not, Lord Justice Devlin advances in *The Enforcement of Morals* the most extreme claims made in England for many years past in favour of the law's right to control private behaviour. He discounts all the time-honoured doctrines upholding individual freedom in a manner strikingly at variance with the historic role of the Bench in championing the liberties of the subject against arbitrary encroachment. Sir Patrick will have performed a considerable (if unintentional) service if he sends more politicians, in their search for the framework which should shape our laws relating to moral questions, back to the first principles of political philosophy. For it is there, as always, that the unending debate about the nature of society continues.

One of the best recent statements of the liberal's outlook on that debate was given by Sir Isaiah Berlin in his brilliant Inaugural Lecture as Chichele Professor of Social and Political Theory in the University of Oxford:[3]

> It may be that the ideal of freedom to live as one wishes – and the pluralism of values connected with it – is only the late fruit of our declining capitalist civilization: an ideal which remote ages and primitive societies have not known, and one which posterity will regard with curiosity, even sympathy, but little comprehension. This may be so, but no sceptical conclusions seem to me to follow. Principles are not less sacred because their duration cannot be guaranteed. Indeed, the very desire for guarantees that our values are eternal and secure in some objective heaven is perhaps only a craving for the certainties of childhood or the absolute values of our primitive past. 'To realize the relative validity of one's convictions', said an admirable writer of our time, 'and yet to stand for them unflinchingly, is what distinguishes a civilized man from a barbarian.' To demand more than this is perhaps a deep and incurable metaphysical need; but to allow it to guide one's practice is a symptom of an equally deep, and far more dangerous, moral and political immaturity.

This bold assertion that freedom entails pluralism of values, and that without such pluralism there can be no democratic society, is surely the ultimate answer to those who seek, even in these latter days, to justify use of the law as a weapon for the enforcement of morals.

In a later issue of Man and Society *(No. 6, Autumn 1963), I reviewed Professor H. L. A. Hart's* Law, Liberty and Morality,[4] *in which he comprehensively criticized Lord Justice Devlin's thesis – incidentally pointing out that laws prohibiting consenting sexual relationships are themselves fundamentally immoral, because far from preventing or alleviating suffering, they 'create misery in quite special ways and in a special degree', doing more harm than good both to individuals and to society. I concluded my review by saying:*

This indeed is the crux of the matter. While it is fascinating to read and appreciate the abstruse arguments of Mill, Stephen, Devlin, Hart and the others; and while we can anticipate with intellectual pleasure much more clever talk about liberty and morality as long as our country remains a democracy – while this cosy debate goes on and bad laws remain unreformed, human misery is multiplying every day. For the laws against unorthodox sexual behaviour are not, as their defenders sometimes try to pretend, merely a symbolic paper denunciation of what is unacceptable to the orthodox; they are savage penalties enforced by policemen, courts, and sometimes imprisonment, often with appallingly wasteful consequences in terms of human suffering. And where prison sentences are imposed, their effects do not end with release, but affect the whole future life of the victim. In addition, these laws have a harmful effect upon those who support and administer them – for they foster attitudes of bigotry, hypocrisy, ignorance, and downright cruelty in society at large.

A short spell of duty in the Albany Trust's offices listening to some of the shocking stories of personal misery and social injustice which reach us almost daily should convince anyone that the operation of the criminal law as an instrument for the suppression of sexual immorality is in fact far more evil and immoral than the behaviour at which it is aimed. It is time that Lord Devlin and many other members of his profession cleared their minds on this point.

Notes

1. Report of the Committee on Homosexual Offences and Prostitution (HMSO, September 1957, Cmnd. 247).
2. 18 March 1959. Published by Oxford University Press.
3. 31 October 1958. Published by Oxford University Press.
4. Oxford University Press, 1963.

Promised Land?

ARENA THREE,[1] FEBRUARY 1967

Anyone who believes that the passage into law of Mr Leo Abse's Sexual Offences Bill, on which so many hopes are set, is going to bring the male homosexual into the promised land of legal equality with his lesbian sisters – or with heterosexual philanderers – had better have another think. For the more one considers the details of Mr Abse's Bill, the less adequate it appears to those of us who work with homosexuals and know something of their lives and problems.

There must be sincere admiration and gratitude to Mr Abse, Lord Arran, and Mr Humphry Berkeley for all that they have done to make the possibility of any sort of reform a live political issue. But unless one accepts the dubious proposition that any reform is better than none, strenuous efforts should be made to get the Bill improved during its Committee Stage – which, as the tortuous progress of abortion reform is currently demonstrating,[2] may in any event prove hazardous.

So far the only amendment mooted to the Abse Bill is the exclusion (for some obscure reason) of merchant seamen from its provisions in the same way that members of the Armed Services are already exempted. The wisdom or need for either exception is debatable. But there are other and more important points which ought to be raised. First and foremost, in the view of many of us who are concerned for the wellbeing of young people, are doubts concerning the suitability of so high an age of consent as 21 – especially in conjunction with the way in which the Bill deals with people under that age. The Bill aims, laudably, at protecting vulnerable youngsters from homosexual seduction by older men. But, incomprehensibly, it seems blind to the elementary social and biological facts that young men's sexual capacities, desires – and nowadays performances – do not remain dormant until their twenty-first birthdays.

If all homosexual acts committed by those under 21, even with their contemporaries, are to remain criminal as the Bill proposes, how are homosexual youngsters to be helped, or encouraged to confide their situation, any more readily than at present? Indeed, their position will in some ways be worsened by the creation of a sort of teenage homosexual ghetto. Faced as we are nowadays with lots of teenagers busily getting into sexual muddles – often only temporary ones, but liable to become permanent unless timely help is at hand – it seems singularly inept of Parliament to retain severe laws which are unlikely to deter young people's sexual activities but will certainly hamstring the social worker.

The Bill, indeed, does little to make the social freedom of even the adult homosexual more secure. It contains severe provisions against a third party who 'procures' homosexual acts which are themselves legalized under the Bill: and 'procuring', which has a nasty sound, might be stretched by some courts to cover the social introduction of two known homosexuals, or throwing a party, with no question of financial gain entering in. Then there is Lord Dilhorne's amendment, incorporated into the Bill by the House of Lords, which makes the privacy of a homosexual act – and therefore its legality – depend not upon where it takes place, but on whether anyone else besides the two participants is present. This could quite easily prove as oppressive, and as conducive to blackmail, as was the original Labouchère Amendment of 1885.

As Iris Murdoch wrote to Esmé Langley in September 1963, 'Anything to do with "special relations with the police" . . . must be got away from. What needs to be recognised is that homosexuals are perfectly ordinary people and vary as much as heterosexuals.' Such a recognition seems to have been sadly absent from the minds of those who drafted Mr Abse's Bill which, welcome though it is, remains a woefully hesitant step towards that comprehensive overhaul of all our laws and attitudes about sex ('normal' or 'abnormal') which is called for in the second half of the twentieth century.

Notes

1. *Arena Three*, the first British publication concerning itself with lesbianism, was edited by Esmé Langley for the Minorities Research Group.
2. David Steel's Bill to liberalize the abortion laws, which was going through Parliament at the same time as the Sexual Offences Bill, had become bogged down in seemingly interminable Commons Committee sittings. Thanks to Mr Abse's deft tactics, the Sexual Offences Bill cleared its Committee Stage in a single day.

The Citizen in the Street

SUBSTANCE OF AN ADDRESS TO THE JOSEPHINE BUTLER SOCIETY,[1]
16 JULY 1969

The law as it affects the citizen in the street is a veritable jungle: a major codification of it is urgently necessary, unless the civil liberty of the subject to go about his or her lawful business unmolested by officialdom is not to remain seriously endangered.

Most of us cordially dislike the Street Offences Act of 1959.[2] As that Act is concerned with the preservation of order and seemliness in the streets and public places, rather than with the regulation of sexual behaviour *per se* or the enforcement of morals, we have to consider it in the context of public order. This is also the case in relation to section 32 of the Sexual Offences Act of 1956.[3]

The following are the main provisions controlling or affecting the citizen's behaviour in the streets. First of all, overt behaviour. In general, anyone can pass through the streets freely so long as he does not obstruct the highway; behave in a manner likely to cause a breach of the peace; use insulting words or behaviour whereby a breach of the peace may be caused; or obstruct a policeman in the execution of his duty.

As to the first of these offences – obstruction of the highway – it is a Common Law offence of public nuisance for any person or collection of persons to act in a way *likely* to prevent members of the public from exercising their right to pass along or cross the street. That word 'likely' is very important, because it is not necessary to prove that anyone was actually impeded; but there must be evidence of intention or recklessness, and it was held in George Clark's Case that the defendant's use of the highway must be 'unreasonable' in order to constitute the offence. As it is a Common Law one, punishment is at the discretion of the court. But there is also section 121 of the Highways Act 1959 which provides that it is an offence, punishable with a fine of up to £50, if a person 'in any way wilfully obstructs the free passage along a highway'.

For conduct likely to cause a breach of the peace, anyone may be bound over by the justices, under the Justices of the Peace Act of 1360 (re-enacted by the Magistrates' Courts Act 1952), to keep the peace and be of good behaviour or go to prison for six months. You will note I said 'anyone': he doesn't have to be up on any charge, and in a recent case which caused considerable disquiet two 17-year-old schoolboys who appeared as prosecution witnesses in an affray case were bound over by the magistrates for their pains and had to appeal to Quarter Sessions to get the stigma removed. This ancient catch-all enactment has been used in a great miscellany of situations, some of them relating to street behaviour such as sitting down in the road, wearing the other sex's clothes, using the other sex's lavatory (difficult and delicate situations, these two, in the case of a transvestite or a would-be candidate for sex change surgery who, psychologically speaking, regard themselves as belonging to the opposite sex from their anatomical one), and – inevitably – obstructing the police. It has also been used in even more bizarre ways to enforce public (or private) morals, as when a girl was bound over on condition that she did not sleep at an hotel with a man to whom she was not married.

Obstructing the police is itself an offence punishable with a fine of £20 and/or one month's imprisonment. While a defendant can plead that he had no intention of doing so, his ignorance of the policeman's status is no excuse.

Insulting words or behaviour whereby a breach of the peace may be occasioned have been punishable in London since 1839 under the Metropolitan Police Act, and in various other towns and cities under local Acts and bye-laws; since 1936 they are also covered nationally by section 5 of the Public Order Act which (as amended by section 7 of the Race Relations Act 1965) provides that:

> any person who in any public place or at any public meeting (a) uses threatening, abusive or insulting words or behaviour, or (b) distributes or displays any writing, sign or visible representation which is threatening, abusive or insulting, with intent to provoke a breach of the peace or whereby a breach of the peace is likely to be occasioned, shall be guilty of an offence.

The penalty upon summary conviction is a fine of £100 and/or three months' imprisonment, and upon indictment, £500 and/or twelve months. The offence covers any conduct with *intent to provoke* or *likely to occasion* a breach of the peace: again, intent does not need to be proved if the courts consider that a breach of the peace would, in the eyes of a reasonable man, have been a likely consequence of the conduct complained of.

These offences of course commonly crop up in connection with public meetings, which are lawful in themselves subject to local Acts and bye-laws that often include the requirement of prior notification to the police of proposed procession routes. Some of these Acts give the local authority concerned, or the Secretary of State, special powers to ban processions; and in the Metropolitan area there are numerous special bye-laws and regulations controlling meetings within a radius of the Palace of Westminster while Parliament is in session. The Ministry of Works is responsible for regulating meetings in Hyde Park and Trafalgar Square.

Poster parades, loudspeakers and bands, and the distribution of leaflets in the streets are all controlled by various local Acts and regulations. While posters are usually only regarded as 'insulting' if they are exceptionally offensive or provocative, the unauthorized sticking of handbills is virtually entirely prohibited nowadays under the Town and Country Planning Acts. The Metropolitan Streets Act of 1867 provides that:

> no print, board, placard or notice may be carried or distributed by way of advertisement in any street within six miles of Charing Cross except in such a manner as may be approved by the Commissioner of Police for the Metropolis or the City of London.

The courts have held that the distribution of leaflets is a 'notice by way of advertisement', for which police permission is required. So much depends upon the respective discretion of a leaflet distributor and the police if the former is not to find himself in court either under this Act or for obstruction or insulting behaviour. And while there are no explicit laws against the collection of signatures for a petition in a street or public place, obstruction again looms. As for the collection of money in the streets, the insulting flag-day collector who cropped up so frequently in the recent Lords debates [on the Street Offences Bills] is only in the street at all on sufferance of the police: in London, for instance, the Commissioner has an advisory committee which recommends licenses for not more than one collection a week in a locality, and from whose decision there is no appeal. Unless you are a large and well-organized charity, these regulations make *bona fide* street collections a troublesome and unattractive way of raising money.

So much for overt behaviour. But one does not have to be blatantly nefarious in order to incur suspicion and arrest in the streets these days. While it is still true that, in general, the police's powers to stop and search anyone are limited to situations where open or violent crime occurs, there is a growing number of exceptions and qualifications to this. In London, a policeman may arrest anyone loitering by night who cannot give a satisfactory account of himself. And under the Prevention of Crimes Act 1953 he may arrest without warrant any person whom he reasonably believes to be unlawfully carrying an offensive weapon in a public place. Since the 1839 Metropolitan Police Act, it has been possible for the police in Greater London to stop, search and detain any person who may be reasonably suspected of having or carrying in any manner anything stolen or unlawfully obtained. They may also search vehicles under this power. Such wide 'stop and search' provisions were almost entirely confined to London until a couple of years ago, but they have now been extended throughout the country by two recent Acts, one at least of which is giving rise to major concern because of the threat that it poses to civil liberties.

The first of these acts is the Firearms Act 1968, which permits a policeman to detain and search any person whom he has reasonable cause to suspect of having a firearm in a public place. The second – the Dangerous Drugs Act 1967 – has greatly enlarged police powers to stop and search citizens in the street. Section 6 of that Act provides that:

> If a constable has reasonable grounds to suspect that any person is unlawfully in possession of drugs, he may detain and search that person, or stop and search any vehicle in which he suspects drugs are being carried, and may seize and detain anything which appears to be evidence of a drugs offence.

This section has come under heavy criticism, and as the National Council for Civil Liberties' *Handbook of Citizens' Rights* points out, 'while the conviction rate for drugs offences may have increased as a result, one of the damaging consequences has been the harassment of ordinary citizens going about their ordinary business'.

In this context, it seems that long hair and 'hippy' type clothing are sufficient to arouse suspicions in some constables' minds which they, if not the courts, regard as 'reasonable'. To quote the NCCL *Handbook* again:

> The police will be within their legal rights in searching you in the street or ordering you to open your bags only if they have reasonable suspicion. Unfortunately, it is by no means clear what circumstances must exist before a court will hold suspicion to be reasonable. A scruffy but honest citizen walking aimlessly by night in an area frequented by drug users may well feel aggrieved if stopped and searched, but the circumstances might induce a court to hold the policeman's suspicions to be reasonable.
>
> The police greatly value the wide scope of these powers, but the very nature of the powers often leads to abuse. The problem for the individual is that he may be perfectly innocent but that would not necessarily prevent the police having a reasonable suspicion, for there might have been a robbery in the vicinity, in which case anyone carrying a large bag might be open to suspicion.
>
> It is therefore wise to ask the policeman in question why the request to search is made and then refuse to be searched if his answer seems unsatisfactory. If innocent, you would be quite within your rights in walking away. If he was sure of his ground you would then run the risk of being arrested, but if he could not satisfy the court as to his reasonable suspicion you might have a right of action for damages against him for unlawful arrest.

But while it might be *proper* to ask the policeman why he was searching you, and to walk away if dissatisfied with his answer, I doubt whether it would be *wise*!

Clearly the police have comprehensive – and very diffused – powers to deal with all varieties of street nuisance, including the more objectionable forms of kerb-crawling (despite *Crook v. Edmondson*[4]). Some of these powers have been added to the law since 1959, when the Street Offences Act was passed as being necessary to clear prostitutes off the streets. Certainly there are not so many prostitutes visible in the West End nowadays – but it is perhaps an open question how far this is solely due to the Act, and how far to the changing social conditions of the past decade which have led to new methods of organizing and conducting commercialized vice.

My own personal reaction to the Act in its early days was that I had far less objection to the 'ladies' who used to line certain side streets of Soho than to the seedy, shady men who began sidling up to one in Shaftesbury Avenue and other main thoroughfares asking out of the sides of their mouths if you 'wanted to find a nice girl'. And apart from the practical effects of the Street Offences Act, the injustice of designating a woman as a 'common prostitute' before a case has even been made out against her is common ground among us. The Act may or may not work: it is still unjust; and it is surely not beyond the wit of legislators to devise something more equitable.

Even more objectionable is section 32 of the Sexual Offences Act 1956, which provides that 'it is an offence for a man persistently to solicit or importune in a public place for immoral purposes'. It is perfectly clear from the section's context that it was originally intended to deal with offences relating to heterosexual prostitution: indeed, the Home Secretary of the day, introducing the clause into an 1898 Vagrancy Act, said explicitly that it was meant to catch the prostitute's 'bully'. The penalties it provides are proportionately severe – up to six months' imprisonment summarily, and up to two years on indictment; and until the Sexual Offences Act of 1967, the accused could not claim the right to a jury trial if the prosecution wished otherwise. Yet since at least 1912, the section has been used almost exclusively against male homosexuals, and has by no means been confined to offences of soliciting for homosexual prostitution. Indeed, the great majority of cases brought under this section relate to homosexual activities analogous to the non-commercial 'boy meets girl' kind of pick-up, which I am sure none of us would dream of making subject to any criminal sanction whatever.

Now that the 1967 Sexual Offences Act has expressly provided that it is no longer an offence for a man to procure a lawful homosexual act *with himself*, I should very much like to see a case which tested the validity of the manner in which section 32 continues to be used in such cases. In the first 1968 House of Lords Debate on the Street Offences Bill, Lord Foot gave an admirably succinct summary of the illogicalities which a distinguished Divisional Court had (no doubt inadvertently) imported into the interpretation of section 32 in the *Crook v. Edmondson* case; and I would only add to what he said my dubiety at that Court's assumption that the section's unaltered inclusion in the 1956 Sexual Offences Act – which was a consolidating statute – implied a tacit parliamentary acceptance of a usage which was not contemplated by its original enactors. I should not have thought that this necessarily followed.

I rate the entire repeal – or at any rate the radical recasting – of section 32 as an extremely high priority in any attempt to bring about a more just state of affairs. While it may be necessary to have some provision for adequate punishment for the type of ponce who is a bully in fact as well as in name (and do we really know whether there are many such men nowadays?), the chief evil of the section as it at present stands is that the threat of an expensive prosecution upon indictment, with all the consequences that an adverse verdict will bring, can be held over the hapless man who is arrested in circumstances which in fact amount to infringement of some minor bye-law concerning park regulations and so forth for which the penalty is a £5 fine, and to which a plea of 'Guilty' is thus all too easily obtained.

Prosecutions for this type of offence have undoubtedly been stepped up lately. The position of the Homosexual Law Reform Society regarding them remains what it has always been – namely, that the presence wherever practicable of uniformed constables at known trouble-spots is both more economical and fairer to the police than the employment of plain-clothes vice squads in circumstances which inevitably give rise to suspicions of *agent provocateur* tactics, whether such suspicions are well-founded or not; and that the requirement of independent evidence of annoyance from a member of the public is at least as essential in homosexual importuning cases as it is where heterosexual street offences are concerned. Perhaps we shall one day reach the situation of New York, where I am informed that (in contrast to some other American cities, where police attitudes to such offences are still very punitive) no solicitation prosecutions are now being brought by the police themselves and the only cases are those which result from public complaints.

This brings me to the question of what essential elements should be incorporated in any legislation that we eventually succeed in getting on to the Statute Book to deal with street offences. First of all, do we still need to think in terms of a special street offence because the conduct complained of was either explicitly sexual in nature or designed to facilitate or invite sexual behaviour elsewhere? I have always been dubious about this, and would prefer a broader reform which dealt with street offences as a whole. This is also the view of the National Council for Civil Liberties.

I hope, therefore, that a broader drafting group will be convened to review the entire range of the law as it relates to conduct in the streets, and to produce a uniformly applicable, national Statute which will either sweep away altogether, or at any rate standardize, the various piecemeal and local provisions for which there is really no rhyme or reason. This is a radical and ambitious proposal; but if it is beyond the powers of a privately constituted voluntary group to produce the necessary draft, I would hope that the Government's attention can be drawn to the need for such a reform.

Any acceptable law to regulate importunate or insulting street behaviour should not discriminate between the sexes or between classes of persons, and should hinge essentially upon *nuisance*, with either intent to commit a nuisance or persistence in doing so as basic elements of the offence. In all cases, proof of actual annoyance by evidence independent of that given by the police should be required. The nuisance should result from the actual conduct complained of, and should not be inferred simply because of the specific purpose of behaviour not otherwise offensive.

None of this may seem particularly original – but it is essential if the law concerning street behaviour is to be put upon a sensible footing. I cannot conclude without acknowledging my indebtedness to two invaluable sources of information – the NCCL's *Handbook of Citizens' Rights* I have already referred to, and the admirable pamphlet *The Street Offences Bill – A Case for its Amendment* which was produced by the Church of England Moral Welfare Council in 1959 while the Government's Street Offences Act of that year was still being debated in Parliament. This provides some of the most effective criticisms of the Act's provisions, together with some carefully thought out observations on the whole problem.

My theme has been that 'the laws regulating the conduct of the citizen in the street are too numerous, have been increasing, and ought to be revised'. With this I think your illustrious founder, Josephine Butler, would be in accord, for it was she who wrote:

> Our laws do not permit, and it is hoped they never will, the arrest of persons, either men or women, because they are known to the police to be persons of immoral character. Our laws permit, and justly so, the arrest or warning of persons guilty of any disorderly conduct in the streets.[5]

Notes

1. The Josephine Butler Society, to which I then belonged, was primarily concerned with reforming the laws relating to prostitution.
2. This Act substantially enacted the proposals of the Wolfenden Committee for the regulation of prostitution.
3. This section made it an offence for a man 'persistently to solicit or importune in a public place for immoral purposes'.
4. This 1966 Appeal Court case decided that persistent soliciting or importuning contrary to section 32 of the Sexual Offences Act 1956 was only an offence if committed by a man towards another man, but not if done by a man to a woman.

5. Nearly thirty years on, the rights of the citizen in the street are narrower and less secure than when I gave the above address.

Privacy and the Outsider

ADDRESS TO THE PARLIAMENTARY CIVIL LIBERTIES GROUP,
17 JULY 1969

It is two years since the Sexual Offences Act of 1967 provided a measure of relief for adult male homosexuals. In healthy contrast to the Abortion Act, little has been heard since the reform about the working of the new Act or the need for possible revisions. But this does not mean to say that it is a final or completely satisfactory piece of reform: it has merely placed the male homosexual in a somewhat similar legal and social position to that of the 'common prostitute'. Nor has the operation of the unreformed parts of the law become less harsh. Indeed, since the early part of this year, we have had a clear impression of a deliberate campaign by the law enforcement authorities to tighten things up.

Recently, the HLRS/Albany Trust counselling service has had a much higher rate of legal cases than at any time since the reform Act – and some of these cases are as unpleasant as those one remembers in the early 1950s, when police methods of arrest, investigation and questioning aroused considerable public distaste. Also, these pressures would appear not unconnected with those upon other minorities. Freedom is indivisible; and anyone who has the notion that in today's climate of law enforcement as it affects unorthodox minorities we are living in an over-permissive society is, I'm afraid, leading a pretty sheltered life.

For with regard to homosexuals, what are we doing? Well, we no longer say (as the old pre-1967 law used to) 'It's all right to *be* one, as long as you don't *do* it'. I suppose we can at any rate be thankful for that: but we seem to have substituted the scarcely less fatuous attitude of 'Well, do it if you must – but not if we can help it'. The basic problems of homosexuals are, of course, social; but lack of acceptance by families, non-homosexual friends, and employers is formidably bolstered by the law, even today.

Do we make it easy, legally or socially, for homosexuals to meet one another? We do not. If they are knowledgeable or brazen enough, they can go to so-called 'gay' pubs. . . . Theoretically – and I use that word advisedly – clubs should be safer. But homosexual clubs are still being regarded by the police as 'disorderly' if those who frequent them betray their inclinations in a non-heterosexual manner. The legal status of single-sex dancing between men, for example, is dubious; is it 'disorderly' or 'indecent' *per se*, or only if there is behaviour which would constitute such an offence if committed by a man and a woman?

At a case concerning a homosexual club in the Midlands which was raided by the police last year, it was stated for the prosecution that the behaviour witnessed by police officers (who had taken out membership of the place for the purpose of carrying out their observations) was 'of a disgusting nature, comparable with the activities of Sodom and Gomorrah'; and the Recorder, fining the licensee £500, said that 'what was going on was intolerable by any standards, heterosexual or homosexual'. Evidence from several club members – some of them professional people – that they had witnessed nothing disgusting at the club, and that the kind of dancing which went on was what could be observed at any ordinary club and mostly in the modern style where the partners did not touch one another, was disregarded.

So an evening out at a 'gay' club may not prove either safe or pleasurable. What, then, does the lonely homosexual do? Advertise for friends? In view of what we've been hearing about *International Times*, this sounds like rather a hollow joke.[1] I should like to say a word about that matter. I find it very curious that if the police particularly object to the advertising columns of *IT* – as distinct from its editorial matter, which I should have thought is on occasion a good deal more provocative – they should have concentrated so heavily upon the homosexual advertisements. *IT* of course carried similar advertisements of a heterosexual nature. With the awful example of Mr Shaw of *The Ladies' Directory* and Conspiracy to Corrupt Public Morals fame[2] before them, even this may have been a foolish thing to do. But section 4 of the Sexual Offences Act 1967 specifically provides that it is no longer an offence for a man to procure a homosexual act with himself, if that act is not itself an offence; and so I cannot see why the 'Males' column of *International Times* is interesting the police quite so much. But it is. I gather that a CID sergeant has been detailed upon a year's assignment to travel the country following up all the advertisers and respondents whom he can trace, and that several have already been visited with a *pro forma* questionnaire and invited to sign statements and give evidence, if required. The possibility that people seeking partners for private sexual gratification in this way may receive an official tap on the door more than a year afterwards is, I hope you will agree, extremely repulsive and indeed alarming: Big Brother is stalking with a vengeance – and I, as a taxpayer, strenuously object to footing his expenses.

So far as censorship is concerned, I believe that it is always ultimately (even when unconsciously) political. I myself don't find *International Times* a particularly interesting or amusing paper. It certainly doesn't strike me as being seriously subversive. But its point of view has a right to be heard. That it should be intimidated – or that its printers should be intimidated – is utterly wrong; and that those who advertised in it should also be intimidated (whether incidentally or not) is intolerable. And this *IT* business is not the only instance we have had of adults who have made contacts through 'pen pal' clubs being visited by the police and questioned about their private correspondence and sexual lives – sometimes as long as two years after they had written the letters in question.

So if you are a homosexual and you don't like the idea of a club raid or a police visit about your letters to pen pals, what do you do? Go for a walk? Not if you're wise! This is not the occasion for a major discussion of the infamous section 32 of the 1956 Sexual Offences Act – the 'persistently soliciting or importuning in a public place for immoral purposes' clause which has brought so many unguardedly smiling citizens to grief. Our case files show no diminution in the type of public lavatory case where the sole prosecuting evidence is that of plain-clothes vice squad men who in certain towns appear to be most assiduous in frequenting places of relief, and whose evidence, although most invariably accepted by the courts, is frequently completely at odds with the defendant's version of events.

Plain-clothes police also seem to have been deployed in considerable numbers late at night in parks and open spaces recently – and in the daytime too. No one wishes to complain at police activities designed to preserve the decency and salubriousness of municipal parks for the public at large; but when one hears stories of special sub-stations being set up in park potting sheds, and bevies of special duty officers in mufti arresting strolling men, one does begin to wonder what is going on. The strolling men may indeed have wanted a pick-up: but it is hard to believe, in most of the numerous cases of this sort that I've heard of, that their behaviour became sufficiently offensive to warrant arrest without some provocation having been offered to them. In one instance I heard of recently, no one else was in sight except the arresting officer, and it took ten minutes for the police car which he summoned by walkie-talkie to arrive: yet the charge was 'insulting behaviour whereby a breach of the peace may have been occasioned'.

Are such tactics – while possibly within the letter of the law – really in accordance with its spirit? The law, in this context, is surely primarily concerned with preserving public order and decency; and as the Homosexual Law Reform Society has said many times before, this would be much more effectively maintained, and at a lesser cost in police manpower and court time, by the presence of uniformed police patrols as a preventive measure at known trouble-spots. Arrests on these charges carry with them such dire social consequences: loss of jobs, evictions from lodgings, expulsion from study courses and other such misfortunes are by no means unknown after a man has been in court on an importuning charge – sometimes even if he has been acquitted. I do not consider that such arrests ought to be made unless the culprits are *in flagrante delicto* to the annoyance of identifiable members of the public who are prepared to give evidence. In these days of rising crimes of violence and theft, a little less police attention to victimless crimes would be welcome.

While these matters may only seem to be the concern of minorities (and unpopular ones), in the end they affect each one of us. For if the generally high standards of British justice decline so that minorities are no longer protected and allowed to live without unreasonable harassment, every man and woman in this country will suffer in the end.

Notes

1. *International Times*, an 'alternative society' paper, was being prosecuted for 'conspiracy to corrupt public morals', because it had published some explicit gay contact advertisements; and in 1973 the House of Lords affirmed by a majority that this common law crime did exist [*Knuller v. DPP*]. ('Knuller' – the name of *IT*'s publishing company – is Swedish for 'fuck': I doubt whether even the prosecution realized this!)
2. Shaw had published a *Ladies' Directory* of Soho prostitutes, and was convicted of the hitherto unheard-of common law crime of 'conspiracy to corrupt public morals'. His conviction was upheld by a majority of the House of Lords in 1961, despite a strongly dissenting judgement by Lord Reid. This judicial lawmaking on the hoof posed a serious threat to freedom of sexual information which could be construed as 'immoral' and therefore 'contrary to public policy'.

Compulsory Virtue

NEW SOCIETY, 5 APRIL 1973[1]

Today's social climate, with nearly a hundred Conservative MPs clamouring for the return of the death penalty and jeremiads resounding from all sides about the 'permissive society', seems a far cry from the reformist days of the mid-1960s when Parliament abolished capital punishment, conditionally legalized abortion, and relieved male homosexuals from some of the penalties hitherto visited upon them.

Since then, the Abortion Act has been the target of continuous criticism. Homosexual law reform, in contrast, has aroused little comment except from the committed Gay Liberationists who – with some degree of justice – regard society as being still almost as hypocritical and oppressive towards homosexuals as in pre-1967 days, and seek further reforms.

This week the Campaign for Homosexual Equality holds its first annual conference, and will consider a paper on The Law and Homosexuality which poses the question: 'What next?' The fact is that the law still discriminates against homosexuals over the age at which they may legally have relationships; it still entirely prohibits such relationships in Scotland and Northern Ireland, the armed services, and the merchant navy; and it restricts legal homosexual behaviour in private to circumstances where only two people are present.

What is the best way forward towards the removal of such discrimination? Should we (the CHE paper asks) seek further piecemeal reforms, or should we at once seek to sweep away the whole hotch-potch of muddled law about sexual offences and replace it with something more comprehensible and in line with what ought to be contemporary thinking?

The Sexual Law Reform Society's working party, which has been studying this problem for over two years, has little doubt that the latter approach is both more logical and ultimately more likely to succeed. We started from the premise that since we live in a pluralistic society it is not the law's job to enforce a specific code of morals – at any rate in the sphere of sexual taste and behaviour. It seems clear to us – in the words of the Society's chairman, Bishop John Robinson – that the function of the law in society is not to prohibit but to protect, not to enforce morals but to safeguard persons, their privacies and freedoms.[2]

If we are correct in conceiving society as pluralistic rather than paternalistic / permissive, the whole notion of the law as policing morals falls to the ground. We are left with the much more relevant and less contentious function of safeguarding individuals' liberties: their rights to please themselves so long as they do not harm or interfere with others; their rights to protection from harm or assault; their rights of privacy.

Sexual law at present (or anti-sexual law, to be more accurate) is contained in a number of statutes. The main one, the Sexual Offences Act of 1956, consolidates numerous laws passed since mid-Victorian times. A reading of this Act conveys the distinct impression that (marriage apart) most things to do with sex – not only rape or actual assaults – are Very Nasty Indeed. While our working party is still finalizing its detailed proposals, it is already clear that these will be based upon the principles that the law only has cause to interfere with people's sexual behaviour and preferences where these involve activities where (1) there is not freely given mutual consent; (2) there is not full responsibility on the part of one or more of the partners (for example, where one is mentally defective); or (3) members of the public (other than policemen) testify that they have been offended.

At present, the law is defective in all these respects. First, it still prohibits much sexual activity (both heterosexual and homosexual) which is in fact fully consented to by all concerned. Second, it assumes that whole categories of people – e.g. girls aged under 16, youths under 21 behaving homosexually, and men of any age doing so if they are Scottish, Northern Irish, serving members of HM Forces or merchant seamen – are not sexually responsible enough to be permitted to choose what they do or don't do. Third, many sexual activities which are not in fact observed by or annoying to members of the public are illegal (and frequently prosecuted) if they occur in a public place, however unlikely the public are in fact to go there.

The real need is, surely, for the law not to victimize, but to protect and to rehabilitate. It is because of their recognition of this that bodies such as the Society of Friends' Penal Reform Committee and the National Secular Society, and individuals like Bishop Robinson, have raised the question as to whether the age of consent should not merely be lowered but possibly abolished as a criminal concept, and replaced by an 'age of protection' involving social care. Opposition to lowering the age of consent from 16 for girls has come from other quarters, such as the British Medical Association working party and the Josephine Butler Society, for precisely similar reasons – because they feel that to lower the age of consent would reduce the protection currently afforded to young girls from traffickers in prostitution and other forms of corruption.

On another aspect of the law – that concerning street offences – there is a weighty body of evidence that the existing state of affairs is unjust and discriminatory. A law that gets rid of the specifically sexual crime of soliciting and treats all misbehaviour in the streets as a public nuisance is thought to be necessary by the Josephine Butler Society, the National Council for Civil Liberties, and many other groups. Lord Chorley has twice unsuccessfully introduced a bill to this effect in the House of Lords, and it is to be hoped that provisions along these lines will eventually be enacted. In particular, it should be a requirement before a man or woman is convicted of such an offence in a public place that an identifiable member of the public (other than a policeman) must appear in court to testify that they have been annoyed or pestered. This would prevent the type of conviction – still all too frequent – that is based upon unsupported police evidence of sexual misbehaviour in a street or a public toilet. All too often, when no independent public evidence is given, allegations are made that the police themselves provoked the misbehaviour in order to make an arrest.

In reforming the law so as to eliminate its inappropriately moralistic aspects it will be necessary to go beyond the specifically sexual laws so as to ensure that the statutes relating to obscene publications, and the common law relating to conspiracy, are not used to circumscribe sexual freedom. The current preoccupation of police, magistrates, and judges with the sexual content of 'obscenity' is alarming.

There is therefore much to be done, first in educating the public and ultimately by Parliament, before the law concerning sex can be said to have attained a rational basis. Needless to say, feelings run deep on this issue. We are most of us – both reformists and conservers – moralists in our various ways. We all wish to quell violence and to protect the weak and inexperienced. But in sexual matters is the inexperience which results from prohibition or from fear to be equated with virtue? Perhaps the ultimate question to ask those who seek to enforce personal morality through the weapon of the law is: What moral value is there to be found in *compulsory* goodness?

Notes

1. *New Statesman* © 1973.
2. The Rt Rev. J. A. T. Robinson, *The Place of Law in the Field of Sex*, The Beckly Lecture for 1972 (published by the Sexual Law Reform Society).

Homosexual Law Reform

FROM *THE TACTICS OF PRESSURE*[1]

I have told the story of the 1960s law reform campaign in Quest for Justice. *What follows is a brief account, written much nearer the time, and so of interest for its contemporary impressions of what stood out in my mind at the time.*

To secure a change in the law relating to sexual behaviour is a task fraught with peculiar difficulties. Nevertheless, in the Parliament of 1966 not one but several such changes were enacted – notably those relating to divorce, abortion and homosexuality. Having been closely connected with this last reform during the whole of the ten-year interval between the publication of the Wolfenden Report in 1957 and the passage into law of the 1967 Sexual Offences Act which embodied its main recommendations, I am perhaps well placed to assess the role and limitations of pressure groups operating in the more delicate and emotion-charged areas of social change. As Secretary of the Homosexual Law Reform Society (1962–70) I saw democracy at work at close quarters. It was a strenuous and sometimes disconcerting experience; and if I had known at the beginning all that was to be entailed, I might have thought twice before taking it on.

For where sex is concerned, one is up against not merely the ordinary prejudice and misinformation which surrounds any political topic; there is an altogether deeper dimension of emotionally held attitudes which impel those on each side to espouse their causes with a high degree of self-righteousness and consign their opponents to the devil. I think this was especially true over abortion and homosexuality. We received surprisingly few abusive letters at the HLRS, and most of those which did arrive were anonymous, the writers apparently being apprehensive as to the wisdom of giving their names and addresses lest some awful fate should befall them. The campaigners for liberalizing reforms regard themselves as crusading to end inhumanity and injustice; their opponents look upon them as contributing to the moral downfall of society and 'opening the floodgates' to rampant licentiousness.

How was it, then, that between 1966 and 1969 so many sensitive social issues were tackled by Parliament? Partly, I think, because there were an unusually large number of liberally (small 'l') minded MPs of all parties in that Parliament; but also because the changes they enacted reflected a majority view in the country that the time was right for reform in these matters. The Labour Government reacted by providing sufficient parliamentary time for several important Private Members' Bills to become law on a non-party, free-voting basis.

Pressure groups such as ALRA (the Abortion Law Reform Association) and HLRS undoubtedly played a significant role in this result. How significant? Here I am treading upon delicate ground, having recently incurred the 1967 Sexual Offences Act's parliamentary sponsors' displeasure by inadvertently remarking on television that 'it took me nearly ten years' hard work to get the law changed', when I should of course have said 'us'. But while I would (needless to say) be very far from claiming that 'alone I (or HLRS, or ALRA) did it', I must risk further displeasure by asserting that without the hard and persistent work of HLRS and ALRA over a period of years before homosexuality and abortion became live parliamentary issues, the Sexual Offences and Abortion Acts would almost certainly not yet be on the Statute Book.

From the plains, a mountain peak looks distant but startlingly simple and dominant. When you stand upon it, you may find yourself merely on the brink of a range of foothills with much more challenging and arduous goals still ahead. The social reforms of the 1960s may be viewed in this way. Mostly, they embodied recommendations made several years (usually at least a decade) previously which had in the intervening time been the subject of fierce controversy. By the time they were enacted they were all, in some respects, irrelevant to some pressing contemporary needs – yet in the eyes of many of the protagonists, they represented a 'solution' to the problems with which they were concerned. To deny that this was in fact so is in no way to belittle their significance or to underrate the signal achievement of those who succeeded in manoeuvring them through the cumbrous parliamentary machine.

The results, however, do underline one feature of the role of pressure groups which those seeking to emulate them would do well to face at the outset. This is that, while a pressure group can be, and frequently is, instrumental in achieving its broad objective, it usually has far less influence over the details – or even the general scope – of the legislation in which it is interested than may be thought. This can perhaps best be explained by reviewing the campaign for homosexual law reform historically, as it passed through several successive stages.

First, the pressure group's formation. In our case, this came about some six months after publication of the Wolfenden Committee's report, whose principal recommendation was 'that homosexual behaviour between consenting adults in private be no longer a criminal offence' (para. 62).

Although the House of Lords debated homosexuality and prostitution – the two subjects dealt with by the report – within three months of its appearance, there was no sign of active interest in the Commons and it became clear that the then Conservative Government had no desire to promote legislation along the recommended lines. Yet the report had had a predominantly sympathetic reception from the press, church spokesmen and professional organizations; and public opinion polls taken shortly after its appearance showed that some 40 per cent of the population accepted its findings while just over 50 per cent opposed them.

In the spring of 1958 there was a recurrence of old-style 'chain' prosecutions of consenting adult homosexuals at assizes in various parts of the country. This directly precipitated the formation of the Homosexual Law Reform Society, which arose out of correspondence in various newspapers calling for active steps to promote the Wolfenden reforms. On 7 March 1958 the following letter appeared in *The Times*:

HOMOSEXUAL ACTS

We, the undersigned, would like to express our general agreement with the recommendation of the Wolfenden Report that homosexual acts committed in private between consenting adults should no longer be a criminal offence.

The present law is clearly no longer representative of either Christian or liberal opinion in this country, and now that there are widespread doubts about both its justice and its efficacy, we believe that its continued enforcement will do more harm than good to the health of the community as a whole.

The case for reform has already been accepted by most of the responsible newspapers and journals, by the two Archbishops, the Church Assembly, a Roman Catholic committee, a number of Non-Conformist spokesmen, and many other organs of public opinion.

In view of this, and of the conclusions which the Wolfenden Committee itself agreed upon after a prolonged study of the evidence, we should like to see the Government introduce legislation to give effect to the proposed reform at an early date; and are confident that if it does so it will deserve the widest support from humane men of all parties.

Yours, etc.

N. G. ANNAN; ATTLEE; A. J. AYER; ISAIAH BERLIN; †LEONARD BIRMINGHAM; ROBERT BOOTHBY; C. M. BOWRA; C. D. BROAD; DAVID CECIL; L. JOHN COLLINS; ALEX COMFORT; A. E. DYSON; †ROBERT EXON; GEOFFREY FABER; JACQUETTA HAWKES; TREVOR HUDDLESTON CR; JULIAN HUXLEY; C. DAY LEWIS; W. R. NIBLETT; J. B. PRIESTLEY; RUSSELL; DONALD O. SOPER; STEPHEN SPENDER; MARY STOCKS; A. J. P. TAYLOR; E. M. W.

TILLYARD; ALEC R. VIDLER; KENNETH WALKER; LESLIE D. WEATHERHEAD; C. V. WEDGWOOD; ANGUS WILSON; JOHN WISDOM; BARBARA WOOTTON.

Notwithstanding the distinction of the letter's signatories, the Government showed no inclination to take their advice. On 19 April *The Times* published a further letter supporting the Wolfenden recommendations, signed by fifteen eminent married women. Most of the signatories to these two letters, together with others who were now approached by A. E. Dyson (the university lecturer who was the moving spirit in forming the HLRS), became founder-members of the Society's 100-strong Honorary Committee – a very distinguished band which was somewhat sourly referred to by one of the London evening papers as 'the pick of the lilac establishment'. A smaller executive committee, with the late Kenneth Walker – a well-known surgeon and sexologist – as Chairman, began planning a political campaign. As Mr Walker later wrote, 'We all agreed that the law as it stood was archaic, grossly unfair and ineffective. Some of us would have put the matter far more strongly than this.'[2]

During its early months the Society had no permanent office, and the bulk of its clerical work was done by voluntary helpers at the home of two of them. As these two – Len Smith and Reiss Howard – were, in fact, living together in a homosexual relationship, their action in letting the Society use their address was as brave as their work for it over a period of years was efficient and dedicated. By the autumn, enough funds had been collected to enable a paid Secretary to be appointed and an office to be opened. The Revd A. Hallidie Smith became the Society's first Secretary at 32 Shaftesbury Avenue, London W1, which remained its headquarters for the entire reform campaign.

This much success brought its own problems. Previously the Society's contact with supporters and other members of the public had been almost entirely through correspondence. Now, with an office to be telephoned and visited, the volume of work descending upon the Secretary rocketed – not least in the form of unscheduled callers with personal problems, many of them urgently requiring advice and practical help. This aspect of the work has always consumed a great deal (some would say too much) of the staff's time and energies. The press, too, demanded information and articles. Various organizations and groups requested a speaker. Soon the office was overburdened (a state which remained chronic throughout my own tenure, despite a staff expansion which at its peak in 1965–67 totalled seven full-time paid employees), while the voluntary helpers' team was still coping with most of the routine enquiries.

This, not unnaturally, led to criticisms of the office; internal dissensions were happily rare within the HLRS, but it has not always been plain sailing for the incumbent of the 'hot seat', whose critics usually have little conception of the pressures involved in running an intensely busy, precariously financed operation of this sort. Money is a recurring headache for all voluntary organizations. My own view is that responsibility for raising it should be assumed by the governing body – if necessary through a separate fund-raising committee – and should not be imposed upon the chief executive, who has his hands more than full carrying out the day-to-day work of campaigning. At the height of the law reform activity in Parliament, I found myself having to spend almost half my time extracting funds from sympathizers to avoid the Society's imminent collapse at a time when it was in daily consultation with many Members of both Houses of Parliament.

Readers of this essay will doubtless be familiar with the limitations placed by the Charities Acts upon political activities. This presents problems for campaigning organizations whose primary purpose is to ameliorate social problems and who seek changes in the law towards this end. As I have already mentioned, the HLRS found itself operating willy-nilly as a social casework agency from the time its office opened. In order to qualify for charitable grants and tax relief in connection with this side of its work, some executive committee members formed the Albany Trust, a registered charity whose objects are 'to promote psychological health in men by collecting data and conducting research; to publish the results thereof by writing, films, lectures and other media; to take suitable steps based thereon for the public benefit; to improve social and general conditions necessary for such healthy psychological development'. As time passed, the functions of the Albany Trust became more extensive than those of the HLRS and were by their nature more long-term, if not permanent. After the reform Bill became law, the HLRS was more or less dormant, but the Albany Trust saw new horizons of social work ahead. Yet the mistaken notion that the reform of 1967 had largely solved the problems of homosexuals obscured this fact in many quarters which ought to have been better informed, with the result that the Trust is now burdened with a case-load of some 3000 people a year which is still growing, while its income has declined.

This points to the need for continuous education of the public as to all aspects of the problem with which one is dealing. To oversimplify by crystallizing upon a single issue, such as the passage of a parliamentary Bill, is sometimes unavoidable but may in some ways be counter-productive.

The second phase of the Society's life stretched from the autumn of 1958 through to mid-1964. It might be labelled 'the long haul'. The Society's executive committee realized that there was little immediate hope of legislation. The Home Secretary, Mr R. A. Butler (as he then was), had said in the first Commons 'Wolfenden' debate in November 1958 that time was needed to educate the public towards general acceptance of the report's recommendations, and the Society regarded itself as the chief instrument of public education. At this stage it mostly kept away from Parliament and concentrated upon the press and the public. The circulation of its pamphlet *Homosexuals and the Law* to all MPs before the 1958 debate, coinciding as it did with similar distributions (unknown to the Society) from other sources of Peter Wildeblood's book *Against the Law* and Eustace Chesser's *Live and Let Live*, had given rise to a parliamentary outcry by opponents of reform that the Commons was being subjected to the attentions of 'a rich and powerful lobby of perverts' (who never existed: if they had, the Society's task might have been less hazardous. In fact, the mythical cohorts of wealthy 'queers' eagerly pouring money into the Society's coffers remained mythical).

One result of this scare was that the MPs on the Society's executive – notably Mr Kenneth Robinson (later to be Minister of Health) – advised strongly against any further early direct approaches to the Commons, as the debate of November 1958 had made it quite apparent that early legislation could not be expected. As Kenneth Walker has written:

> It was clear . . . that a long and arduous fight lay ahead. To 'educate' the public upon such an emotional topic as homosexuality to the extent that the Wolfenden proposals might become palatable to politicians who feared, apparently, a massive constituency backlash from those who were totally ignorant of the subject, was a formidable task for a small and slenderly financed voluntary organisation such as the HLRS. Nevertheless, we set out to obtain as much publicity as possible for the need to change this law, and the Revd Hallidie Smith . . . began addressing numerous meetings of constituency political parties, university societies and discussion groups ranging from church organisations to humanists – an activity which his successors have continued at an increasing tempo. I believe that there have now been hundreds of such meetings addressed by representatives of the Society, and that at not one of them has a predominantly hostile audience been encountered. Indeed, motions in favour of homosexual law reform are repeatedly carried in university unions and debating societies up and down the country, and not a single one has been lost. So much for 'public opinion' as we have encountered it face to face. In press correspondence, too, the letters published are predominantly in favour of reform. With one or two exceptions, opponents of the Wolfenden recommendations are remarkably inarticulate and unwilling to engage in public discussion of the matter.[3]

The next parliamentary airing of the Wolfenden proposals was in June 1960, when Mr Kenneth Robinson took the first opportunity following the 1959 general election to move a Commons motion calling on the Government 'to take early action' on the report's recommendations. Despite a number of strongly sympathetic speeches (mostly from the Labour side), the Home Secretary, Mr Butler, again made a temporizing speech and the motion was defeated by 213 votes to 99. But even some of its opponents admitted in their speeches that reform must eventually come.

This debate was the first major occasion for the HLRS to practise the techniques of supporting a parliamentary initiative; a 'trial run', as it were, for the main campaign of 1965–67. The Society's activities in this respect have been flatteringly described in some quarters as 'sophisticated'. I would prefer to characterize them as 'discreet'. What we did – then and later – never amounted to a mass lobbying operation of the blunderbuss variety which some organizations assume (wrongly, in my view) to be required: we had learned somewhat painfully from the 1958 debate that blanket circulations of all MPs are almost certainly a mistake.

Consequently, we were largely guided in what we did by the advice and requests of our chief parliamentary sponsors – at this stage Mr Robinson, later Lord Arran and Mr Leo Abse. We endeavoured to carry out, to the best of our ability, what they required of us. This involved the supplying of information which they needed and, when necessary, research into points of detail. There was also a good deal of routine clerical work in connection with the 'whipping' letters which they personally circulated to their voting supporters before each debate, the keeping of comprehensive lists of all MPs on record as having spoken or voted in favour of or against homosexual law reform, and so forth – but very rarely the making of direct approaches by the HLRS to Members of either House who were not already known to us. As a result, those who wished to help (and on some occasions even those who opposed the reform!) tended to come to the Society for information; so that by 1966 we probably had a much wider range of parliamentary contacts than we would have acquired by 'badgering' unknown MPs out of the blue.

This combination of assiduous but quiet rallying of support within Parliament by the Bill's sponsors there, assisted by our office acting as 'general staff', proved singularly effective. I am sure that any attempt by the HLRS to operate independently of the parliamentarians (a role which some pressure groups aspire to) would have been a mistake, both in principle and in practice. There were occasions during the Bill's passage when the Society could have wished that more attention had been paid to its viewpoint; but these were genuine differences of opinion about what was practicable rather than disagreements as to ends, and the degree of understanding and smooth co-operation between the parliamentary and extra-parliamentary wings of the reform movement remained generally close throughout.

The month before Mr Robinson's debate the Society had held its first (and largest ever) public meeting at the Caxton Hall (on 12 May 1960, the second anniversary of the Society's foundation). Despite some difficulties – later to become tediously familiar – over advertising, enough posters and handbills were distributed before the event to produce an audience of well over 1000, and an overflow meeting had to be hastily arranged in one of the smaller halls in the building in addition to the main one. Speakers included the Bishop of Exeter, Mrs Anne Allen JP, Kingsley Martin (editor of the *New Statesman*), Dr Neustatter and the Revd A. Hallidie Smith. The meeting was interesting in that it revealed a wide variety of attitudes about homosexuality and towards homosexuals, both among the speakers and members of the audience: yet all agreed that the legal reforms supported by the Society were necessary. The Bishop of Exeter's description of the then prevailing law as 'a monstrous injustice' summed up the feeling of the meeting, which with only three dissentients carried a resolution urging the Government to implement the Wolfenden findings 'without further delay'. Immediately after the meeting, a letter signed by the Chairman and Secretary was written to the Home Secretary, in which the result of the meeting and the predominantly favourable reception given to the Society's campaign throughout the country was recorded. Mr Butler replied before the June debate that he still considered legislation would be 'premature'. Despite the meeting's success, it received hardly any press publicity: the time had not yet come when homosexuality and homosexual law reform was regarded by the press as a topic of general interest.

The next bout of reformist activity came somewhat later in the same Parliament, in March 1962, when Mr Leo Abse (Labour MP for Pontypool, and already well known for his interest in social causes) introduced a Sexual Offences Bill which deliberately omitted any reference to the controversial legalization of homosexual acts between consenting adults in private but sought to enact some of the subsidiary proposals of the Wolfenden Committee – to ensure that men complaining of homosexual blackmail should not themselves be prosecuted, that 'stale' charges relating to homosexual offences more than twelve months old should be prohibited, and that all cases against 'consenting adults in private' should be brought, if at all, by the Director of Public Prosecutions.

This attempt to mollify the main current of opposition with legal compromise met with little favour; the Bill was 'talked out' by opponents who were as vehement against it as if it had embodied the main Wolfenden proposal. They wanted none of what one of them called 'Wolfenden watered down'. Another objected to these 'abominable' offences being muddled up with 'more respectable' sexual crimes in the Bill's title, and expressed the hope that neither that nor any future Parliament would go one inch along the path of legalizing homosexuality, which he described as 'particularly repugnant to the vast majority of people in this country'.

Notwithstanding such extreme views, it became known in July 1964 that the Director of Public Prosecutions had 'requested' Chief Constables to consult him before prosecuting men for homosexual acts committed in private with another consenting adult, and also in respect of offences more than twelve months old or revealed because of blackmail complaints. It was pointed out by the Attorney General at the time, and also by Home Office spokesmen in subsequent parliamentary debates, that this did not imply that any change in the law had taken place through administrative action, or that the law was never to be applied against consenting adults. Nevertheless, this directive (whose cause remains somewhat obscure) was the first sign of official concern at the operation of the existing law.

It had been preceded, in the spring of 1964, by another parliamentary initiative – the last of that Parliament – from an unexpectedly right-wing quarter. Sir Thomas Moore, the High Tory MP for Ayr and 'father' of the House of Commons, was well known as an extreme supporter of the death penalty and of corporal punishment. But he was also a supporter of the

Wolfenden proposals because, as he once told me, he had known some men of upright character whose lives had been made miserable because of this law. As a result of a summary of case histories circulated by the Society at the end of 1963, he asked the Home Secretary (Mr Henry Brooke) when he proposed implementing the Wolfenden Report; and on receiving a negative reply, Sir Thomas tabled a motion in April 1964 calling on the Government to legislate on the grounds that this 'would tend to prevent much danger of blackmail and many personal tragedies'. He requested the Society to ask those MPs who had supported Kenneth Robinson in 1960 to sign his motion, but only about two dozen did so: several of them considered that it was too near the end of that Parliament's life for such a gesture to be fruitful; others may have been unwilling to march under Sir Thomas's banner. He himself was disappointed at the paucity of support, and privately expressed the view that with a general election in the offing, those with marginal seats were unwilling to sign anything which might be used against them in the forthcoming campaign. As he was retiring from Parliament, he had no need to worry. Nevertheless, his initiative may have played some part in bringing about the Director of Public Prosecutions' subsequent directive; in any event, Sir Thomas Moore deserves an honourable mention in the annals of homosexual law reform.

The opponents of reform remained in a majority (though a much smaller one) in the Parliament of 1964–66. Mr Abse's 'half-way' Bill had convincingly demonstrated that opposition to even minor alterations to the law would be just as strenuous as to a 'whole-hog' measure, and the Society accordingly decided that it would endeavour to obtain a sponsor for a full Wolfenden reform as soon as possible after the general election of October 1964. This brought Labour into power, but with such a tiny majority that a further general election within a few months seemed inevitable, and the MPs on the HLRS executive were dubious as to the usefulness of a full-scale parliamentary effort before this took place.

However, the Earl of Arran got in touch with the Society soon after the new Parliament met and said he intended to take an early opportunity of raising the question of the Wolfenden reforms in the House of Lords. Lord Arran had never been (and never became) a member of either the Honorary Committee or the HLRS executive, and acted quite independently and on his own initiative, taking full and final responsibility for all the decisions which he had to make, although he consulted closely with us throughout the campaign which now commenced. There is no doubt that the main parliamentary credit for achieving homosexual law reform is his; for while the Bill would not have got through the Commons without Leo Abse's skilful tactical generalship, it was Lord Arran's dogged perseverance and sensitivity to the mood of the Upper House in 1965 and 1966 which paved the way to ultimate success in 1967.

This was not Lord Arran's first sortie into the field of homosexual law reform; before the general election he had written to the then Prime Minister (Sir Alec Douglas-Home) urging the case for the implementation of the Wolfenden proposals by the Conservative Party in the interests of compassion and personal freedom, but he had received a discouraging reply: this was not a nettle which Conservatives cared to grasp. However, with a new Government in office and an influx of younger, more radically minded MPs, Lord Arran felt that an initiative in the Lords would be worthwhile. He was right. On 12 May 1965 his motion 'drawing attention' to the Wolfenden Committee's report on homosexuality (which the Peers had not debated since 1958) was supported by a distinguished array of speakers, including the two Archbishops; sixteen Peers spoke in favour of reform whilst only three opposed it. The Labour Government's spokesman maintained neutrality, as his Conservative predecessors had done – but this time a positive neutrality rather than a negative one, with clear hints that if the House took a favourable decision in favour of reform the Government would not seek to frustrate its wish.

The form of the motion precluded a vote, but two weeks later a simple one-clause Bill tabled by Lord Arran, providing that homosexual behaviour between consenting adults in private should not be a criminal offence, was given a Second Reading by 94 votes to 49. This symbolic victory of almost two to one signalled a breakthrough, and was a personal triumph for Lord Arran. With drafting help from the Government, he steered a full Bill embodying the substance of all the Wolfenden Committee's recommendations through its detailed Committee and Report stages to receive its Third Reading in October 1965 by 116 votes to 46.

Inevitably, there were some minor setbacks. The Bill's opponents tabled a series of 'wrecking' amendments, and succeeded in carrying one of these – a much narrower definition of 'in private' than that envisaged by the Wolfenden Committee – into the Bill. (The Committee had contemplated that whether a homosexual act was 'in private' or not should be decided by the courts, *pari passu* with their decisions in heterosexual cases of behaviour alleged to be offensive to public decency; the Act as finally passed provides that a homosexual act is regarded as not 'in private' – and therefore remains unlawful – 'when more than two persons take part or are present', thereby substituting a quite different concept.) On a number of other points, the Government's draft clauses differed from what the Society would have liked. But Lord Arran was not willing to jeopardize the continuation of Government assistance in the provision of technical advice and parliamentary time, so the Society asked other supporters of the Bill to table amendments embodying its views.

These – notably one on conspiracy ably moved by Lady Wootton on two occasions – covered some important legal points and produced interesting discussions, but were generally not successful because of Home Office opposition. This resistance was usually in fact to the substance of the amendments, but most of the objections were ostensibly directed to what was said to be their 'defective drafting'; so in the result the Government got its way in a somewhat backhanded manner (especially as it was officially 'neutral' towards the Bill). Lord Arran, as he was fully entitled to do, preferred their views on most of these points to those of the Society, but it was unfortunate that he somewhat too readily assumed a lack of technical competence on our part in drafting clauses which in fact embodied principles which the Government were unwilling to accept – though they were frequently in closer accord with the recommendations of the Wolfenden Committee than the final terms of the Bill. It was also disappointing and rather frustrating to the Society that at no time were they invited by either Lord Arran or Mr Abse to a drafting conference with the Government draftsman who assisted in drawing up the Bill. Perhaps as a consequence of this omission, it is noteworthy that all the points at which the 1967 Sexual Offences Act departs from the letter of the Wolfenden recommendations are in a more restrictive direction than that envisaged by the Committee.

These, however, are comparatively trivial discomfitures when set against the great achievement of passing the Bill; and I only mention them at all in order to demonstrate that 'pressure groups' – even well-organized ones – are by no means omnipotent in relation to the parliamentary sponsors of legislation in which they have an interest. Even the friendliest and best-disposed of sponsors rightly tend to emphasize that the final decisions as to parliamentary tactics and terms must be their prerogative. Politics is 'the art of the possible', although there is room for legitimate differences of opinion as to what is in fact possible in any given situation. Where such differences occur, those within Parliament, and not those outside it, must inevitably have the last word.

In contrast to the Peers, the Commons remained reluctant to accept reform. In May 1965, two days after the Second Reading of Lord Arran's Bill, MPs refused Mr Abse leave to bring in a similar Bill under the Ten-Minute Rule by 178 votes to 159 – a significantly different hostile majority (19 votes) to the 114 of 1960. Public opinion was also swinging in the right direction. National Opinion and Gallup polls published in the autumn showed that over 60 per cent of the respondents now agreed that homosexual behaviour between consenting adults in private should no longer be a criminal offence. This change in the balance of opinion since 1959 followed an intensive phase of press publicity and public speaking, in most of which the HLRS was directly involved. Since the spring of 1964, press requests for information and articles had multiplied, and numerous speaking engagements were undertaken.

The press breakthrough came, in my estimation, when within a few weeks of each other three of the most prominent women journalists in the country approached the Society saying they wished to write about homosexuality as they felt it was time that the veil of genteel ignorance was ripped from their female readers' eyes. They did so, frankly and sympathetically, and this successful invasion of mums' and girlfriends' magazines started a process of more forthright dealing with sexual topics in their columns which has continued ever since. In the public speaking field, a great many university debates occurred on the Wolfenden proposals during 1964, 1965 and 1966, in most of which HLRS spokesmen participated and in none of which were the reformers defeated. Usually they won by overwhelming majorities. (Their opponents were, indeed, hard put to it to find coherent arguments for retaining the *status quo*. Sometimes they themselves could not be found, and at least one debate took place in which the leading 'opponent' was in fact a supporter of reform who stood in at the last moment for a bashful 'anti' MP.)

Lord Arran's Bill had only passed through the Upper House when the session ended, and it was therefore necessary for it to pass again through all its stages in both Houses in order to become law (there being a convention that all legislation dies if it is still 'in the pipeline' at the end of the annual parliamentary session). Immediately the new parliamentary year started in November 1965, therefore, Lord Arran reintroduced his Bill in the Lords. In the Commons there was also a new and more hopeful start: Mr Humphry Berkeley, the Conservative MP for Lancaster, drew second place in the annual ballot for Private Members' Bills and announced his intention of introducing a Commons Bill similar to Lord Arran's. He did so in close consultation with the HLRS, and after a five-hour debate his Bill succeeded in obtaining its Second Reading by 164 votes to 107 on 11 February 1966, after a speech from the Labour Home Secretary, Mr Roy Jenkins, expressing his forthright support for the measure (in marked contrast to his predecessor's hesitant stance). Unfortunately, after this promising start, national politics supervened and Parliament was dissolved in March 1966, so the Sexual Offences Bills in both Houses automatically lapsed.[4]

When the new Parliament, which had a substantial Labour majority, met, Lord Arran once again introduced his Bill in the Lords. It was given its Second Reading on 26 April by 70 votes to 29, its Third Reading on 16 June by 83 votes to 39 and passed by 78 votes to 60. Leo Abse now brought his (identical) Bill into the Commons under the Ten-Minute Rule procedure: it was approved by 244 votes to 100, the size of the reformist vote reflecting the more liberal views of the new intake of younger Labour and Conservative members. (About 60 Conservatives consistently voted for the Bill and ensured its majority throughout its passage.)

This victory, and the moral support of the Lords' votes, enabled Mr Abse to secure enough Government time to permit the Bill to pass through all its remaining stages in the Commons. The Second Reading debate took place on 19 December, technically without a division, although a vote on a procedural Motion to enable the debate to continue after 10 p.m. obtained the support of 194 members against 84. Mr Abse's next success was in persuading the Government business managers to appoint a separate Standing Committee for the Bill so that it would not be held up in the queue of Private Members' Bills already waiting to be examined by the Standing Committee assigned to deal with them, and which was currently wrestling with the lengthy intricacies of the Abortion Bill.

Mr Abse's Bill passed through its Committee stage at a single sitting on 19 April 1967 – a remarkable feat, in striking contrast with the marathon Committee stage wrangles which had held up the Abortion Bill for three months and were threatening to jeopardize its passage into law. In order to avoid a repetition of this state of affairs, Mr Abse's supporters deliberately avoided a lengthy discussion of amendments, and the opponents were nearly all absent from the Committee's first and only sitting. Nevertheless, some important amendments were made to the Bill in Committee, and a number of controversial points were aired – several of them by supporters of the Bill at the HLRS's behest, notably that of the age of consent: 21, many of us felt, was too high to be realistic and the penalties laid down by the Bill for committing homosexual acts below that age were too severe. Such a law, said the Hon Nicholas Ridley (Conservative, Cirencester and Tewkesbury), would make no sense at all in the minds of the young men of generations to come who would grow up being expected to observe it, and it would be a disaster to make a mistake over this.[5] Mr Abse, however, stood firm for 21 and another influential Member of the Commons who supported a lower age (Mr G. R. Strauss, Labour, Vauxhall) urged his colleagues to suppress their doubts and worries about some of the Bill's details at this stage of its precarious life so as to ensure its passage onto the Statute Book.

One major new clause – inserted with Mr Abse's agreement to mollify the only organized lobby of opponents which had manifested itself during the most recent series of House of Lords debates – excluded the merchant navy from the provisions of the Bill. Representatives of the National Maritime Board and of the National Union of Seamen had held discussions with Mr Abse and their spokesmen had objected to his Bill on Second Reading on the grounds that it failed to provide a similar degree of 'protection' for merchant seamen to that given to members of the armed services (whose total exclusion from the benefits conferred upon civilians by the Bill ran counter to the recommendations of the Wolfenden Committee but had been accepted by Mr Abse to meet the belated wishes of the Service Ministries, who had abandoned their earlier position of neutrality and moved to a more restrictive attitude). Somewhat to the surprise of the Bill's opponents, Mr Abse had, between Second Reading and Committee stage, acquiesced to the insertion of a new clause – now Section 2 of the Act – whose effect was to provide that a homosexual act between two consenting adults in private remained an offence if committed on board a United Kingdom merchant ship between a crew member of that ship and another crew member of the same or any other United Kingdom merchant ship. The fact that such acts, if done on a ship by a member of its crew with a passenger or a foreign merchant seaman, are apparently not illegal under the terms of the clause, seems to have escaped its supporters! (Although Mr Ben Whitaker [Labour, Hampstead], who favoured the Bill as a whole, pointed out the illogicality of the new clause and said it would bring the whole of English law into ridicule.) The HLRS remained a passive and somewhat bemused spectator of this seafaring skirmish, which was conducted virtually singlehanded by Mr Abse; it was a highly successful tactical foray on his part, which successfully drew the sting of opposition to the Bill at its Committee stage.

The opposition, however, rallied for the Report stage and kept up a determined filibuster throughout the extra Friday allotted by the

Government. Strong pressure brought upon the Leader of the House by the Bill's friends (strengthened by the Home Secretary's sympathetic attitude towards it) enabled the debate to be resumed after 10 p.m. on Monday, 3 July, and after an all-night sitting it was given a Third Reading by 99 votes to 14. In all, there had been thirteen divisions during the Report stage, and on four occasions Mr Abse's supporters successfully voted the closure, which necessitated the presence of at least 100 of them; the opponents never exceeded 40. Mr Abse's Bill was then sent to the Lords, who gave it a Second Reading by 111 votes to 48 and formally passed it through its remaining stages to receive the Royal Assent on 27 July 1967. As a chronicler of this and other social reforms of the 1966–70 Parliament has written: 'To secure the enactment of a major Bill is a great political achievement for a back-bencher.'[6] The Sexual Offences Act of 1967 was the joint achievement of Lord Arran and Mr Leo Abse, both of whom combined persistence with parliamentary skill to a marked degree.

How satisfactory was the campaign from the HLRS's point of view? Personally, I have always regarded the legislative process as a fundamental part of public education, and there is no doubt that the series of parliamentary debates between 1965 and 1967 helped considerably to educate the public mind about the existence and nature of homosexuality, although a high degree of ignorance still remained after the law was changed. As Professor Richards has pointed out, 'a feature of the parliamentary debates on this subject is that the fundamental moral issue was consistently avoided'. Practically without exception, supporters of the reform conceded that homosexual acts were intrinsically undesirable, and some maintained that they were unnatural. Is this really true? A frank debate was not forthcoming because (to quote Professor Richards again) 'clearly it was not in the interest of the reformers to raise contentious issues of this sort. Their task was to arouse Christian compassion, not Christian controversy. Their tactic was to keep public and parliamentary debate as rational and moderate as possible because of the danger that an upsurge of emotion and prejudice would ruin their chance of success.'

As a consequence of this continuing unwillingness of politicians to face up to the needs, in the first instance for any action at all, and subsequently for a really frank and searching debate, the discussions which did take place in Parliament between 1965 and 1967 contained elements of unreality and to that extent were in fact irrational. How far could the course of these debates have been influenced by more effective (or different) tactics on the part of the HLRS? I do not believe very much. The Society's chief contribution had been made before the debates of 1965 began, in creating the climate of opinion in which they could be held at all. It is perhaps in the nature of pressure groups that this should be so. Once an issue comes before Parliament, its parliamentary sponsors take charge – and they are unlikely to pay undue attention to outside influences (even friendly ones) unless they are unusually modest or timid souls, in which case they would be unlikely to be piloting a Bill through Parliament. Indeed, there is a discernible tendency on the part of most MPs and Peers to discount organized opinion from any quarter, just because it *is* organized. Perhaps this betrays a subconscious resentment on their part of the nowadays all but universal Party Whip.

What, then, were the salient features of the homosexual law reform campaign, seen from the Homosexual Law Reform Society's standpoint? First and foremost, I would say that the more intensive a pressure group is, the more it experiences a sensation of pressures being focused upon itself – from friends as well as from opponents. In the early days, the pressures derived from being virtually the sole channel of reforming activity, from 1958 until 1964, and the brunt of opinion-forming (in accordance with Mr Butler's behest) was compounded by the intensive pressures imposed by a growing number of individuals direly in need of help: a facet of the work which was maintained and indeed grew throughout the busiest period of parliamentary work. The phase of active reform brought new insights, some new frustrations, but also an elevating sense of achievement which sustained all concerned. The frustrations derived from the realization that the Society's efforts were undeniably essential, but nevertheless not central enough in the minds of the Bill's parliamentary champions to mould either the tactics of debate or the detailed shape of the resulting legislation as much as we might have wished. (But their hands, too, were tied by the need to ensure that Government 'neutrality' was benevolent as regards the provision of debating time and drafting assistance.)

The resulting blurring of certain issues led (as Professor Richards has pointed out) to a less satisfactory reform than might otherwise have been achieved – notably in its civil liberties aspects, where the desirable and equitable objective of equality before the law for homosexuals and heterosexuals was negated in several additional respects beyond those conceded by the Wolfenden Committee. One especially unfortunate failure was the lack of Government response to Lady Wootton's amendments (twice tabled at the HLRS's request) seeking to ensure that conspiracy charges should not be brought against people committing, seeking to commit, or facilitating, homosexual acts legalized by the Act. The foreseeable outcome of this has been the 'conspiracy to corrupt public morals' charges brought (successfully) against the publishers of *International Times* and (unsuccessfully) against those of *Oz*. In this and other respects – notably with regard to the age of consent; the heavy penalties still incurred by some homosexual behaviour between consenting parties if one or both is under 21; the complete exclusion of Scotland, Northern Ireland, and serving members of the armed forces from the benefits of the reform; and the restrictive definition of 'in private' – the 1967 Sexual Offences Act stands itself in need of amendment.

But I should like, in conclusion, to make it plain that in saying this I am expressing a personal opinion rather than a collective HLRS one (because the Society's successor, the Sexual Law Reform Society, is currently making a detailed study of further changes in the law which it may wish to propose); and that I in no way wish to derogate from the signal achievement of Lord Arran and Mr Abse. Theirs was the brunt and theirs the victory. We at the Society helped as best we could – and in the event, I hope, not too clumsily. Whether or not the Act which our combined efforts obtained is destined to be an enduring solution, it was at least the first and essential step along the road towards a greater degree of justice and humanity in our sexual laws and mores.

Notes

1. Ed. Brian Frost (Galliard, 1975).
2. *Sexual Behaviour, Creative and Destructive* (Kimber, 1966), p. 242.
3. Ibid., p. 244.
4. Humphry Berkeley lost his seat in the ensuing general election.
5. Ironically, Nicholas Ridley was the Cabinet minister whose department was responsible for the 1988 Local Government Act into which the notorious 'Clause 28' was inserted. At that time, I wrote him a pained personal reminder of his more libertarian younger days; he sent me a lame reply (presumably drafted by his civil servants), claiming that the rogue clause was necessary to prevent homosexuality being 'glamourised'.
6. Peter G. Richards, *Parliament and Conscience* (Allen and Unwin, 1970).

Reforming the Law on Sexual Offences

COMMENTS TO UNIVERSITY OF LEEDS FRANK DAWTRY SEMINAR, SPRING 1981

The Seminar was held while the Criminal Law Revision Committee was still engaged upon its review of the laws relating to sexual offences, and the main speaker was Professor J. C. Smith, QC, a member of the CLRC. I was invited to contribute as Secretary of the Sexual Law Reform Society.

Sexual offences are a most important – and a peculiarly intimate – area of the criminal law. Our sexual thoughts, feelings, desires, behaviour, and relationships are among the most personal and private aspects of the lives of each one of us. Every person's chances of happiness hinge to a large extent upon how we each experience and deal with our sexuality. But sexuality and sexual relationships are obviously of social concern as well as being a personal matter. What should be the role of the criminal law in this respect? Professor Herbert Hart has said that:

> interference with individual liberty . . . is itself the infliction of a special form of suffering – often very acute – on those whose desires are frustrated by the fear of punishment. This is of peculiar importance in the case of laws enforcing a sexual morality. They may create misery of a quite special degree. . . . The suppression of sexual impulses generally is something which affects the development or balance of the individual's emotional life, happiness and personality.[1]

What is the law's legitimate role? The law, of course, can only deal by means of punishment or deterrence with the external aspects of behaviour. It cannot prohibit or punish thoughts and fantasies (although, in the case of obscenity and pornography, it goes to considerable lengths to prevent their publication). What kinds of sexual behaviour should the law seek to prevent? Certainly, we have made a good deal of progress in our thinking about this matter during the last 100 years. In mid-Victorian days, when the laws about sexual offences were largely consolidated within the 1861 Offences Against the Person Act, the prevailing attitude was that all sexual activities outside marriage were shockingly sinful and indecent, and that it was right for the State to punish severely such 'unnatural' conduct as homosexual behaviour between consenting parties. The law was also very sexist, in always seeing women and girls as the passive partners in sexual activity and as the potential sexual victims of sexually predatory males.

By and large, this attitude prevailed until the publication of the Wolfenden Report in 1957. I am pleased that the Criminal Law Revision Committee have adopted as their working guide the 'Wolfenden principle' that the law's proper functions of preserving public order and decency, protecting the citizen from what is offensive and injurious, and providing sufficient safeguards against the exploitation and corruption of those who are vulnerable, ought not to extend to intervention in private lives to enforce any particular pattern of behaviour that does not breach these concerns.

However, I find the tenor of some of the CLRC's working paper proposals disappointingly unadventurous: they might be described as 'Wolfenden and Water' – with a good deal more water than Wolfenden! I had hoped that they would have grasped more firmly some of the nettles with which this field is strewn.

I particularly regret that the chance has not been taken to dismantle the archaic and prejudicial terminology in which many sexual offences are described. Why, for instance, has 'indecent' been so overworked by Parliament and the lawyers as legal shorthand for 'sexual' that they make it sound as if all sexual behaviour is an intrinsically indecent or at any rate undesirable activity, and all discussion of sex is obscene?

Sexual acts which are trivial, non-violent, and in some cases consensual, are classified by the law as 'indecent assaults' – which makes them sound much more horrid and anti-social than actual assaults committed with hostile violence but without sexual motives. Mutual masturbation – whether in public or in private, and with or without consent – is 'gross indecency' in legal parlance. People can be – and often are – charged with this offence without any grossly indecent behaviour (whatever *that* may be) having taken place: the term has been so widely interpreted by the courts that it covers behaviour which is in fact consensual, unobtrusive, and in private.

Why should the law regard any behaviour as 'indecent' *just because* it is sexual? Must we really continue to think of sex as being in itself 'indecent' (at any rate outside marriage), even in legal terminology? I believe that nothing sexual which people *want* to do together, and consent to (and, hopefully, enjoy!), is actually indecent, whatever the law may call it. So why can we not move forward to a more objective and neutral description of those categories of behaviour which the law still needs to proscribe?

As for legal fictions, I fear that the conservative approach adopted by the CLRC to the crucial topic of consent will make their perpetuation inevitable, even if there is some redesignation of offences. I do not think it answers the objections of those of us who oppose the whole notion of making anybody criminally liable for sexual behaviour to which they have *in fact* consented (provided, of course, that it is not publicly offensive) to say that an 'age of consent' law is not a fiction but merely makes the consent of one or more of the parties irrelevant. For that is precisely what I object to: consent should *never* be irrelevant.

And I find it interesting that, having turned down the alternative way suggested by the Sexual Law Reform Society for dealing with adolescents at risk in relation to their sexual behaviour within a non-criminal framework of protection orders and injunctions, the CLRC itself moots a similar procedure to enable the decriminalization of sexual activities with mental defectives. Surely, such retarded adults are even more liable to the risk of sexual exploitation than most averagely bright post-pubertal teenagers are?

This issue of consent is crucial to the law's legitimate role in this area. The question I continually ask myself is: 'Who owns my body?' To judge from the way a good many lawyers, and some doctors, talk and behave, *I* don't – at least, not entirely. I find this difficult to accept, and even to comprehend, in a supposedly 'democratic' society. I believe the criminal law has the proper function of protecting people from sexual behaviour which they don't desire and haven't consented to, and from the sexual activities of third parties which invade their privacy. I do *not* believe, as the CLRC apparently does (despite its lipservice to the 'Wolfenden principle') that the criminal law has any rightful role of 'protecting' people *from themselves*, or of punishing them, or their sexual partners, for behaviour which they in fact desired and participated in willingly and even eagerly. I regard this whole paternalistic approach as profoundly mistaken. It removes the incentive for young people to take charge of themselves and to assume responsibility for their own lives and relationships. It infantilizes them – and when the law appears to those whom it impinges upon as thoroughly unreasonable and even tyrannical – as, for instance, in the case of teenage homosexual behaviour – it may well embitter some of them for life and make them genuinely antisocial and accepting of activities which are indisputably criminal. I believe that when it is necessary – and it is sometimes necessary – to provide protection against sexual exploitation for immature and inexperienced adolescents, this can and should be done in ways which do not involve criminal penalties that treat consent as irrelevant. It behoves the law to look well at its boundaries, if it is to retain people's respect.

I also regret that the CLRC has not wielded a bolder broom around sexual behaviour taking place (actually or technically) in public. I think it would be beneficial to abolish specifically sexual offences of this nature, and to include such behaviour under a broad 'public nuisance' provision dealing with all types of public misconduct.

In our Working Party's report (submitted as our main evidence to the CLRC) the Sexual Law Reform Society set out the following positive principles on which we believe that future legislation should be based:

(1) There should be a general freedom, upheld by the law, for individuals to engage in such sexual activities as they may freely choose, subject only to restrictions which are clearly socially necessary.

(2) These restrictions arise, and arise only, from the need to protect those who by reason of their age or condition are not fully responsible; to avoid the infliction of involuntarily received pain, anguish or physical damage upon participants; and to punish affronts given to third parties, whose complaints are held by the Courts to be justified.

(3) It follows that only those sexual activities should be illegal (a) which are not willingly consented to or which are subject to restriction on grounds of age or limited responsibility; or (b) which result in clinically demonstrable mental or physical damage or suffering; or (c) which have given rise to reasonable complaints from a member of the public.

(4) It should also be an offence to indulge in any sexual activity or display where this is observed by others and causes them actual annoyance; but it should be a defence that no such observation could reasonably be expected, or that the observer did not object.

(5) Where an offence contravening any of the above principles is alleged, the burden of proof should in all cases lie on the prosecution.

In his book *Sex Law*,[2] the Regius Professor of Civil Law at Oxford, Tony Honore, proposes that a right of sexual freedom should be included in any Bill of Rights which may be enacted in the United Kingdom, and that the following principles are involved:

(a) The right to sexual freedom consists in the right to use our own bodies as we choose and to touch others with their consent, together with accessory rights to ensure reasonable sexual opportunities.

(b) Sexual freedom may be exercised by those who have reached maturity. The age of maturity is also the age of full responsibility (18).

(c) The principle of sexual freedom or self-rule is a principle of conduct, not of education. (In education, parents, teachers, officials and, so far as concerns them, courts are entitled to give effect to the moral preferences of society.)

I believe that both these sets of principles, seen as an extension of the Wolfenden approach, provide a sound basis for modern, realistic sex laws.

Notes

1. In *Law, Liberty and Morality* (Oxford University Press, 1963).
2. Duckworth, 1978.

Modernizing the Sex Laws

FREETHINKER, JULY 1981

The sex laws have long been a battleground between the (usually religious) upholders of an authoritarian, State-imposed moral code and those – often freethinkers – who take the libertarian view that individual citizens have the right and responsibility to make their own sexual choices freely so long as they do not harm or involve unwilling others.

In Victorian times, puritanical influences on the criminal law reached a high-water mark. A husband's sexual rights over his wife were absolute (and even today he cannot be charged with raping her[1]). Divorce was unavailable, except to the very rich, throughout most of the nineteenth century. Abortion was outlawed under the 1861 Offences Against the

Person Act, male homosexuality by the 1885 'Labouchère Amendment', and incest in 1907. The dissemination of birth control information was fraught with legal risk, as the trial of Besant and Bradlaugh demonstrated. All this moralistic lawmaking was done under the guise of 'protection', with the result that a variety of sexual activities which in fact happened with the willing consent of the participants became classified by the law as 'indecent assaults' and even more serious crimes.

Reform in this area is notoriously difficult. Because many people think there ought to be a law against whatever they dislike, disapprove of or are disgusted by, it is often wrongly assumed that those of us who recognize sound philosophical and legal reasons for decriminalizing consenting sexual behaviour which does not interfere with the rights or privacy of others are actively in favour of whatever we don't think should be crimes – although in fact we may strongly disapprove of some such activities. Indeed, merely to seek an open and rational public debate of such emotive topics as paedophilia exposes one to accusations from such moral malaprops as Mrs Whitehouse of 'promoting' it! Such mental muddle (or, perhaps, calculated muddying of the real issues) makes the task of the would-be reformer arduous and thankless.

However, there have been victories – passage of the Sexual Offences Act and the Abortion Act in 1967 and some other minor piecemeal reforms during the 1970s. And now the Wolfenden Report – which was itself highly controversial when first published in 1958 – seems to have set a new fashion in current jurisprudential orthodoxy: both the Williams report on obscenity and film censorship and the Criminal Law Revision Committee's working paper on sexual offences preface their arguments with acceptance of the 'Wolfenden principle' which held that the correct role of the criminal law in the sphere of sexual conduct was 'to preserve order and decency, to protect the citizen from what is offensive or injurious, and to provide sufficient safeguards against exploitation of others', apart from which it was not the law's proper function to intervene in private lives or to seek to enforce any particular pattern of behaviour.

Even this common-sense philosophy is under raucous attack from the frantic foes of 'permissiveness', who perceive the law's task as the erection of an all-embracing system of moral signposts saying 'DON'T!' But their viewpoint is unlikely to prevail, if only because the practical problems of enforcing the sort of laws they at heart desire would necessitate a Big Brother bugging device in every bedroom in the land – a prospect which should make even the most moralistic policeman quail.

The signals which have so far emerged from the Criminal Law Revision Committee's review are rather mixed. While the Committee's espousal of the 'Wolfenden' approach is welcome, they seem reluctant to apply it wholeheartedly. Although they and their Policy Advisory Committee have evidently made a big effort to look at the subject with realism, compassion and a genuine concern for the best interests of sex offenders, every now and again they have experienced revulsion and moral disgust at what they were contemplating (such as 'an act of bestiality in a cowshed committed by a man of low intelligence and witnessed only by a police officer who was peeping through a chink in the weather-boarding'), and have in effect pitched the 'Wolfenden principle' overboard by refraining from taking its implications to their logical conclusion. For instance, they go to considerable lengths to devise ways to catch naughty goings-on in homosexual clubs, even if nobody present is likely to be offended. This is surely inconsistent with their own declared stance.

In 1974 the Sexual Law Reform Society submitted evidence to the CLRC in which we urged two important matters of principle. First, that the whole concept of 'sexual offences' could usefully be done away with, as its main effect is to create stigmatizing prejudice even before a case comes to court, and all the sexual misbehaviour which the law should properly prohibit and punish could be reclassified as assaults, invasions of privacy, or nuisance. Second, that the terminology of the law, which (for instance) refers to even quite trivial, and sometimes consenting, behaviour as an 'indecent assault' (if one of the parties is below the age of consent), and describes mutual masturbation as 'gross indecency', should be scrapped and replaced by neutral descriptions of prohibited behaviour. But the CLRC have turned down these suggestions. Nor have they been notably liberal in their attitude to substantive reform. To propose lowering the minimum legal age for male homosexual behaviour from 21 to 18 is scarcely adventurous in the light of modern social, medical, and psychological knowledge and in view of the fact that a growing number of European countries now have ages of 16, 15, and even lower.

Indeed, the CLRC's whole approach to the crucially important issue of how best to protect adolescents smacks of wistful paternalism. They seem to think that sex is something young people need guarding against; that 'premature' sexual experience is a major hazard facing most young girls, and that the lure of homosexual seduction is a menace to lots of potentially heterosexual boys. Insofar as there is a grain of truth in such fears, it is largely because the sex education of teenagers is still woefully deficient. And I do *not* mean by 'sex education' merely the 'plumbing' or 'how to do it' bits, but the informed awareness of facts as opposed to fantasies about all aspects of sex (including homosexuality and paedophilia), and the appreciation of the moral and social issues involved in being maturely responsible about one's own and other people's behaviour.

What the Sexual Law Reform Society would like to see is a low 'age of consent' for both heterosexual and homosexual behaviour – we proposed 14 – with an effective 'age of protection' up to the legal age of majority (18), so that during the crucial years of puberty and its immediate aftermath young women and men could be taught the meaning of sexual and moral responsibility, and encouraged to practise it, without the threat of the criminal law hanging over them and their consenting partners, but with civil sanctions in reserve to safeguard the especially vulnerable. For we believe that freedom to choose and the development of a sense of responsibility go hand in hand; and that the best way to instil self-respect and consideration towards others is not to brandish legal or moral

'*Verboten!*' notices at the young, but to encourage them to develop responsive self-awareness.

While the CLRC's Policy Advisory Committee found our proposals 'challenging', they maintained that the criminal law has an important protective role to play. Their final report on the age of consent is a dismayingly unimaginative document. It leaves a long way to go to the elimination of 'victimless crime' and the creation of a positive attitude to teenage sexuality.

It is a serious weakness of the CLRC system (it is a standing committee of the Home Office) that it takes no oral evidence. It only receives written submissions and delivers written reports. I believe that if – on this topic, at least – the CLRC had given its witnesses a chance to meet with it, to discuss face to face the thorny topics it considered, and to be heard 'in the flesh', it might have reached somewhat different conclusions.

For sex, and sex law too, is not a dry, abstract topic. It is a flesh-and-blood matter, arousing strong passions and sparking off spontaneous ideas which need to meet and mingle to produce fresh, constructive insights. Almost a hundred years ago one of the first campaigners against the infamous Labouchère Amendment, the bisexual Victorian literary critic John Addington Symonds, wrote:

> Good Lord! In what different orbits human souls can move. He talks of sex out of legal codes and blue books. I talk of it from human documents, myself, the people I have known, the adulterers and prostitutes of both sexes I have dealt with over bottles of wine and confidences.[2]

Notes

1. This remained the law until 1992.
2. 19 July 1890: *Letters*, vol. III, p. 476. ('blue books' – i.e. Government reports.)

Sex and the Law –
Some Questions for Libertarians

FREE LIFE,[1] VOL. 3, NO. 1, 1982

What should be the law's function?

Our sex laws are in a thoroughly messy state, and need to be drastically recast. Historically, the law's task was seen as the enforcement of a moral code which was derived from religious belief and imposed with the backing of severe criminal sanctions. In a modern, pluralist society this is no longer appropriate. As the Wolfenden Report said in 1957, 'Unless a deliberate attempt is to be made by society, acting through the agency of the law, to equate the sphere of crime with that of sin, there must remain a realm of private morality and immorality which is, in brief and crude terms, not the law's business'.

The Criminal Law Revision Committee have emphasized the primarily protective function of the law in their interim reports on sexual offences. So the next question is:

Who is being protected?

The Wolfenden Committee saw the law's role as being to preserve public order and decency, to prevent offensive or injurious behaviour, and to safeguard the vulnerable against exploitation or corruption. This implies that adult citizens have the right and the responsibility to make their own decisions about their sexual behaviour, so long as they don't harm others. As J. S. Mill pointed out in his essay *On Liberty*, it is going beyond the generally acceptable framework of the criminal law to use it to protect people *from themselves*.

Who is harmed?

Obviously anyone who is physically sexually assaulted, or coerced into sexual activities against their will, is harmed and their assailants should be punished. But is a person who inadvertently stumbles upon people having sexual intercourse in what they believe to be private circumstances, and who is shocked and offended by what she or he sees, sufficiently harmed to justify criminal penalties? Different people have different views as to what is sexually harmful, and to whom. At what age should young people be considered by the law as being old enough to make responsible sexual choices for themselves about their behaviour and its likely harmfulness? And does a prohibitive law itself do harm to a young person who, out of positive desire or mere curiosity, engages in experimental sexual behaviour classified as unlawful? Should there be 'victimless crime' where sexual activity is concerned?

Whose consent?

At present, the law forbids – because of the participants' ages, and/or the circumstances in which the activities take place – much sexual behaviour which is *in fact* consented to, but which *in law* is punishable as 'indecent assault', 'gross indecency', etc. Apart from the loaded legal labelling (for which the Sexual Law Reform Society would like to substitute neutrally factual definitions), the question of principle here is whether *any* sexual act which is, in fact, consented to by the participants should ever be punishable (unless others are unwillingly involved or affronted). If the CLRC's view that the mere fact that sexual conduct is consensual should not always be decisive against its criminality[2] is to be upheld, the Sexual Law Reform Society believes that the burden of proof that prosecutions really are in the public interest in such cases should always rest upon the prosecution, and should be strict and narrowly defined. Libertarians will, I hope, agree that people who have attained puberty should generally be free to decide for themselves what they want to do sexually with their own bodies. . . .

Whose privacy?

The law has traditionally taken the view that some behaviour which is legal in private should be punishable if done in public, because it is offensive to others. Usually the law achieves this result by defining what is a 'public place' (there are different definitions for different purposes) and laying down national and local regulations about conduct in such places. Thus many sexual activities which are acceptable in private – which is a narrower concept than 'indoors', because many indoor premises are public places – are designated by the law as 'indecent' and punishable if done in public. This is so whether uninvolved third parties are actually present and offended or not. The result is that people are frequently brought to court on indecency charges when the only witnesses of their 'indecent' behaviour have been the police. Such a system lends itself to abuse, and lawyers working in this area are all too familiar with allegations of *agent provocateur* tactics and police perjury which, though difficult to verify, indicate that those laws could advantageously be reframed.

Unfortunately, the CLRC has not yet grasped the opportunity to do so. Its Working Paper, whilst recognizing that those who wish to engage in sexual activity in the open air (e.g. in a secluded private garden) are entitled to their privacy provided that they take reasonable precautions not to be overlooked, suggests that the law should properly continue to punish the sexual behaviour of adults on premises which are 'places of common resort', such as clubs, even if all those present and consenting are members, on the ground that such behaviour is intrinsically 'grossly indecent' and that therefore the mere knowledge that it may be taking place is seriously offensive to members of the public who *aren't* present. Such an attitude regresses from the Wolfenden principle, is largely unenforceable without police infiltration and haphazard raids upon suspected premises, and is an unwarranted interference with personal liberty. The moralistic attitudes enshrined in the sex laws die hard, and this proposal reflects the distaste many British people feel at the idea of places which are, in effect, brothels. But such places have always existed, and they will continue to exist whatever the law may say because (however deplorable the fact may be) they meet a demand.

Where the protection of privacy is concerned, a balance has to be struck between the privacy of those who wish to indulge freely in consenting sexual behaviour (whether heterosexual or homosexual, 'moral' or 'immoral') in a secluded place – even though not legally defined as 'in private' – and the privacy of those who are offended by such behaviour. The SLRS believes that a fair and practical solution would be to make the commission of actual nuisance, rather than quibbles about what is technically 'in private' or a 'public place', the guideline for the law in this respect. If 'nuisance' became the test, it would be necessary, in order to secure a conviction, to produce witnesses other than the police who were prepared to say in court that they had been offended by something which they had unintentionally witnessed. The issue would become one of factual offence – not of hypothetical disgust. Suitable provision could be made to prohibit sexual behaviour in specified places primarily used or habitually frequented by children. Such a law would also be a much fairer way of regulating street offences such as soliciting by prostitutes, instead of the harshly unjust laws we now have which allow them to be sent to prison after sufficient previous police cautions and convictions.

Whose permission?

The sex laws raise deep philosophical issues about the nature of society and the claims of personal freedom. It is fashionable these days to attack 'permissiveness' as the source of social and moral ills, and to clamour for stricter laws regulating personal morals, sexual behaviour and freedom of speech. It seems bizarre that such calls mostly come from those who, in other respects, advocate greater economic *laissez-faire* and a robust individualism as the antidote to Britain's material troubles.

The notion of 'permissiveness' begs the all-important question of who has the right to 'permit' or to withhold 'permission' from others to behave as they wish sexually in the first place. Those who speak in this way seem to assume that there are, and should be, authoritative social controls, appropriately enforced by law, over everyone's personal and private choices; and that these controls have laxly been allowed to slip. (The speakers, of course, always see themselves as the eager controllers, and never as the unwillingly controlled.) This model of society is surely totally unacceptable to Libertarians.

The only effective control over personal – and especially sexual – behaviour is the inner one which the more old-fashioned amongst us call conscience. Externally imposed laws can never be a satisfactory substitute for the internal claims of self-respect and concern for others. Of course, too many people may lack a sufficient degree of these qualities; and so the law has a rightful place to function in protecting everyone – and especially the weaker members of society – from physical abuse or psychological coercion. But laws which set out to protect people from themselves, and to impose externally defined 'permissions' upon freely made mutually consenting sexual choices, are self-defeating and ultimately antisocial. By vainly seeking to impose compulsion in spheres of personal behaviour where truly ethical choices can only be made in freedom, the law becomes the enemy of those very values of personal responsibility which it should promote, and creates 'victimless crime'.

Who is victimized?

If the purpose of the law is to prevent people from being sexually victimized, it must ensure that nobody is victimized *by the law* for making what are essentially personal and private choices about their own sexual behaviour. By all means let the law punish – and, where necessary, punish severely – those who violate others' sexual freedom by rape, actual assault, or mental coercion. In doing so, the law is rightfully protecting the sexually victimized. But let the law cease to punish – as it is now doing by the hundreds if not thousands every year – those who, merely because their sexual preferences and choices are unorthodox, or regarded by some as being 'immoral', fall foul of a code which is no longer appropriate in today's modern, pluralist society. For these people are cruelly victimized by the law. And let society be clear-minded and unhypocritical about who the real victims of the existing situation are.

Whose life? Whose rights? Whose responsibility?

Libertarians will, I hope, agree that the questions raised by the application of law to sexual behaviour concern the very roots of social justice. The basic question is: *What sort of a society do we wish to live in?* One where each individual is seen as uniquely important in his or her own right, and in which positive regard and compassion for others are valued as much as our own wants; or one in which flesh-and-blood people are sacrificed to abstract principles. Who owns my life? Who owns my mind? Who owns my body? To believe that *my* life is the most important business in the universe to me is not antisocial selfishness: it is, on the contrary, the right starting point and the surest foundation for me to become socially concerned, and useful to others. Such a mutually involved, yet liberty-loving, society can only exist in an atmosphere of social, political, and legal freedom. This is more than a mere matter of balance – it is a question of belief. If you believe profoundly, as I do, that the first and foremost possession to which each one of us is rightfully entitled is *ourselves* – our minds and our bodies – with all the moral and practical consequences of responsible ownership which flow from that, you must be aware that sexual politics – the business of securing proper recognition within society of individual sexual freedoms – is an essential component of a Libertarian attitude to life.

Notes

1. Journal of the Libertarian Alliance.
2. CLRC Working Paper on Sexual Offences, 1980, para. 10.

Lessons of Section 28

OPEN MIND,[1] AUTUMN 1988

Now that Section 28 of the Local Government Act[2] has, alas, reached the Statute Book unscathed by all the widespread criticisms during its parliamentary passage, what lessons can we learn from this episode to promote future more successful campaigning for equality? The following occur to me for a start.

Ignorance about, and prejudice against, homosexual people is at least as widespread today as it was twenty years ago. The essential task of public education, which should have been embarked upon after the 1967 Sexual Offences Act decriminalized the private behaviour of two consenting men aged over 21, has been shirked by successive Governments and has been beyond the resources and competence of gay organizations or of wider sex education groups. This is not just a gay matter: accurately informed and sensible attitudes to other people's sexuality, as well as to one's own, is essential for happy living in a healthy society. How can we get this firmly onto the national agenda?

Being sweetly reasonable is not enough. I am not suggesting that we should not go on arguing our case logically and politely – but we have to recognize that many of our homophobic opponents have such an irrational fear of homosexuality that their loathing of homosexual practices spills over into loathing of anyone whom they know or think is homosexual. Unpleasant though it is to realize, they regard us as evil, antisocial people undeserving of equal citizenship simply because we are who we are. And they have demonstrated their political power.

In advocating equality we have few stalwart friends amongst politicians or the media. Even the Labour Party's front bench had to be dragged kicking and screaming to belatedly attack Clause 28 in the Commons, after initially pronouncing themselves satisfied with it. So much for party conference votes! Vocal Tory opponents of the clause were almost as scarce as snowstorms at the equator. Apart from television news, the press virtually ignored the massive public protests against the clause – although one would have thought that 20,000 people marching peacefully in Manchester and more than 30,000 in London would have been newsworthy.

Whether cynically or from conviction, this Government is prepared to pander to populist prejudice against unpopular groups. In the shadow of AIDS, this is deeply worrying: if a similar attitude is maintained against drug misusers, prostitutes, etc., the outlook for public health will be extremely grave. The exclusion from Section 28 of 'anything done for the purpose of treating or preventing the spread of disease' is irrelevant and illogical: what health educators 'promote' is safer sexual practices, regardless of the gender of those engaging in them. (Doubtless the bigoted moralists behind Section 28 would like to ban this too: their simplistic, sovereign remedy is to say 'Don't'!)

The Government was unwilling to amend the clause so as to reduce the conceptual and semantic muddles underlying it. I find this dismaying. It is a primary precept of good legislation that it should be as clear and precise in its meaning as the skills of parliamentary draftsmen can make it. Yet despite repeated complaints that no one really knew just what 'promoting homosexuality' actually meant, Government spokesmen persisted throughout in adhering to this cloudy formula, and even resisted amendments designed to exclude from it activities intended to discourage discrimination against or to protect the civil rights of anyone. Their Alice-in-Wonderland reasoning for this was that even activities intended to combat anti-gay prejudice would constitute 'promotion' of homosexuality, since they would discriminate in its favour! I find this quite bizarre. Ministers also maintained that there was a sinister move afoot to 'glamourize' homosexuality. If, looking at the current social climate as a whole, they really believe that, they are capable of believing anything.

Section 28 is based on a bogus prospectus, but expresses real concerns. The bogus pretext was a handful of trumped-up and largely fictional cases of alleged 'promotion' of homosexuality by a few left-wing councils who had appointed gay rights committees, anti-discrimination study groups, and so forth. Part of the problem arose from genuine misunderstanding about the way in which language was being used – a frequent cause of political and social conflict. The gay liberationist jargon which is still so assiduously used by left-wing gay activists is now somewhat dated and is never going to get a fair hearing from traditionalist opponents, who find the concepts ludicrous and the terminology abhorrent. Somehow, a constructive dialogue has to be opened up with fair-minded politicians, educationists and others who are willing to comprehend the fears and anger of both homophiles and homophobes who evidently feel so threatened by each other.

The gay response to Section 28 has been magnificent, but needs stronger political clout. I am not one of those who turns up their nose at all the articulate anger that has been generated against the clause. The huge, well-behaved protest marches have been impressive and splendidly organized. If we can thank Dame Jill Knight MP and her cohorts for anything, it is for mobilizing far more gay energy and anger than on any other issue that I can remember. But we do need to beware of the lure of street theatre as a substitute for much duller and more traditional forms of political action. Parliamentary abseiling and chaining oneself to newsreaders' legs makes a spectacular point, but is unlikely to shift politicians' attitudes. Those of us who are dedicated not merely to erasing the infamy of this tawdry little clause, but to ensuring that a social climate is created as rapidly as possible in which the homosexual people of Britain are candidly accepted by others as equal and worthy fellow citizens, have more serious political work to do.

I cannot do better than to end by quoting my friend Dr Franklin E. Kameny of Washington, a veteran American gay activist, who wrote this almost twenty years ago:

> We ask for acceptance as full equals, not as poor unfortunate creatures in need of compassion and some crumbs of sympathy. We ask for nothing that is really more than or different from what everyone else asks – and what in our culture everyone is brought up to expect as a matter of course: our basic rights and equality as citizens; our human dignity; acceptance of us and judgment of us, each upon his own individual merits and by criteria reasonably relevant to the context of the judgment; the right as human beings to achieve our full potential and dignity, and the right as citizens to make our maximum contribution to the society in which we live; recognition that our right to the pursuit of our happiness is as inalienable as the right of all others to the pursuit of theirs; and the right to love whom we wish, how we wish – all while being true to ourselves as the homosexuals that we are and that we have the absolute moral right to be.
>
> We recognize the changes in traditional attitudes which are needed to accept us in this way, and the difficulties inherent in the making of such changes; but we are increasingly firm in our justified insistence that such changes be made, and quickly, because they are essential to the fundamental prerogatives of citizenship and of humanity, of justice and of morality – and of Christianity in its truest and most meaningful sense.[3]

Our response to Section 28 must launch from a self-respecting platform such as this. There is no less that we can demand.

Notes

1. Journal of the Conservative Group for Homosexual Equality.
2. This section of the Local Government Act 1988 states that a local authority shall not 'intentionally promote homosexuality or publish material with the intention of promoting homosexuality', or 'promote the teaching in any maintained school of the acceptability of homosexuality as a pretended family relationship'.
3. Franklin E. Kameny, 'Gay Is Good', in *The Same Sex*, ed. R. W. Weltge (Philadelphia: Pilgrim Press, 1969), pp. 129ff.

PART TWO

POLITICAL/SOCIAL

Why Not?

Save for Joyce Grenfell's comically respectable middle-aged old-tyme dancing ladies doing the military two-step 'bust to bust' because of the scarcity of male partners, same-sex dancing in public was quite unthinkable in 1950s and 1960s Britain. Where it did occur, at least between men, and however discreetly, it frequently gave rise to prosecutions for 'disorderly behaviour'. So for the mid-century English homosexual, a visit to the gay clubs of Amsterdam was like a breath of fresh air. The novel flavour of such foreign freedom is conveyed in the following piece, written in 1960.

Men. Dancing together. Women dancing together is OK: we're used to that. But *men*. Dancing *together*!

At first the sight of men dancing together astonishes an Englishman. And yet: why not?

On a recent visit to the Netherlands I had the opportunity to see for myself the effects of legal acceptance on a homosexual community. Dutch law recognizes two age groups – from 18 to 21, and 21 and above[1] – within which homosexuality is legal for both sexes, and in Amsterdam there are two clubs which provide social functions for adult members.

The first thing to be clear about is that both clubs are well conducted. And they exist with the approval of the police. After all, homosexuals are going to meet somewhere, and the fact that they have these clubs enables the authorities to clamp down on any objectionable public behaviour the more firmly because they know there is somewhere that homosexuals can meet in a pleasant atmosphere without causing offence to anyone.

Neither club advertises, and their premises are unobtrusive and discreetly labelled. At the clubhouse of the main Dutch homosexual organization (COC) you go in through the side door at what appears to be the entrance to a warehouse block. Inside, your passport is examined at the reception desk, and for Fl.2.50 (about 5 shillings) a tourist's weekly entrance permit is supplied. Full membership for residents is strictly supervised; people wishing to join have to prove their respectability and *bona fides* – no prostitutes or other doubtful characters are allowed – and to be over 21.

In the club hall is a pleasant bar, above which hangs a portrait of Queen Juliana. There are tables at which coffee and drinks are served – and the dance floor. Women homosexuals belong here as well as men, and the club has a female strength of about 220 out of the 1300 Amsterdam members, but there are rarely more than two or three mixed couples on the floor, which is usually crowded with pairs of the same sex dancing together and obviously enjoying themselves.

On first arriving I suppose most tourists sit down to digest the scene and have a drink. You see: it's so normal. So ordinary. The company consists of well-behaved, soberly dressed, average looking people. The drinks are good and quite cheap – no clip joint this – and the waiters will never ask you to buy. Nor, indeed, can you expect to be approached by anyone else. The Dutch all seem to speak excellent English, but they are nervous about trying it out uninvited. And mostly they are with small groups of their own friends, though usually willing to dance with a visitor who is prepared to ask them.

This club, which also has television and billiard rooms and a library, represents only one side of the organization's work. The other is centred at their office near the main railway station. Here people come to discuss their problems and to arrange for legal, religious or psychiatric advice.

Most legal troubles apparently arise from the law's restrictions on homosexual behaviour between people of over and under 21. Formerly the age of consent for boys, as for girls, was 16, but it was raised in 1911 by a clause which was introduced into parliament late one night by a Catholic minister and passed by an almost empty House. (One cannot help being struck by the resemblance to our own Labouchère Amendment on hearing this.) The COC say that this provision creates some difficult situations for people in their late teens and early twenties, but feel that it would be politically impossible to alter it.

Unfortunately there are cases of adults interfering with young children in any country; and with such incidents involving an adult and a child of the same sex in Holland, the organization is often officially asked to help and to give advice. This it always tries to do, though the problem is quite a distinct one from normal homosexual relationships and it must be difficult for any well-adjusted adult to understand how another person can be sexually interested in young children.

Good relations with the probation services and with the churches have been the result of hard work over many years, as the organization's president, Bob Angelo, explained. He is an impressive man, with a clear sense of mission, and must have needed immense courage when organizing the club just after the war. From the beginning he sought, and obtained, police sanction; and once the idea caught on, membership grew rapidly. It is now about 3000, and branches have been started in most of the other large towns of Holland besides Amsterdam.

But even success has its drawbacks. Three or four years ago one of the committee members apparently decided that the social side was now so flourishing that he bought the building which then housed the club in order to run it on purely commercial lines. Consequently there was a split, and the original premises is now another homosexual club which, though run for profit, is very pleasant too.

It serves excellent food. But there also one will not be pressed to eat and drink, and – what would be foolhardy in Britain – in both places dancers leave their cigarette lighters, drinks, and even wallets, unconcernedly on their tables to reserve their places. The general verdict seems to be that, if this second club has the better floor and decor, the first one is far more closely linked to its members' welfare.

And what effect has all this had on Amsterdam? Most people are probably unconcerned, as they should be. Dutch homosexuals, though, seem to be better adjusted to life and to lack the tenseness so common over here. They can relax, accept themselves, and deal with the genuine problems which life presents without being distracted by the knowledge that they are technically criminals. And in contrast to London, there are hardly any signs of homosexuality in the streets or public lavatories.

Returning to England one finds it hard to understand why something similar cannot be done over here. Surely it is in everybody's interest? Mr Butler[2] wants 'vice' off the streets; the police want their present unpleasant tasks eased; the general public want to forget a squalid, boring tale of injustices; and homosexuals want somewhere to meet their own kind freely and sociably as people rather than sordidly and furtively as criminals.

Well, why not?

Notes

1. Following the Speijer Report (see pp. 176ff. below), Dutch law was changed in 1971 to provide a common age of consent of 16 for homosexual and heterosexual behaviour.
2. The Rt Hon R. A. Butler, the Home Secretary.

Towards a Sexually Sane Society

ALBANY TRUST WINTER TALK, 5 MARCH 1963

For several years during the early 1960s, the Albany Trust held a series of well-attended Winter Talks in central London. To conclude the first series, I spoke about the social aspects of the Trust's work.

I have called this talk 'Towards a Sexually Sane Society' because I believe that the society we are living in today, at any rate in this country, is not a particularly sane one in this respect. It might even be described as a sexually insane society, or at least one that is mad about sex in various ways. This, I think, is an unfortunate state of affairs which we should try to put right.

I believe it was Bernard Shaw who said that there has been more nonsense talked about sex than about any other subject; and if one reads the newspapers or listens to debates in Parliament, one certainly gets the strong feeling that this is true. I once talked to an eminent member of the House of Lords who had previously sat in the Commons for many years,[1] and he said to me: 'You know, when those fellows get up and talk about sex they completely take leave of their senses. From the way they carry on, you would think that every girl was a shrinking young virgin and every young man was a brute who wanted to rape the first woman he came across, and it is terribly difficult to get them to be in the least balanced or sensible about anything of this kind.'

Sex, of course, is just one aspect of life. It is a very important aspect – indeed, a fundamental appetite, like sleeping or eating or thinking – and one cannot ignore it. By trying to ignore it or suppress it, one merely succeeds in making it into an overwhelmingly important thing which gets out of all proportion in life, and lots of people nowadays make far too much fuss about it, usually in quite the wrong ways. Three main categories of these spring to mind. First of all, there are the puritans – the people who think the whole thing is dirty and ought to be suppressed. These are the people who provide the censors and the punishers, and unfortunately they still dominate our law-making and law-giving. Second, there are the people who set out to exploit sex in a commercial way; not just the people who live on prostitution and make big profits out of that, but the sexual titillators, among whom I would include not merely pornographers, but also the sensational press, who do it under the guise of preaching good behaviour and saying 'How shocking all this is', while all the time they are really creating more relish for it. And then there are the unfortunate people who as a result of all this titillation and repression become so sexually obsessed that . . . their whole thought and life-drive is dominated by the unsuccessful search for satisfactory sex.

I think that all these English attitudes are particularly unbalanced and immature; in fact, we are quite rightly regarded as the laughing-stock of the Continentals in this respect (although I wonder whether they are all that much better than we are). You may have read Mr Malcolm Muggeridge in this week's *New Statesman*, commenting on the recent report *Towards a Quaker View of Sex*.[2] He says: 'Sex, to the French, remains pleasurable or humorous. They cannot grasp it as a duty. The wrongs of homosexuals condemned to seek their pleasures in public lavatories, which so harrowed the Quakers, leave them cold.' So those who seek a healthier and more matter-of-fact approach are themselves sensationalized in this sort of way. The Quaker report has been commented upon in the press in ways which are simply a grotesque garbling of what they did in fact say.

The more one tries to do social work to help people who have sexual problems, the more one realizes that workers in all the fields of family difficulties and sex matters come up against a mountain not merely of prejudice, but of wilful ignorance. People don't want to know about sex; they not merely don't know about it, they actively don't *want* to know. This is especially true of homosexuality, because homosexuality is a subject about which one either knows a good deal or else one knows nothing at all; and those who don't want to know will not be told. I have heard of an 18-year-old boy who was troubled about his homosexual feelings, and who, having hesitated for months, came down to breakfast one day and said to his parents: 'I've got something very important to tell you: I'm homosexual.' His mother, who was pouring out the coffee, did not even bother to look up. She said, in reproving tones: 'Don't be silly, dear, that's not a funny joke at all.' In other words, 'This couldn't possibly happen to *my* child – it's always those nasty people down the road'. I have also had the extraordinary experience of discussing this subject with one of the Members of Parliament who had expressed himself most violently against the Wolfenden Report in a House of Commons debate, and who, after some quite friendly and reasonable conversation with me, suddenly looked very puzzled and asked: 'Is it really true that these homosexuals actually find the idea of going to bed with a woman distasteful?'

This is the basic problem which we at the Albany Trust are up against. Almost in spite of ourselves, we are becoming a social service agency for quite a lot of our time, and in the process we are learning quite a lot about all sorts of people. The ignorance which exists about homosexuality is quite appalling. I have heard of a couple of cases only this week of parents who have been so shocked and upset by finding that their children had homosexual tendencies that they either turned them out of the house or assaulted them. And the children, the people who come to us for advice, will often say: 'Well, I have lived with my parents for ten, fifteen or twenty years, and I don't know what to do, and life is very difficult.' Usually I ask them whether their parents have any idea about their homosexuality, and they reply: 'Oh, no – I couldn't possibly tell them. I would not know how to start.' This is a very difficult problem, which everybody has got to solve for themselves, but which far too few are making any attempt to solve at all.

These attitudes are of course largely due to the law, which is why we want to change the law; but it is not the only factor. I believe that quite apart from any question of the law, there is a genuine fear among the population at large of the unknown, and a dislike of the different. However silly it may be, there are many people who feel that homosexuals are a threat to their security – to their emotional security, if not their physical security – and that is why it is not sufficient for us to speak of 'persecution', and to present homosexuals as a minority which has a legitimate grievance, in order to get the law changed. This is, of course, true; but we have got to take a more positive approach, and somehow to make society surer than it is at present that the homosexuals in its midst are not a danger to it.

How are we to move towards a more sexually sane society? First of all, I think that everyone who wishes to do so could usefully begin by making an honest self-criticism of their own lives and characters, seeing if they could be more objective about them and moving towards a better outlook in themselves. And those who are homosexual must be sufficiently honest with themselves to think seriously about some of the most common criticisms of homosexuals which are made by the public at large, in the press, in Parliament and so forth, even if they feel that these criticisms are largely unfounded and born of ignorance. I would ask everyone, nevertheless, to try and think what they can do about these things, both as individuals and as members of a community; and in discussing them, I would like people also to speculate how far the situation with respect to these matters will or ought to be different a few years after the law has been changed?

The first of these very common criticisms is that far too many homosexuals are indiscriminately promiscuous, and that they positively enjoy indulging in furtive and sordid sexual activities, often in public places – not merely because they are forced to do this, but because they prefer it that way and get a kick out of it. Possibly there are far worse things than promiscuity; and much of the public misbehaviour which goes on may not bother anybody else. But, to say the least, it does not help to improve the public's idea of homosexuals one little bit; and I think we should lose no opportunity of stressing that the present state of the law against private relationships tends to increase the amount of promiscuous and public misbehaviour, rather than to curb it.

Then there is the common belief that homosexuals are a danger to youth, because they would all like to seduce teenagers if they got the chance. This also may be a wild exaggeration, but I cannot help being conscious that behaviour of this sort does go on. Of course, it is unrealistic to expect that teenagers who are homosexual will happily refrain from all sexual activity until they reach their twenty-first birthday; and it may be that implementation of the Wolfenden Report will create a difficult situation for youngsters if the law is altered to make 21 the consenting age. As you know, the Homosexual Law Reform Society stands for the Wolfenden Report, and for this particular recommendation; but I think there is no harm in discussing its possible consequences. Perhaps, with the spreading frankness that there is these days about heterosexual teenagers' sexual activities, there may also come about a greater degree of frankness and understanding about homosexual teenage behaviour as well. But it would surely be a good thing for anyone who does have contact with teenagers in this category to think very hard about the desirability, in their own best interests, of discouraging them from a path which we all know is fraught with personal difficulties and dangers, and also with some inevitable unhappiness.

In *Towards a Quaker View of Sex*, the authors deny the notion that all homosexual relationships are necessarily sinful just because they are homosexual. This is rather a remarkable view for a Christian body to put forward, and some of the press commentaries on the Quaker report have said, quite rightly, that it is not remarkable so much for what it says, but it *is* remarkable because of the people who are saying it, as this is the first time that a Christian group has come out so clearly and explicitly in favour of revising entirely our ideas about what is and what is not sinful. To the Quakers, what matters is the quality and depth of any human relationship – the extent of sincere care and feeling for the other person. It is this which determines whether or not any relationship, whether heterosexual or homosexual, is good or evil.

> Members of this group [they say] have been depressed quite as much by the utter abandon of many homosexuals, especially those who live in homosexual circles as such, as by the absurdity of the condemnation rained down upon the well-behaved. One must disapprove the promiscuity and selfishness, the utter lack of any real affection, which is the stamp of so many adult relationships, heterosexual as well as homosexual. We see nothing in them often but thinly disguised lust, unredeemed by that real concern which has always been the essential Christian requirement in a human relationship. But it is also obvious that the really promiscuous and degraded homosexual has not been helped by the total rejection he has had to face. Society has not said 'if you do that, that is all right, but as to the other, we cannot approve of that'. It has said 'whatever you do must be wrong: indeed you *are* wrong'. We must consider whether it is not the relationship that matters, rather than the acts that it may involve. Then homosexuals will be helped to face the implications of thin selfish relationships and society will accept homosexuals as human beings.

This brings me on to my third critical talking point. It has been said that homosexuals can usually have some lovers and plenty of acquaintances, but they have very few friends. Is this true, and if so need it be true? Is there anything, in other words, in the essential nature of a homosexual which makes him inevitably bound to be more self-centred and less capable of friendship than a heterosexual is, because he is unreliable, or even downright dishonest, in his treatment of other people? I do not think so, and I know a lot of homosexuals who are the opposite of all these things. But there are also a great many who *are* like this, and what can we do to persuade them that it is unnecessary, and a mistake, both for themselves and for everyone else?

In Holland, there exists an organization called the COC, which you may have read about recently in the *Observer*.[3] It has worked for sixteen years with considerable success to foster a degree of *esprit de corps* among both men and women homosexuals in a way which unfortunately is still impossible here until the law is changed, but which points a way ahead. This is more than just a social club, although there is quite a good clubhouse. They aim at helping people to resolve their personal problems in the most fruitful and constructive way that they can; and wherever possible, to establish permanent relationships based on affection in place of casual, promiscuous ones. And not only do they encourage people to face up to their own position and accept themselves honestly; they also help them to establish franker and more sincere and honest relationships with their families, with their employers, even, and with the community around them. Their whole aim is not to separate off homosexuals from society and bring them together in a little cliquish group, but to integrate them with the community. In other words, they do not encourage them to live the whole of their social lives within the homosexual group; they rather try to provide an atmosphere of background relaxation which will enable their members not only to be friendly amongst themselves, but to be more sociable with other people and to mix in heterosexual society. This, I think, is a good thing – this aim at personal integration into the community, rather than at separating the homosexual's life as a homosexual from the rest of his life. If the Dutch can do it, why is it so impossible in this country? Even if it cannot yet be done in an organized way, because of the law, why is it impossible for people to attempt it individually, by bringing more of this spirit into their own lives and into the lives of others?

I ask this because I do feel that the sort of attitudes and behaviour that one finds among numbers of English homosexuals are not particularly healthy, or particularly helpful to other people. At the Albany Trust we do come up against some hard cases, and one cannot help seeing what a large part human selfishness plays in creating a lot of needless unhappiness. The callousness with which so many people treat others, when they ought to be only too aware from their own experience of life how vulnerable other people can be, is quite lamentable. Over the past month, for instance, I have seen about twenty people whose basic trouble was the same in every case: they were all lonely. And several of them had reached the pitch of depression needed to drive them into our office to talk about it because somebody else had let them down.

I should like to think that most of the Albany Trust's active supporters are not in the habit of letting people down, and that they would even make a point of seeking out – instead of running away from – the difficult person who presents a bit of a problem, and trying to repair some of the damage. I do think that a lot of the personal problems which homosexual people have in their lives, and the dangerously nervous states which many of them get into, are caused by the legal and social attitudes of our society, because these cause a 'splitting off' of the sexual part of a homosexual's nature, and of his sex life, from all the rest of it – his working life and his family life – so that everything becomes unnecessarily difficult and confused for him. In these circumstances, it is scarcely surprising that some homosexuals develop rather fragmented personalities, and become incapable of sustaining a really deep, mature relationship with anyone.

Now, you may fairly ask me, 'What are you doing about it at the Albany Trust?' . . . I believe that our main achievement in the five years that we have existed is to make it possible to discuss this subject openly at political meetings, university union debates, rotary clubs, religious groups, and sometimes even Mothers' Unions. Until about five years ago, homosexuality was totally unmentionable, and it is a very good thing that it is now an accepted topic for the average discussion group's winter programme, so that over this winter we have been getting requests for about two talks a month.

The Albany Trust is pursuing three main aims – those of education, research, and social help. In the field of education we publish, besides *Man and Society*, various pamphlets and literature aimed at parents, teachers, magistrates, doctors, and other people who have influence or authority, and who should know about this problem, with the aim of making them better acquainted with the facts (as distinct from the myths) about homosexuality. We have just co-operated with the National Council for Civil Liberties in producing a booklet called *Arrest*, which is a guide to the citizen's rights if he is taken into custody by the police.

As regards research, we have two projects in blueprint, and are only waiting for the necessary funds in order to get them started. (Fundraising is a long and difficult business, and one has to be patient, however unwillingly.) The first of these research projects is for a study of court cases during a specified period in the London area, and also in a provincial centre. The second proposed research would attempt to find out what public opinion about homosexuality is, as distinct from what we are told it is. We are always being told, by Home Secretaries and Members of Parliament and other 'knowledgeable' persons, that there is a terrific weight of opposition to this reform. Yet whenever we go around speaking, we always win debates by huge majorities: we always find everybody we talk to agrees with us once we have put the case for reform to them, and they are often quite indignant that the law has not been changed long ago. Perhaps we would find, through some research, that most people who have not had it drawn to their attention have no strong views on the subject at all, but are probably mildly hostile on the strength of reading or hearing occasional things such as court reports. A lot of these people probably know very little about homosexuals, and it would be very useful to find out if this is so, and what their impressions are.

In the sphere of social help we have, as I said earlier, a continuous stream of people coming to us at our office, whom we try to help as best we can by putting them in touch with suitable doctors, clergymen, lawyers, and other advisers. If we had sufficient time and money to advertise the fact that we help people in this way, we would get more than we could cope with. The fact that all the people who come to us just arrive, without our doing any advertising to bring them in, does make us feel that there is a great need for very much more positive social help than exists at present for people who are puzzled and worried about their sexual lives. Some of the people who come to us are in quite dire straits, and we have had men admitted as in-patients to psychiatric hospitals within 24 or 48 hours; but most of them are just people who feel much better for a friendly chat, and go away after it with a rather more balanced outlook on life. Our counsellors in this work give a great deal of time and trouble to it – far more than we could do ourselves. We are especially grateful to people like the Camberwell Samaritans, who have been a great help to several people with quite serious problems just recently, and also to bodies such as the Voluntary Hostels Conference, who had a very interesting symposium on homosexuality a few months ago, attended by a great many probation officers, hostel wardens, and others who wield a great deal of influence in the social work field.

We find that people who have been in prison and come to us asking for help in finding jobs are a big problem, because unfortunately there is more prejudice against ex-prisoners who have been in prison for a homosexual offence than there is against somebody who has merely stolen a few thousand pounds from the petty cash, for instance. This is a fault in social attitudes which is going to take a long time to put right, but we do what we can for ex-prisoners, even if it is not very much – I know of some professionally qualified men who have been six or nine months without succeeding in getting even the most menial job after they have come out of prison.

Growing out of these small beginnings, there is a very healthy realization among social workers of all kinds that homosexuals are human beings with problems – not people who automatically deserve punishment; that in this respect the law is an ass, and that the social and human problems of homosexual people have got to be coped with regardless of what the law theoretically demands. All this growing awareness of the problems that homosexuals are up against is a hopeful sign, and it has made us feel that the time may be riper now than it was two years ago (when we first suggested it) to get funds and backing for the idea of a psychosexual out-patients' clinic, where not only homosexuals but anybody with sexual difficulties and problems can go for help which is skilled, sympathetic, and inexpensive. The Albany Trust convened some meetings about this at Church House two years ago. They came to nothing, unfortunately, but we are now trying to revive the idea and get wider support for it.

From what I have been saying, you will see that there is a great deal to be done and not nearly enough people, time or money to do it with. I have been helping the Albany Trust and the Homosexual Law Reform Society in one capacity or another ever since they started, and I am more than ever convinced as a result of doing so that law reform is an essential step towards a sexually sane society. I have also come to realize that law reform by itself is not enough; it will be merely preliminary to the real job which the Albany Trust must continue doing after the law is changed, of helping everybody in this country who has a sexual problem, whether it is a heterosexual one or a homosexual one, to find the way towards a happier, a healthier, and a fuller life. After all, our lives here on earth are very short, and we should not be having to waste a minute of them on unnecessary or artificially created problems.

Notes

1. Lord Brabazon of Tara (d. 1964).
2. *Towards a Quaker View of Sex*, ed. A. Heron (Friends Home Service Committee, 1963).
3. 13 January 1963.

Time for Sanity

WOLVERHAMPTON EXPRESS AND STAR, MAY 1963

I had many requests for articles from the national and local press during the 1960s. The editors wanted me to deal with the hitherto 'unmentionable' topic of homosexuality in a manner which would be acceptable at the middle-class breakfast table. This and the following example – curiously, from the same town in the same month – are fairly typical.

The Vassall case[1] has again brought homosexuality into the news. Speakers in both Houses of Parliament made the obvious point that law reform on the lines advocated by the Wolfenden Committee would remove a fruitful source of blackmail from the espionage agent's armoury in this country; yet this suggestion is still viewed with a marked lack of enthusiasm by many MPs whose attitude towards homosexuality remains fixed in the tradition of unrealism which immortalized the courtiers of King Canute.

It has been well said that Parliament can do anything except turn a man into a woman; but in regard to sexual behaviour, some of our politicians seem to imagine that Victorian laws framed in psychological ignorance before Freud had ever been heard of are good enough for Britain in the 1960s. The grandmother of parliaments has said: 'There shall be no homosexuals', and that must be that.

If Dr Kinsey's figure of 4 per cent of the US white population who are exclusively homosexual throughout their lives is halved for safety and applied to this country, it would indicate that there are probably at least 1.5 million men and women in Britain who are capable of emotional attachments only to their own sex. In addition, a much larger number are bisexual in varying degrees.

Here is a sizeable social problem. What causes homosexuality is far from agreed by the medical 'experts', but even if a single biological or psychological reason for it could be found (and in fact, the causes probably differ from person to person), the task of remedying the situation for everyone concerned is obviously out of the question. Only a tiny proportion of homosexuals ever receive medical attention, and even those who want desperately to be 'cured' often have to wait as long as six months before there is a vacancy for them to begin treatment, which is usually lengthy, and whose success is by no means a foregone conclusion.

So most homosexuals must face the prospect of living out their lives as they are. Even with a more tolerant law, their personal and social problems would still be considerable. Homosexuals are often blamed for being promiscuous, fickle and unstable. But how many marriages would last as long as they do if there was no legally binding tie and no strong social pressure to maintain the family? When the law says that *all* sexual acts between consenting male homosexuals, whatever their age and even if committed in the privacy of their own homes, are serious crimes, it is surprising, not that so many homosexual relationships fail to endure, but that in spite of the legal and social antipathy, so many people still make the attempt to live with a companion as their emotional drives impel them to do.

But what is not surprising in these circumstances is that a lot of homosexuals are highly strung, neurotic and troubled people. The laws which make their private lives a public crime are responsible for far more psychological disturbance and general ill-health among them than is their homosexuality itself. If allowed a minimum of legal toleration and social acceptance, many of them would live much more stable, happy and constructive lives than they do at present.

It is true that relatively few homosexuals get prosecuted for their behaviour in private. But the constant threat of police investigations into the most personal aspects of their lives is a perpetual nightmare to many quite harmless people, some of whom develop persecution mania as a result. And when the police do start investigations of this kind, the methods used to obtain confessions and corroborative evidence concerning private acts are sometimes disturbing and distasteful to those of us who believe that English justice should have equal regard to the liberty of everyone, even if he belongs to a minority which is viewed by some people with disfavour.

Their legal position unquestionably makes homosexuals vulnerable to blackmail and other forms of thuggery. When the homosexual occupies a responsible or confidential position (as many do), this impinges directly upon the security of the State. But in more mundane circumstances, the effects for individuals can be just as serious. Sometimes, people who are not themselves homosexuals are victimized too. Recent cases I have heard of include that of a man who was robbed by two youths who broke into his flat and ransacked it, saying: 'We know you're queer, so you won't dare tell the police' (he did, and was told there had been a dozen similar cases recently in that district); an undergraduate who was blackmailed to purchase for £50 a tape recording alleged to have been made when he rashly accepted an invitation to a homosexual party; and a man who has had all his clothes and other personal belongings stolen under threat of being falsely accused of homosexual conduct by a bedless stranger in London to whom he had good-naturedly offered a couch for the night.

It is now nearly six years since the Wolfenden Committee reported, all but unanimously, that homosexual behaviour between consenting adults in private should no longer be a criminal offence. Their recommendation has been strongly supported by many church leaders (including both Archbishops and the Bishop of Birmingham), doctors, social workers and newspapers. There can be no possible justification for continuing to keep a law which is so discriminatory, harmful and spasmodically enforced, and it is surely the duty of those who are responsible to grasp the nettle of reform without further delay.

Note

1. Involving a homosexual civil servant in the Admiralty who was blackmailed by the Russians into spying for them.

Ignorance Is Not Enough

WOLVERHAMPTON CHRONICLE, MAY 1963

The British are a kindly race. Their benevolence to people and animals in distress is evidenced by the multitude of voluntary welfare societies and good causes which thrive in our country. We like to feel, and on the whole rightly, that when a need is made known, we can count ourselves among those who will make an effort to help.

Some such needs are obvious. Others are controversial, or at any rate they have to be explained. The relief of those handicapped by an abnormal sexual temperament is a social need of this kind, but one which is coming to be seen by increasing numbers of people as a very important aspect of mental health.

Until a few years ago, homosexuality was never openly discussed, and the condition itself was barely acknowledged to exist, apart from occasional cryptic references in court reports to men charged with 'a serious offence'. But first Kinsey, and then the Wolfenden Report, opened the way to public discussion of this problem.

Most people are now at least vaguely aware that homosexuality – attraction to one's own sex – is an involuntary condition, and that homosexuals comprise a sizeable segment of the community. There are probably about two million men and women in Britain today who are exclusively or predominantly homosexual in their emotional make-up.

The first reaction of many people to the Wolfenden Committee's recommendation that homosexual behaviour between consenting adults in private should no longer be a criminal offence is perhaps one of distaste. But if we try not to allow ourselves to be swayed only by our feelings, and instead consider the subject dispassionately, the logic of the Wolfenden proposal is impressive.

Not only is the existing law arbitrarily severe in singling out for punishment this one group of sexual sinners, but its social effects are undoubtedly evil and unhealthy. It is these social effects that everyone, and especially parents, should consider in judging the matter for themselves.

The time of puberty is always a stormy and difficult one for youngsters. How much more emotionally turbulent it must be for the many boys who first of all realize that, unlike the majority of their fellows, they are not growing up to be interested in girls, and then become aware that this personal peculiarity, which they did not ask to happen to them, will make them be treated as criminals unless they lead a life of complete chastity.

There are very few people who are austere enough voluntarily to renounce all thoughts of love, and its pleasures, and to do without the close emotional companionship that human beings naturally seek, merely because the law says they must. Rather, such a law invites secrecy, furtiveness and anonymous sexual adventures on the part of those affected by it, and thus encourages the very promiscuity and public misbehaviour which everyone dislikes. It also, of course, makes most homosexuals exceedingly anxious to avoid even a breath of suspicion, and renders them sitting targets for blackmail. This unhealthy state of affairs will persist as long as it remains illegal for homosexuals to live together, however discreetly and faithfully they do so.

Again, the law and the fear which it generates deter far more young men from seeking early help than it frightens into doing so. Psychological help at the adolescent stage, before the personality has matured, has a better chance of successfully guiding a boy towards normality than is the case once he is into his twenties. It is folly to scare such boys away from the help which they need.

Public understanding is slowly but surely growing, but there is still a very long way to go. Too many parents are still completely ignorant of the possibility that, through no fault of their own, they may have a homosexual son or daughter. If they understood the facts, they would surely want to give that child as much love and comfort as it is in their power to do. But all too often they do not.

Recently I have heard of a mother who beat her son about the head when she discovered his homosexuality, until she was fortunately convinced of her mistake through the intervention of the local vicar, to whom the boy turned for help; of a father who threw his son out of the house after realizing why he was undergoing psychiatric treatment; and of complacent parents who, when their 18-year-old son at last screwed up his courage, after months of worry, and told them that he was homosexual, ticked him off for making silly jokes.

There is an ancient legal maxim that 'ignorance is no excuse'. A few years ago, a young mother, whose husband had been fined for some minor homosexual offence, killed their baby 'so that he should not grow up to be a pervert like his father'. Such tragedies can be prevented only through the dispelling of ignorance; through abandonment of primitive reactions of horror and revulsion to abnormalities, even if they seem to us strange and unpleasant; and by a general recognition that homosexuality is an undesirable handicap, but one which can be made much more tolerable and harmless, both for the individuals affected by it and for the community in which they live, by a consciously constructive and humane attitude on the part of everyone of goodwill.

English Attitudes to Homosexuality

FROM A TALK GIVEN TO MEMBERS OF THE DUTCH COC,
AMSTERDAM, APRIL 1963

. . . The present British laws against male homosexual behaviour are responsible for a great deal of neurosis and some severe mental illness. These difficulties result primarily from fear and a degree of repression which makes sex a problem that is impossible for the homosexual individual to solve with peace of mind. For the young, especially, such a law has a disastrous effect in deterring them from seeking advice at a time when they could most easily be helped. The effect on the general public is also bad; because of the law, they look upon homosexuality as a crime or an infectious disease which must be forcibly stopped from spreading.

Elements in prevailing social attitudes which combine to hinder progress towards law reform include a large degree of *ignorance* – much of it irrational: many people not only do not know about homosexuality; they quite deliberately do not *want* to know. This is partly the result of *fear*. Most human beings tend to be instinctively conservative, and where emotional situations or sexual behaviour are concerned, they are likely to manifest a fear of the unknown and a dislike of the different. Such people often regard homosexuality as a threat to themselves – an emotional threat, if not a physical one. The idea of it is strange and foreign to them, and they perceive it as a menace to youth, to family life and to the birthrate.

It is a common reaction for those who hold such views to maintain that homosexuality is so unnatural, disgusting and dangerous that it cannot possibly be tolerated – and then to add (without pausing for breath) that if the laws against it are relaxed, it will 'spread like wildfire'. This tendency to be fascinated by what also horrifies, with its accompanying implication that, given free competition, the attractions of homosexuality will prove superior to those of heterosexual love for a large section of the community, may be an interesting phenomenon to the psychologist, but is a very real stumbling block to the law reformer seeking to instil a more rational attitude into public opinion. However illogical these fears in fact are, they must somehow be assuaged, and the public at large brought to realize that homosexuals, if left alone in peace, would constitute no threat to society.

Another largely irrational element in public attitudes towards homosexuals is a conscious or unconscious feeling of *envy* towards the sexual 'freedom' which they are popularly supposed to enjoy. It is true that a homosexual relationship cannot be reinforced by the marriage tie, and that 'faithfulness' does not characterize all such relationships. Possibly all men, whether heterosexual or homosexual, desire to behave promiscuously at times – but the path of promiscuity is positively forced upon the homosexual by hostile social attitudes and laws which make it dangerous for him to cultivate permanent relationships, so that casual 'affairs' seem easier and safer. Then, having driven him in this direction, society commits the double injustice of condemning him as 'immoral', while secretly envying him!

Such envy is not universal. There is also a strong strain of *puritanism*, which in many people is sincere, if mistaken. These folk regard *all* sex as dirty and an unfortunate necessity, and look upon enjoyment of it as wicked, even within marriage. Their attitude stems from a perverted Christianity, and involves a low view of women, who are seen merely as child-bearers and domestic servants, but not as companions or equal partners in a sexual union which should be the source of supreme pleasure. Such superior persons are usually also contemptuous of homosexuals, whom they wrongly regard as 'effeminate'. Yet it has frequently been observed that they are themselves apt to betray latent homosexual tendencies, and that the habit of this ultra-conventional, conservative type of Englishman to congregate for his social relaxation in clubs and gatherings from which women are rigidly excluded demonstrates this. But it is not an argument very likely to convince those concerned!

Besides the puritans, there are also, unfortunately, a number of *hypocrites* in English society who themselves practise homosexuality but would be the last to appear publicly sympathetic or tolerant towards it. Many of them are married men with families, and some occupy high positions. With the law in its present state, their attitude is not surprising; nor can they altogether be blamed for it. Nevertheless, they represent a real hindrance in getting the law changed, and though they have no wish to fall foul of it themselves, their lack of support for reform is a direct cause of suffering to others.

Even less reputable as a factor in some people's attitude towards homosexuality is *sadism*. This, I fear, plays a considerable part in the hostility towards reform displayed by many judges, magistrates, lawyers, and police. Consciously or unconsciously, these people relish their power to punish, and desire to retain their authority over sexual 'wrongdoers' as much as over other types of criminal. For a long time they have been accustomed to look upon homosexuality as a particularly distasteful form of wickedness. It will be a difficult task to convince them that they are wrong.

The exercise of power over frightened and fearful homosexuals may also be an agreeable situation to some members of the medical and psychiatric professions. I do not think most doctors or psychiatrists are guilty of this failing, but there are undoubtedly a few to whom the present predicament of homosexuals is not entirely unwelcome.

Finally, there seems to me to be strong evidence of an active sub-conscious need, even on the part of societies as complex and sophisticated as ours, for a *scapegoat* – a minority group or groups upon whom the community can project its collective guilt and inflict punishment. In the past, Jews were cast for this role; nowadays it is more commonly the Negro and the homosexual.

There is thus a prime necessity to show society that homosexual people do not differ from heterosexuals in any significant moral, mental or physical way: that they are neither criminals, sick, nor necessarily sinners. The latter point has been very effectively made for the first time by a religious group in the recent pamphlet *Towards a Quaker View of Sex*. But it is no use expecting such 'outside' bodies to do all the necessary spadework; homosexuals themselves must help.

They could do this in several ways. First, and perhaps most important, they should try to combat in themselves that 'splitting off' of the sexual from the other aspects of life which is a common phenomenon encouraged by the law. They should cultivate a personal attitude of frankness and honesty in place of their present instinctive habits of secretiveness. This is not to say that they should inform all and sundry of their homosexuality; but it should be possible to enlighten their close friends, and sometimes families, who would be likely to be sympathetic and understanding. They should also try to practise higher standards of social behaviour towards fellow-homosexuals. The too-common habits of breaking dates, not keeping promises, and general unreliability, which characterizes much homosexual life would never be tolerated in other contexts by the very people who perpetrate them. And they should seek to cultivate higher and more conscientious standards of sexual behaviour. Promiscuity, importuning and public indecency are deplorable – if for no other reason than that they are extremely harmful in promoting a bad public impression of homosexuality. As social attitudes progress – and certainly when the law has been reformed – such furtive and sordid habits should come to be viewed as unacceptable and ought to disappear.

Stability in relationships, whether homosexual or heterosexual, is desirable in itself, for the sake of everyone concerned. It makes for happiness of the kind which everybody needs, especially as they grow older. Such happiness is certainly not impossible for homosexuals to attain, and the contrary belief is yet another of the false ideas about them which will only be dispelled eventually by courage, frankness, and personal example.

Attitudes to Homosexuality

MAN AND SOCIETY, NO. 8, SPRING 1965[1]

We are still sometimes told that public opinion is not ready for reform of the homosexual laws. But what is meant by 'public opinion'? There are, of course, many different public opinions; and that expressed in Parliament or in the newspapers is not necessarily the same as will be found in a gathering of social workers or at the local pub. 'Public opinion', as it is expressed in various groups and segments of society, differs sharply on a number of issues, and not only on this one.

One of the things the Albany Trust has sought to do is to find out more about public opinion as regards homosexuality. While there is no clearly consistent pattern, since so much ignorance, fear and myth still surrounds the subject, I think that certain tentative conclusions can be drawn. . . .

A recent pilot survey carried out for the Trust into public attitudes towards homosexuality revealed, in the authors' words, 'a tentative picture of widespread confusion, uncertainty, outright misunderstandings, and contradictory ideas'. These confusions exist not merely about the nature of homosexuality itself – on which even the 'experts' hold more than one view – but also concerning the existing laws about it. Many of those interviewed did not know that the law differed in its attitude towards male and female homosexuals; and when they were told, they considered this to be unfair. A considerable proportion of the sample thought that homosexuality was in fact legal between consenting adults if young people were not involved; in other words, they thought the law was already in accordance with the recommendations of the Wolfenden Committee. Several of them were unable to understand how the law could be any different to such a state of affairs. So the results of our small survey (which admittedly was not on a scale which would allow statistical deductions to be drawn for the country as a whole) would tend towards the conclusion that a good deal of public opinion is unaware of the present law, or indifferent to it, rather than approving of it. Indeed, even people who do not know what the law is tend to accept the ideas of the Wolfenden Committee on the subject as being more in accord with common sense.

One can, of course, approach the issue of law reform from a purely pragmatic point of view, as a reviewer in the 1964 *Howard Journal* purports to do. He says that the whole thing probably boils down to the harm principle: we do not allow this if it is harmful, and there is no reason why we should not allow it if it is not harmful. This is of course a perfectly sound principle. But he then proceeds to ask the following series of questions, which seem to me to betray a very muddleheaded approach to the whole problem:

> Is not the man who sleeps with another man's wife, or with a prostitute, or with his sister, or who practises sodomy upon his wife, or homosexuality, a danger to society? Is he not exhibiting an irreverence and a lack of respect for the other party, even though adult and consenting, and thus, by inference, for all other members of society? Is such a person really a person of integrity and honesty and trust? Is he not as much a corrupting influence in society as the bank robber? Is not society entitled, after anxious reflection, to protect itself against this corruption by the use of the criminal law as an aid to education if in fact it can be shown that such conduct will thereby be reduced and no greater evil created in its place? If the homosexual is otherwise an admirable person who suffers unhealthy sexual repression from the existing law, and the law creates no useful moral climate against his behaviour, then the law has failed. But if the homosexual is shown to be otherwise criminally prone, and will not suffer medically from repression, then the law does counter any suggestion of permission or approval, and the case for the enforcement of morality by the criminal law would seem to be made out.

Now there are a number of quite extraordinary assumptions about the nature of homosexuals in that passage which I need not underline. And these sorts of assumptions appear to be held even by some of the people who sympathize with the case for homosexual law reform. For instance, when the Young Liberals passed a motion by a large majority at their 1964 Annual Conference in favour of reform, the mover of the motion said: 'Private morals must not fall within the ambit of the law. *Alcoholics and gamblers are just as untrustworthy as homosexuals,*[2] but get far lighter treatment.' Again, a Conservative who supports reform, Timothy Raison, who edits *New Society*, wrote in his book *Why Conservative?*[3] of 'the barren hopelessness of homosexual relationships, the impermanence and bitterness that would mark them whether they were legal or not, and the blackmail which would not necessarily disappear if they were legalised' as 'symbols of an unnatural condition which must have brought more misery than joy in its wake'.

Even knowledgeable and sympathetic psychiatrists ask questions like: 'Is there such a person as a happy homosexual?' I had a conversation not long ago with a clinical psychologist who has a great deal of experience in treating homosexuals, and he said that this is a question which occurs to him and his colleagues time and time again, because the people who come to them for help are of course not usually happy people. The 'experts' do not normally come across many representatives of the many homosexual couples of both sexes who have lived happily together for a long time.

And it must be remembered in any case that the proper social analogy for such relationships is not the analogy with a marriage which is blessed by Church and State, but the analogy with common law marriage – a heterosexual relationship which is not recognized by law but where the man and woman live together, perhaps bringing up a family, and which is quite often an adulterous relationship because one of the parties has not been able to obtain a divorce. For in these relationships also all the social, legal and even moral pressures are directed, as with homosexual relationships, to force the parties apart rather than to keep them together.

I could go on almost indefinitely multiplying examples of how even liberal-minded, sympathetic people tend to take a condescending view of homosexuals and the homosexual situation, and make all sorts of unjustified assumptions which keep them on their lofty mental platform and leave the homosexual down in some miserable unsatisfying depth where he has to be given social help or the equivalent of soup from whatever soup-kitchen that particular 'sympathizer' is interested in. The concept of homosexuality as a disease is perhaps the commonest instance. Some homosexuals are of course sick people, who need and can benefit from treatment of one kind or another: others – especially among the younger age groups – may be capable, given suitable help, of achieving a more heterosexual orientation. But the great majority of homosexual men and women, who fall into neither of these categories, are not 'ill' in any medically meaningful sense of the word; and their heterosexual brethren have no intellectually respectable grounds for regarding them in this way.[4]

Being able to patronize the poor unfortunate homosexual (or anyone else) is such an easy way of feeling virtuous for so many people. And the difficulty one is up against in seeking a more objective approach is that whenever it is said that all most homosexuals want is to be left in peace so long as they are minding their own business, the cry is raised that this is really a 'glorification' of the homosexual life: when one says that a homosexual, given equal freedom and equal social conditions and not interfered with by society, could in such circumstances more easily achieve stable relationships which would satisfy him and which would help him towards a more balanced life, many people profess to be outraged by such an 'immoral' suggestion.

In other words, the emotional problems and attitudes of heterosexuals are responsible for a great deal of distortion in much of the current thinking about homosexuality. Not all the sexual problems in life are homosexual problems; there are also a great many heterosexual problems, and these cause some quite unrealistic thinking about all aspects of sex. Possibly the heterosexual's own tensions are sometimes fierce enough to make it emotionally necessary for him to view the homosexual's life and homosexual love as inevitably nasty, brutish and short.

These, then, are some of the current confusions and hypocrisies involved in much of the thought and talk about homosexuality. It is only by everyone – heterosexual and homosexual alike – re-examining their own viewpoints honestly, and questioning the validity of all their (sometimes only half-conscious) assumptions about sex and the nature of sexual relationships that we can hope gradually to attain the more realistic social attitudes which must precede sensible social action to end much of the needless misery which too many individuals are still having to endure in this supposedly enlightened age.

Notes

1. Shortened version of an Albany Trust Winter Talk.
2. My italics.
3. Penguin Books, 1964.
4. The Wolfenden Committee say in their report (para. 30): 'The evidence put before us has not established to our satisfaction the proposition that homosexuality is a disease.'

The Shibboleth of Integration

NEW CHRISTIAN, 14 NOVEMBER 1968

Whatever else Enoch Powell may have done, he has made most of us stop and think.[1] And by making 'liberal intellectual' seem, momentarily at any rate, the most suspect label in the language, Mr Powell has unwittingly performed a much-needed service. For many of the assumptions held and shared – sometimes only half-consciously – by most of us who like to regard ourselves as being reformist and reasonably intelligent are overdue for a long, cool look. If politics are relevant to social ills (and it is difficult to see what other use they are, except perhaps as a perverse sport), we 'liberal intellectuals' cannot escape responsibility for the prevailing national vacillation and ineffectiveness.

This is not a matter of party politics – nor of religious attitude. There are men and women in each party and in none, as well as some Christians and some humanists, who grasp the need for social change, even though their vision of the future is temporarily dimmed. Each party and denomination, too, has its shellbacks who instinctively prefer the past to the present and dread the future. At present, the latter sort seem to be doing most of the shouting. Why? One reason, it seems to me, is that those of us who should be defining new concepts of social progress have become mentally lazy and (until Powell) complacent. At most, we pay uncritical lip-service to slogans conventionally regarded as 'enlightened', whose implications we rarely scrutinize.

I have recently become increasingly concerned about the loose use of one such slogan – that of 'integration', which is the goal of all professed anti-racists. What 'integration' appears to mean, in the mouth of those who peddle it as the ultimate solution to the 'colour problem', is a society in which everyone lives happily together, and nobody even notices the colour of anyone else's skin. Admirable, for sure! But very often there is an unspoken assumption which makes the goal distinctly less enticing to minorities than it appears to the rest of us. This is the notion that an 'integrated' society will behave homogeneously – and that its culture-pattern will be that of the majority.

'Integration', in fact, usually comes to mean assimilation – the nice, safe, acceptable, negro or Pakistani is the Anglicized one who adopts as his own the native British standards of thought, speech, behaviour, and cooking. The story of the perfectly 'integrated' little black girl romping happily in the crowded East London school playground where she was the only non-white pupil, and the visiting African bishop who shook his head over her and murmured: 'How sad! She will grow up with none of her own culture', makes a point. Curiously, it is a less telling one than the now famous legend of the white child isolated (and terrorized?) in an all-black classroom.

Obviously, there are many devoted people working in the temporarily shell-shocked field of race relations who know better than this what 'integration' should mean. But perhaps the most significant indication that many 'integrationists' really believe in majority assimilation of minorities is provided by the disapproving cries of 'ghetto' which arise whenever any minority – racial, religious or sexual – asserts its wish (or its right) to have its own distinct cultural traditions, standards, and way of life. Of course there has to be compromise. All citizens must be equal before the law, and all may be expected to observe community standards of honesty, safety, health, and so on. But why should we resent or fear the natural desire of minorities to congregate, at times, in identifiable groups, and to express values or attitudes which may not always be shared by the rest of us. If they do this are they really (as Mr Powell would have it) a threat to our very existence as a nation?

Take a non-racial example, with which I am professionally concerned. Last year Parliament passed a law relieving adult male homosexuals from criminal penalties for their private consenting relationships. This has predictably led to a greater openness and readiness on the part of many homosexual men to seek advice and help for their personal and social difficulties. Consequently, it is becoming much more widely apparent to clergy, social workers, and others that a common problem faced by men and women who are homosexual is an intense feeling of isolation and social ostracism (actual or potential) within a community which for the most part accepts a homosexual individual only while it remains unaware that this is what he or she is. Because of this very powerful discriminatory attitude on the part of 'normal' society, nearly all homosexuals – especially the young ones – experience at some time in their lives, and sometimes for many years, a deep personal loneliness which is aggravated by the lack of opportunities to meet others like themselves in congenial and wholesome surroundings – at any rate outside London and one or two other major cities.

Unlike coloured people, homosexuals (who are probably as numerically large a minority) cannot be physically identified, and contrary to popular belief they have no infallible means of recognizing one another. Therefore, there is a great gulf between the experienced, gregarious homosexual who knows the social ropes well enough to achieve a degree of social contact with others like himself and the isolated, solitary individuals who undoubtedly constitute the majority of those who experience homosexual emotions and who desperately need constructive, responsible social help to integrate their own lives and relationships.

Not altogether surprisingly, since last year's legislation there has been some discussion of the possibility that homosexuals should now have their own social organizations or clubs which – unlike any of the existing meeting places – would openly state their purpose and endeavour to provide a supportive atmosphere for the lonely homosexual, possibly with professional, medical, religious, and social work guidance available in the background. This suggestion has revealed a sharp division of views. On the one hand, there are those (including some leading advocates of the recent reform) who, whilst anxious to end the legal persecution of homosexuals, regard the idea of social facilities especially for them as a retrograde 'ghetto' manifestation – without, apparently, having any more positive suggestions for helping the lonely ones. Others believe (as I do) that for homosexuals, as for other minorities, recognition of the need to belong to one's own 'in-group', and to be free to demonstrate this belonging, is not inimical to ultimate and fuller social integration but is for many members of a minority group a necessary step towards it.

Sex – perhaps even more than race – is still an explosively emotional topic. But we should not forget that little more than a century ago, demands for freedom of religious worship evoked exactly the same kind and degree of hostility in Britain. To be a 'non-conformist' was not merely a sin but a heinous crime: the civil disabilities suffered by Catholics and Jews, in particular, were only removed hesitantly and reluctantly, with dire predictions of the fate likely to be suffered by society if such disruptive influences were permitted free rein.

Many who were neither Catholics nor Jews fought valiantly for these groups' right to believe, worship, and behave as they wished. In our day, many who are neither negroes nor homosexuals support the concept of a multi-racial society and a more sexually tolerant one. We should beware of interpreting 'integration' in such a manner that we take away with one hand what we profess to give with the other. Toleration inevitably means diversity in living patterns, and not merely theoretical lip-service to an ideal which is abhorred in practice. Freedom necessarily entails choices on the part of some which appear mistaken – or even offensive – to others. Above all, the right of minorities to make such choices, and to work out their own destinies and salvation for themselves so long as they do not harm the rest of us, must be upheld by a society which aspires to be truly integrated and tolerant.

Note

1. In a speech on immigration and race relations in April 1968, Mr Powell had said he was filled with foreboding as he looked ahead: 'Like the Roman, I seem to see the River Tiber foaming with much blood.' The next day, the Conservative leader Edward Heath dismissed him from the Shadow Cabinet.

Sex, Morality and Happiness

BASED ON A LECTURE DELIVERED IN NEW YORK, CHICAGO, LOS ANGELES AND SAN FRANCISCO, OCTOBER/NOVEMBER 1967[1]

We in England are so accustomed to being regarded as socially backward by our economically emancipated Western cousins that it comes as a pleasant shock to find ourselves apparently way ahead of America in our legal, social and religious thinking about sexual laws and behaviour. For whereas in England, since the passage in July 1967 of the Sexual Offences Act which legalized homosexual behaviour between consenting adult males in private, only one form of sexual misconduct – namely incest – remains a crime (save for heterosexual buggery, which is almost certain soon to be struck off the Statute Book[2]), in most of the United States (to quote one of your eminent legal authorities) 'a quick glance at the maze of laws that concern sex and sexual behaviour may well justify the conclusion that sex is not legal'.

In the article to which I have referred (in the *Encyclopedia of Sexual Behaviour*), Mr Robert Veit Sherwin proceeds to examine United States laws about sex, and infers that the only safe advice to anyone, even if they are husband and wife, wishing to perform any sexual act other than face-to-face coitus within marriage is: 'DON'T!' Any variation from this, even between married people, is restricted in all states under one law or another. For you in the United States, therefore, the problem of rationalizing your sex laws is not confined to homosexuality; it is a heterosexual problem too – for your laws would appear to make criminals of 95 per cent of the population.

In Britain, we had a similar problem, in one way. But in another way it was more difficult – because homosexuality is the point at which some of the most violent common prejudices about sex are concentrated. Yet we fought a reforming battle on this issue and won, educating public opinion a good deal in the process. So I make no apology for beginning this address about sex, morality and happiness with a few remarks about law reform, and the relationship of law to morals in the field of sex.

If, in dealing with such a potentially contentious topic as sex, law and morals, I seem somewhat presumptuous, perhaps I have some excuse in that I have recently been in the forefront of the battle which has been waged over the past ten years around the Wolfenden Committee's proposals that the private homosexual behaviour of consenting adults should be removed from the scope of the criminal law. My part has lain largely in the parliamentary and public opinion spheres. It has also involved, almost imperceptibly at first, but of late most importantly, a great deal of social casework which has brought home to me, as nothing else could have done, the real meaning of the law's impact upon some people's most intimate personal lives in terms of human suffering. It is largely because of this casework that I count myself a radical in matters of law reform where private sexual behaviour and morality are concerned.

For I have come to believe that, in nearly every situation to which it can be and is applied, the law is an extremely blunt instrument for making people good in their sexual lives. It seems to me that the very notion of a 'sexual offence' in law is nowadays rapidly becoming as outmoded as the notion of the matrimonial offence appears to many who are concerned to improve the state of the law about divorce.

I have reached this conclusion for what I take to be the most eminently practical reasons: that, as Professor Herbert Hart has put it, whereas one of the best justifications for any law is that it prevents and alleviates suffering, laws prohibiting sexual relationships can create misery in quite special ways and in a special degree, because an enforced suppression of the sexual instincts that is not the product of moral belief or a voluntary act of free will can have devastatingly adverse effects upon a person's entire emotional development; and that virtually all forms of sexual behaviour which are properly and necessarily punishable come under some other heading of criminal law – they are assaults, offences against public decency, or breaches of rules designed to protect children. I would, in fact, be in favour of a reclassification of sex crimes in this way, so that the prejudice and stigma which almost invariably attach to a 'sex offender' could be eliminated before and at his trial.

In saying this, I am by no means ignoring the very important theoretical argument about the law's right to enforce morality which has gone on in England since Lord Devlin gave his famous lecture on *The Enforcement of Morals* in 1959. Indeed, I have been a close student and a minor participant in that debate; and I think that it has been one of the Wolfenden Report's most valuable by-products. But without venturing to weigh the relative strength of the respective arguments put forward by Lord Devlin and his opponents, I still believe that, even if we grant that the law has a *theoretical* right to enforce sexual morality at the level of private consensual adult behaviour, there are some overwhelming *practical* arguments against its doing so.

I by no means underestimate the force of the argument which was so strongly advanced against homosexual law reform – that to remove the private behaviour of two consenting adults from the list of crimes would inevitably weaken moral condemnation of such acts. In the sense that law and morality coexist and underpin each other over wide areas of human conduct, that is undoubtedly true. But even the Wolfenden Committee's distinction between sin and crime, and its dictum that 'unless a deliberate attempt is to be made . . . to equate the sphere of crime with that of sin, there must remain a realm of private morality and immorality which is, in brief and crude terms, not the law's business', begs the all-important question of whether such behaviour between two persons of the same sex is, in fact, always immoral. As someone – a psychiatrist, I believe, and therefore probably not to be trusted in his moral judgements – has said: 'a person's moral value does not depend upon whether he likes men or women'.

I do not deny that the law has a legitimate role to play as the reinforcer of morals; nor do I contend that there should be no laws whatever about sex. What I do say is that wherever the law steps in to *force* people to be good, a lot of the virtue in their goodness is lost; for compulsory virtue is a contradiction in terms. If this sounds like a counsel of perfection, let me refer you to that highly important pamphlet, by a group of Friends, *Towards a Quaker View of Sex*, whose major theme is that the spirit is all-important whereas observance of the letter of the law is not. In this, the message of the 'New Morality' surely has much in common with that of the New Testament.

I am no theologian; but it is striking how quickly the need for a greater self-awareness prompting this Quaker group, the Bishop of Woolwich (Dr John Robinson), and other avant-garde Christians who only a few years ago were decried as shockingly iconoclastic, has spread even to the most traditionalist and orthodox of churches. This has led to new and fruitful debate, by no means yet ended, about the proper relationships between law, morals and religion, and to a growing reacceptance amongst Christians of the fact that if there has to be law for the regulation of intimate human relationships, it must be the Law of Love.

I need hardly say that the law of England, although in some respects becoming more humane, is still far from fulfilling such an aspiration. We may soon see a move forward in the matter of divorce. The Home Secretary recently announced that the Criminal Law Revision Committee was to review the whole of the law relating to sexual offences; and in spite of the recent Act, there will still be plenty for the Committee to look at. So far as homosexuality is concerned, the fixing of the 'age of consent' at 21; the provisions making all homosexual behaviour by youths under that age still a crime – even with one another; the restrictive interpretation of 'in private' as meaning only 'when not more than two people take part or are present', regardless of the actual privacy of the circumstances; the remaining heavy penalties; and the exclusion of Scotland and Northern Ireland from the new Act, all give cause for concern.[3] And there is a wider need for further sex law reforms. Must we still keep all the draconian penalties which stud our Sexual Offences Acts, most of which are unchanged since Victorian times? Is it really socially expedient to retain the present harsh laws about incest? Is our existing attitude to prostitution – making its legal practice a sort of social steeplechase – a sensible and practical one? Are not the various provisions under which public decency is safeguarded ripe for streamlining?

The recent changes in our homosexuality and abortion laws, and the possibility of further changes quite soon in the divorce laws, as well as the trend in government policy towards the provision of more contraceptive advice and better sex education, are all indicative of a changing moral climate. Is this new 'permissive society' becoming too tolerant? Are we in danger of rushing down the Gadarene slope into decadence? Or are we merely becoming more honest, less hypocritical, and readier to accept life's realities?

The basic clash in this area is between individual liberty and authoritarian morals; and while these questions are in no sense party-political, it has always struck me as odd – to say the least – that the very people who are the ruggedest individualists in their political and economic outlook are often the ones who campaign most hotly against free choice in moral values. When the Wolfenden Committee said, in their famous 1957 report, that there was a realm of morality and immorality which was not the law's business, they added:

> To say this is not to condone or to encourage private immorality. On the contrary, to emphasize the personal and private nature of moral or immoral conduct is to emphasize the personal and private responsibility of the individual for his own actions, and that is a responsibility which a mature agent can properly be expected to carry for himself without the threat of punishment from the law.

The discussion which the Wolfenden Committee sparked off as to the need and desirability of reforming our completely prohibitive homosexual laws has played a very large part in educating the public about homosexuality, and indeed about sex in general. It has also promoted some most interesting discussions among lawyers, philosophers and theologians about the relationship of law and morality and about the nature of morality itself. The so-called 'New Morality' movement of South Bank theologians, Quakers and others has begun a serious attempt to rethink the basic Gospel message – an endeavour which has now spread to other countries and to practically every Christian denomination.

o O o

As a counsellor, I have encountered some very heartless homosexuals – and indeed a few depraved ones; but many more who were deeply conscientious, and desiring only to find another of their own kind whom they could love and cherish as tenderly as a person who is normally sexed and averagely moral will hope to love their life's partner.

It is in fact impossible to generalize about the morality of homosexual acts, any more than about the morality of heterosexual ones. It is even less possible, in my view, to judge the strength of the sexual temptations experienced by another human being, or the amount of effort involved in resisting them. Bodily inheritance and make-up, temperament, mental habit, systems of personal values, religious beliefs, all vary so enormously from person to person, and yet these differences often do not become apparent until there is a crisis. Then, what is unthinkable conduct to one is compulsive for another. The normally or the weakly sexed sit too easily and smugly in judgement on their fellow human beings, and another life is blighted: sometimes, destroyed.

When the law does judge and condemn, it should do so with the greatest circumspection, and always liberally tempering justice with mercy. I have seen too many personal tragedies which stemmed solely from the old, bad laws prohibiting any homosexual behaviour between men to do other than fight with all my strength for their repeal. Perhaps the main evil was psychological: the all-pervasive sense of being not only socially handicapped but also an outlaw by reason of his most personal possession – his mode of affection – which has in the past crippled the capacities for happiness of so many a man and youth.

In spite of all the progress in informing the public about these things, and despite law reform, there is still far too little real understanding of the true nature of homosexuality. Very many people, even today, still do not understand that in essence it is about love, and not simply some behaviour which immoral people indulge in 'for kicks'. While unreserved acceptance of the homosexual may seem a legitimate and urgent goal for 'homophile' organizations to campaign for, it is surely unrealistic to expect most people who are not themselves homosexual to regard homosexuality as being other than a personal misfortune, and thus something that ought not to be accepted too readily or easily as part of the normal fabric of life. We have to remember that in many quarters the prevailing attitude towards homosexuality, even on the part of some quite sympathetic people, is still one of fear. Though the belief is unfounded, many people imagine that homosexuality is something contagious – something they, or their children, might get 'drawn into' if it is not socially repressed.

It is necessary for those of us who are working to increase public understanding about homosexuality to assuage such fears – because people are not able to help, to be sympathetic, to realize what other people are going through, unless their own fears are first of all allayed. It is not enough to be rational, or to ask others to be rational. The situation has to be dealt with in emotional terms, by actions and behaviour – and by non-behaviour! – as much as by words.

In our work at the Albany Trust, casework and counselling loom large, and we are very conscious of the need to fashion a carefully thought out and really constructive approach to the provision of advice and practical help for homosexual people. It is still the case that homosexuality is all too often regarded as something which sets a man or a woman apart from the rest of human experience. But many, if not most, of the problems and difficulties which homosexuals face are common to both homosexuals and heterosexuals, even though their manifestations and solutions are different and sometimes quite distinct. I am sure that the right approach to them is one which emphasizes our common humanity, and does not concentrate either upon the differences in direction of sexual desire or the different physical acts involved.

We all of us, whether heterosexual or homosexual, have sexual natures; and we all have our personal solutions (or compromises). Some people find themselves a life-partner to love and live with; others are promiscuous; others choose the path of celibacy, and find in it what they regard as deeper fulfilment than mere physical gratification or even human love could give. But the whole point about celibacy is that its merit depends entirely upon its *voluntariness* – compulsory virtue is really no virtue at all. The greatest evil of laws which prohibit the private sexual acts of consenting adults is that they purport to decree *compulsory* celibacy and thereby make it virtually impossible for those affected by them to consider celibacy, or even continence, upon their merits. My own belief has always been that law reform will help to promote chastity and more stable relationships among homosexuals; and I think that most pastoral and social workers with any experience of the subject would agree.

Just as we are all sexual beings, we are also all social beings; and our lives, even in their most intimately personal aspects, are profoundly affected by society's attitudes and pressures. We can never escape from each other; and utter aloneness is not a desirable permanent state for anyone, any more than constant togetherness is. But there is, of course, a great difference between being alone and being lonely; many very busy people are lonely, while one can be all by oneself yet not lonely at all. Loneliness – as my colleague Norman Ingram-Smith of St Martin-in-the-Fields has said – is nowadays an umbrella word too often used by distressed people to cloak or conceal (even from themselves) a deeper or more specific need. Nevertheless, it is still a very real phenomenon, experienced by a great many human beings – and certainly by a great many homosexuals.

Loneliness and an acute feeling of isolation is, indeed, the most common single complaint of those who seek the assistance of the Albany Trust. They experience a conscious severance from society to an almost unbearable degree, until quite often they are unable to make any really meaningful contact with other human beings. I remember one man, in his thirties, who, after seven years of emptiness following the break-up of his only homosexual friendship, had reached the crippling stage of neurosis at which he was physically incapable of the effort of speech when faced with an unfamiliar person or situation. And he was only an extreme example of a very common plight which for many gets progressively worse with advancing age.

One must beware of generalizing. I know that there are very many gregarious homosexuals, and also those who have achieved happy partnerships. Perhaps as a social worker in the field I see an undue proportion of the others. But they force me to ask myself whether there is anything in the nature or make-up of homosexual people which makes them more prone to this plight of loneliness than non-homosexuals are? Richard Hauser[4] once wrote a provocative article in *Man and Society* called 'The Drug of Self-Pity', in which he accused homosexuals of suffering more from self-pity and self-righteousness than any other minority. An American psychiatrist[5] has called them 'injustice collectors'.

I think these strictures are too harsh – many homosexuals still receive more than their fair share of injustices – but I have been driven (unwillingly) to the conclusion that what too many homosexuals do suffer from is an incapacity to experience and enter into really satisfying and worthwhile human relationships. Of course, this is not an exclusively homosexual phenomenon: many heterosexuals, including married ones, are totally irresponsible and selfish in their attitudes and behaviour towards others. But a high proportion of the homosexuals that one encounters seem unable to commit themselves to anyone; to give, or to love in a relaxed, unselfish way – at any rate for very long.

This, I think, is not due to the much-vaunted Freudian causes of homo-sexuality – over-possessive mother, weak or hostile father, and so forth – so much as to the difficulties inherent in all homosexual relationships, which are of course accentuated by the unhelpful social environment in which most homosexuals have to live. Surprisingly, it often seems to escape the attention of researchers into the psychology of sexual behaviour that men and women differ not only physically, but also in their emotional make-up and needs. A heterosexual relationship – which is a union of opposites – differs in its nature from either a male or a female homosexual relationship. And (what is usually completely overlooked) these two opposite types of homosexual relationships probably have more contrasts than likenesses to each other than either has to a heterosexual relationship, because of their all-maleness, or all-femaleness, respectively. I do not mean to imply in any way that the love which male or female homosexuals are capable of feeling for their partners is different, or inferior, to heterosexual love – I am simply saying that the respective end-products, in terms of living patterns, are bound to be different. Women, for example, are commonly thought to have a far stronger home-making drive than most men do. To the male, promiscuity seems more natural than to the female: and while this may seem morally objectionable to many people, the most cogent objections to it for the homosexual male are probably severely practical – namely, that it usually does not lead to real happiness – rather than moral or theoretical.

In addition, the moral and emotional significance of the physical sex act is of course different for a man and for a woman, not only in their heterosexual relationships but also in their homosexual ones. Adequate attention surely needs to be given to this rather obvious point in any serious system of ethics. It seems to me paradoxical, from an ethical point of view, that so much more fuss has traditionally been made about homosexual 'sins' than about heterosexual ones – which are often much more morally and emotionally damaging in the man–woman relationship than any sexual act is in the single-sex one. Far too much counselling still proceeds on the assumption that the aim for heterosexuals is to help them achieve satisfactory sex, while the aim for homosexuals is to persuade, cajole or bully them into having no sex at all. This is utterly wrong, and urgently needs to be superseded by a more adequate conception of what the homosexual, as well as the heterosexual, is seeking through his need for sexual relationships – namely, the capacity for self-fulfilment through loving closeness to another human being.

Among homosexuals, as with heterosexuals, there is much unrequited love, which can be a cause of deep, and not always temporary, suffering. I believe that one of the functions of counselling must be to help people to cope with the unhappiness caused by such unrequited love; and this help is not only needed by the rejected lover – the beloved who feels good will but cannot return the same degree of affection needs to know how best to behave in these circumstances as well. This way, much unnecessary unhappiness on the one side and anxiety on the other could be avoided: for even where love cannot be mutual, kindness can; and hostility or panic on either side should certainly have no place in such situations.

As I said earlier, the homosexual's problems are first and foremost ones of relationships. Once he grows up and leaves the family circle, this no longer exists for him within his own generation, or with the younger generation, as it does for heterosexuals; and this fact itself creates great difficulties. I sometimes think that one of the worst things the Church's teaching has done in the realm of social policy is to over-emphasize the importance and key place of the family unit in society to the exclusion of all other groups, so that the family and its loyalties has become a sort of sacred cow at the dire expense of Christian neighbourliness. The person with no family is very alone – yet the community outside the family simply does not exist in any meaningful sense for most people in our contemporary urban life.

This creates an especial dilemma for the homosexual. If he has had no happy or deep relationships within his family as a child, there is but little chance of his achieving any when he becomes an adult and leaves it. He has not been taught how to; and with vulgar denunciations of homosexuality as vile and filthy ringing in his ears, he often believes that such satisfying relationships are reserved for heterosexuals and are impossible for him; he ends up kidding himself he doesn't want them, and that sex without love is sufficient. His fate is likely to be a very lonely old age.

My own work has convinced me that, in helping homosexuals, not only individual social and pastoral counselling is needed, but also much more group counselling, involving parents, friends and – sometimes – lovers. So often, what the troubled person is really seeking is *reconciliation*: in the first instance, reconciliation with himself; but ultimately reconciliation with those whom he loves and needs to love him, but who are rejecting and despising him.

In Holland, where the Dialoog Foundation has undertaken some very important and interesting experimental work in collaboration with Roman Catholic and Protestant counsellors, two-day meetings have been held where the parents of homosexual children discuss with each other, with their own children, and with other homosexuals. The parents, too, have their guilt feelings, and the first day of the gathering is sometimes the 'crying day' – for fathers as well as mothers. But the ultimate release of emotions and establishment of mutual confidence is said to be immensely helpful to all concerned. The need for openness – with parents, with friends, with lovers – is one of the prime needs of the homosexual (indeed, of everyone). We are all too afraid of giving ourselves away, and any tentative advance by one person all too often leads to precipitate withdrawal by the other.

Another sphere where greater communication and contact is needed is between the generations. The current commercially exploited cult of the young is leading to a state of affairs where the under-25s tend to regard themselves as so radically different in thought, feeling, sentiment, and behaviour from their elders as to be almost a separate species. The result seems to be a growing loss of kindness between the generations. For homosexuals, in particular, this could be tragic – because the hectic premium on youth in homosexual circles has bitter consequences for the middle-aged and elderly. In the homosexual world, no less than others, sympathetic understanding and helpfulness between younger and older people is an urgent necessity. The continuity of life, and the need for mutual giving, needs emphasizing once again for us all. In this way, the absence of families may ultimately be remedied by the growth of family-substitute units where older homosexuals help the young and the younger care for the old. The homosexual 'Peter Pan' syndrome needs to be broken.

Am I being too idealistic? I hope not. I hope it is not being too idealistic to say that there is more to homosexuality than emotional shallowness and one-night stands; or that a man's moral worth does not depend upon whether he prefers other men to women.

You will see that I believe in the essential similarity of the homosexual's and the heterosexual's dilemma as an individual in society. While there *are* differences – and while not only the homosexual, but also other sexual minorities such as the transvestite and the transsexual, do have their singular and peculiarly acute problems of isolation and emotional stress – the basic fact for us all to grasp and latch on to is that we are all first and foremost human beings: we are all members one of another, or, as John Donne said, 'No man is an island'. We must neither set ourselves apart in, nor relegate others to, a sexual ghetto. For it is only by ultimate integration, and not by sexual apartheid, that we shall all of us realize our humanity to the full.

The task before us remains a formidable one. But if we persevere it must surely bring us all, in the end, to a society which offers a happier, a healthier, and a fuller life for everyone. There are enough unavoidable troubles in the world without the addition of sexual misery. Our lives here on earth are very short, and we should not be having to waste a minute of them on such unnecessary or humanly aggravated problems which greater understanding and tolerance could avoid.

Notes

1. *Man and Society*, No. 11, Winter 1969–70.
2. An over-optimistic prophecy! It was not decriminalized until 1994.
3. With the reduction in 1969 of the legal age of majority, and the minimum voting age, to 18, this remains especially true in relation to the under-21s.
4. A sociologist, brother-in-law of Yehudi Menuhin, and author of *The Homosexual Society* (Bodley Head, 1962) – in my view an idiosyncratic and muddled book.
5. Charles Socarides.

Sex and Sanity

AT WORK, 1977

In 1977, I finally left the Albany Trust after fifteen years in the hot seat. Having done so, I contributed the following leader to the Trust's newspaper, At Work, *but the issue never appeared: the piece is printed here for the first time.*

How far has society's attitude to sexuality changed for the better since the Albany Trust was set up in 1958? While there has been a big swing towards greater frankness about sexual matters – indeed, we are nowadays saturated with sex – much that is said and written about it is superficial, often sensational, and sometimes downright silly. There has also been, resulting from the growth of the so-called 'permissive society' (a term I dislike, for *who* is entitled to permit or to withhold permission from others about how they should live their private lives?), a worrying growth in the political muscle of narrow-minded pressure groups purporting to speak for 'Christianity' – though theirs is a primitive and, in the view of other Christians, a heretical interpretation of the Gospel of Love – agitating not merely for moral restraint but for more severe laws in the sphere of personal behaviour.

There has thus been an increasing polarization between libertinism on the one hand and punitiveness on the other. As always, most people belong to the silent majority in the middle, who want neither to participate in group orgies five times a week nor to lock up consenting adults who do; but middle-of-the-road voices are not being heard loudly and clearly enough in today's clash between noisy extremes.

That seems to me the main difference between 1962, when I became Secretary of the Albany Trust, and 1977. Then, one felt that reasonableness, though not always very articulate, was an attitude favoured by the mainstream of British opinion. Now, one is not so sure as political, economic, social, and sexual polarization proceeds apace.

The essential problems to be dealt with remain strikingly the same. The threefold task of education, research, and social action is as necessary today as in the early 1960s. In March 1963 I gave a talk which I called 'Towards a Sexually Sane Society'.[1] Much of what I said then is just as relevant in 1977. We are still beset by the loud-mouthed people who think that most of the sexual activities and feelings existing in the world are dirty and ought to be suppressed by censorship and punishment. The commercial exploiters and titillators continue to cash in on others' sexual appetites. And there are the innumerable victims of all this repression and stimulation – the sex-obsessed who, because their sexual values have been warped by a conflict between guilt and prurience (both artificially induced), spend much endless time and energy in the frantic search for satisfying sex.

Too many British people's attitudes to sex remain, by and large, unbalanced and immature, often prejudiced and wilfully ignorant. In some respects, such as the greater ability of homosexuals to be more open about their orientation, attitudes have improved: but not nearly as much as one would have hoped ten years after the 1967 Sexual Offences Act. The procession of tense, sad, worried people who bring their problems to the Albany Trust, Friend, Icebreakers, Gay Switchboard and other counselling and befriending agencies continues unabated, and their problems are strikingly similar to those of their predecessors of fifteen years ago: parental shock, employers' prejudice, public ignorance, sometimes actual persecution.

I said in 1963, and repeat now, that the most effective way to help sexual minorities is to defuse the fear of the different which fuels so much of the hostility that exists towards those who are sexually unconventional. While this is in one sense a political issue, it is even more a personal one: for the changes required in society's attitudes can only be brought about by a self-critical – and self-disciplined – approach by those of us who are members of sexual minorities ourselves. Self-indulgent pleas for special treatment because we are 'different' are more likely to result in continuing discrimination and ill-treatment than in improvement. We shall only change society for the better by integrating into it and gaining acceptance of our sexuality by being accepted as what most of us are – whole and wholesome human beings.

Note

1. Reprinted at pp. 63ff.

Being Rational about Being Gay

TALK TO GAY AND LESBIAN HUMANIST ASSOCIATION, JUNE 1980

Being rational and being gay are both very important things for me as a person. There isn't time to say everything I want to about either, but what I want to do is to talk first about the importance of being rational – because not even all humanists or all non-believers always recognize how essential that is, especially in the present state of the world; then to look briefly at the commonest varieties of irrational attitudes towards gayness and gay people which are manifested by all too many who *are* gay as well as by those who aren't; and finally to suggest some ways in which GALHA – which is dedicated to the propositions that reasonableness and gayness are both positive factors in healthy human living – could help to spread some enlightenment around.

First of all, I want to say that being gay, for me, has never been 'a problem'. I am perhaps fortunate in never having experienced the phase of acute self-doubt, or even self-disgust, which so many young gay people pass through about their sexuality and which some never entirely grow out of, even as adults. For me, being attracted sexually to other boys, and not to girls, was always so natural a part of my being from the time I first became aware of it that I couldn't understand how anybody else could doubt its validity even if they didn't share the experience. So I never made that liberating lurch from self-hate to public celebration of my gayness which I know has been such a positive event in a lot of gay people's lives. Perhaps I missed something – but I don't regret having missed the self-hating bit.

What did happen to me was a determination, ever since I was very young, to fight the injustice, prejudice and discrimination which society meted out to homosexual people. And this, of course, led me on to a recognition of many other injustices in society which also needed to be fought. I'm grateful for being gay, because it has made me much more aware of other people's suffering and I am far less complacent about that than I otherwise might be.

During the time that I was Secretary of the Homosexual Law Reform Society I made a point, while fighting a single-issue campaign to get the Wolfenden Report's recommendations made law, of doing as much as I could in other ways by belonging actively to bodies like the National Council for Civil Liberties and the Defence of Literature and the Arts Society, which was how I first came into contact with the humanist movement through meeting Barbara Smoker, David Tribe and Bill McIlroy.

It became increasingly apparent to me during the 1960s, and is certainly crystal clear now, that the basic issues of human rights, civil liberties, freedom to publish, and sexual freedom are inseparable and have to be seen as a whole. Certainly our most vociferous enemies see them that way – they're against the lot! What concerns me increasingly today is the sort of society I'm going to be living in in 1990 and 2000, if I'm still here then. I passionately want it to be a free society. So, I believe, do most other Britons, of whatever political persuasion. So I'm not quite so worried as some people about the lurch towards authoritarianism – my worries being more about the repressive resources modern technology makes available than because I fear deliberately malignant intentions on the part of the majority of my fellow-citizens.

And this is where the importance of being reasonable comes in. If we are reasonable, if we are rationalists, we make certain assumptions about human nature. Everyone, in fact, does this whether they are aware of it or not. One of the main reasons why I am not a Christian is because (quite apart from my scepticism as to the existence of the kind of God they claim to believe in) I do not share their assumptions about human nature. The belief that all human beings are born radically evil because of original sin, and are only endowed with some redeeming good qualities through belief in an incredible creed and acceptance of a personal Saviour who was God made man, is one which I cannot accept because it is contrary to the evidence. Goodness is not confined to believing Christians; nor are such people more immune to evil behaviour than anyone else. The belief that the contrary is so is perverse and irrational and flies in the face of history. If we have to choose between believing that all human beings have potential for good and that most of them recognize that goodness and happiness are connected in ways which have nothing to do with any supernatural power, or else that people are born with a natural inclination to be evil unless they are 'saved' by religion, I know that the first seems most sensible to me. So I am an optimist about humanity – though not, I hope, a naïve one. To believe in the humaneness of humanity is not to deny that there is evil in human relationships, or that some individuals can be very evil indeed.

A lot of the trouble lies in our propensity to project negative concepts onto those we dislike or disagree with, and then to lump them together into a faceless group and dehumanize them: 'All Jews are . . . all blacks are . . . all gays are . . .'. Yes, and 'All Christians are . . .' too! This is what seems to be happening, to an increasing extent, in our public life. Yet there was never a time when rationality, and the search for reasonable solutions to social ills, based upon good will, logical thought, and scientifically assessed knowledge, was more urgently necessary. A most alarming symptom of today's society is the spread of irrationalism and the amount of attention paid to the views of people who are, in some respects at least, cranky and even quite simply barmy. For example, our old friend Mary Whitehouse doesn't accept Darwin's theory of evolution because it contradicts the book of Genesis. Yet an increasing number of people seem to accept her as a serious social critic! She and the bunch of rabid evangelical biblical fundamentalists who are increasingly permitted by the Churches to masquerade as the spokespersons of 'Christian morality' are quite incapable of distinguishing truth from falsehood – and I sometimes suspect they aren't concerned to make any such distinction, because it would be so inconvenient for them. They remind me of something André Gide said in his book *The Coiners*:

> The deeper the soul plunges into religious devotion, the more it loses all desire, all love for reality. . . . The dazzling light of their faith blinds them to the surrounding world and to their own selves. As for me, who care for nothing so much as to see the world and myself clearly, I am amazed at the coils of falsehood in which devout persons take delight.

Hard on the heels of Whitehouse's still unapologized for denunciation of the Albany Trust for its – totally fictitious, need I say? – 'promotion' of paedophilia, we now have Mrs Valerie Riches of the grotesquely named 'Responsible Society' stomping the country accusing the Family Planning Association of 'educating children in promiscuity'. These shameless people . . . obviously don't accept A. E. Housman's belief that 'accuracy is a duty and not a virtue'. Even if they do regard it as a virtue, they make absolutely no attempt whatsoever to be virtuous!

Irrationality about sex is even more pervasive than irrationality about most other things. I suppose it is inevitable that something so bound up with emotion should invite a rush of blood to the head (if to nowhere else). In the preface, written in 1899, to the first edition of Part I of his *Studies in the Psychology of Sex*, Havelock Ellis says:

> It may safely be said that in no other field of human activity is so vast an amount of strenuous didactic morality founded on so slender a basis of facts. In most other departments of life we at least make a pretence of learning before we presume to teach; in the field of sex we content ourselves with the smallest and vaguest minimum of information, often ostentatiously second-hand, usually unreliable.

And a more recent commentator, Kinsey's colleague Dr Wardell Pomeroy, has said: 'There is probably more nonsense written about homosexuality, more unwarranted fear of it, and less understanding of it than of any other area of human sexuality.'

I had hoped that some of the sillier myths about homosexuality which were common coin in the 1950s and 1960s would have been dispelled by now. However, most of them are sadly still alive and seemingly quite well; so here's a check-list together with some of the more obvious responses:

It's unnatural.

It occurs in nature. What about shaving, wearing clothes, eating cooked food? If all of these *are* 'unnatural', so what?

It's sick.

This has been endlessly disposed of, but people go on and on saying it. Let me repeat: numerous psychological researches have shown no statistically significant differences between the psychological health and successful social functioning of homosexual and heterosexual people. There is no more point in asking what makes anyone homosexual than there is in asking what makes anyone heterosexual. Anyway, we're all potentially bisexual. As Kevin O'Dowd – a psychotherapist specializing in sexuality – has said: 'Research into "causes" and "cures" of homosexuality is a complete waste of time and money. Why does this particular form of sexual activity make such an assault upon other people's sensitivities?'

It's sinful.

I leave this one to the Christians, for whom sin and sexual pleasure commonly seem synonymous. I'm sorry for the poor Gay Christians, batting their heads against the brick wall of centuries' old tradition and prejudice. Yet I feel quite impatient with them too, because they are self-oppressive Uncle Toms and Aunt Sallies. As Michael De-la-Noy – who used to be the Archbishop of Canterbury's press secretary – once said to me, you need to be schizophrenic to be gay and a Christian.[1]

It's criminal.

There's still quite a long way to go before most people will realize that the law's legitimate place in regard to sexual morality is minimal. The law should do three things, and three things only. It should punish assaults; punish public behaviour that is justifiably offensive to others; and protect the immature or inadequate from predatory sexual exploitation. Apart from these, every limit which the law places upon people's freedom to choose how they behave sexually diminishes their responsibility and is therefore ethically corrupting.

Gays are a danger to children.

With the John Saunders case,[2] we now have the extraordinary situation that an official tribunal has given a binding ruling that, even if this particular prejudice is totally without foundation, the mere fact that enough people believe it makes it a 'reasonable' cause for dismissal from employment. If ever there was a wilful perversion of the concept of 'reasonableness', this is it; and it is greatly to be hoped that enough MPs will be outraged by such idiocy for some steps to be taken towards anti-discriminatory legislation.

Gays are all like the comic stereotypes.

So people can say 'I've never met one in my life'.

Some irrational gay responses:

'I must be vile/sick/perverted/criminal/sinful. So must my sexual partners. I can't be gay – I don't like drag queens. Gay is better. Passing is safer. (But the double life isn't!) I must stay within my limits (ageism, fetishism, fantasy, SM). Etc., etc.'

We need to liberate ourselves – not just as a political act but, much more significantly, as human beings. This is perhaps even more important for gay people than for others, just because of all the negative bilge we've had dumped on us and are still getting. In the type of humanistic counselling work that I am increasingly involved in these days a lot of store is placed on 'authenticity' as a valuable component of healthy human functioning. Genuineness isn't always easy to define: but I believe that most of us do in fact know in our gut when we, and other people, are being genuine and when we're being phoney.

Not all the phoneyness is deliberate – I'm willing to take at any rate some of what the Bible-bashers say about 'truth' and 'love' as being sincerely meant – but the hash they make of their relationships with others on a human level speaks more loudly than such mere words. My own quite futile efforts to establish some straightforward, mutually sincere dialogue with various characters associated with the Festival of Light and similar bodies have led me to the inescapable conclusion that straightforward, mutually sincere dialogue is not their stock-in-trade.

Constantly having to combat irrational and dangerous thinking is strenuous and sometimes tedious, but not necessarily boring. It can be fun. And as no one else is doing it as consistently and effectively as necessary, I hope that GALHA will concentrate on a demolition job of much of the silly rubbish that is still spouted about homosexuality. To spur us on, here's a quotation from an utterly unimpeachable source:

> It's the uniqueness of each individual that contributes to the variety of life. Free choice is ultimately what life is about, what ethics is about. The whole of the case for freedom is a moral case because it involves choice. Do away with choice and you do away with human dignity. That is why I hate all forms of political extremism. . . . We seek to promote, not destroy, the uniqueness of the individual.

Guess who said that? Margaret Thatcher! But for my very last word, I quote a famous American civil libertarian lawyer, the late Morris Ernst. He wrote in 1936: 'When countries go to the right politically, women go back into the kitchen, books are burned and taboos fence off new frontiers against human adventure.'

Perhaps they're both right, in their different ways. Or am I being unreasonable?

Notes

1. Endorsed by E. M. Forster's comments in his posthumously published gay novel, *Maurice*, that 'between [a homosexual] temperament and [the Christian] religion there is a secular feud', and that those who base their conduct upon what they are must always throw Christianity over in the end.
2. Saunders was a maintenance man at a Scottish teenagers' holiday and training camp who was dismissed after he had admitted to being gay, although he had committed no offence, and his work was acknowledged to be satisfactory. His dismissal was upheld by an Employment Appeal Tribunal, and confirmed by the Edinburgh Court of Session, on the absurd ground that, while there was no objective proof of any such risk, his employers were justified in getting rid of him on the basis of popular prejudices about the danger that homosexuals supposedly posed to children.

Permit Me If You Dare!

ASK BULLETIN, NO. 1, SPRING 1982[1]

The permissive society gets my goat. Just where the grotesque notion that anyone requires somebody else's 'permission' to make their own choices about their personal, and especially their sexual, lives comes from I don't know. But I do know that for the past dozen or so years 'the permissive society' and 'permissiveness' have been cunningly exploited as controlling catchwords by a bunch of people who don't like the personal choices that others are not only making but are daring at long last to be open about.

Whether they realize it or not, these 'anti-permissives' are enemies of human freedom, responsibility, and happiness. In their own warped minds, of course, they see themselves as the (self-appointed) guardians of precisely these values – they are very fond of contrasting 'liberty' with 'licence' and of proclaiming that they alone possess the revealed wisdom that knows the difference. Like all authoritarian parent-figures, from Plato's Guardians down through the ages to Hitler, Stalin, Paisley, and the Pope, they know what's best not just for themselves but for me, for you, and for all those others out there.

Do *you* want to live in a permissive society? I don't. I don't want the Holy Punk of Ulster, the Bigot of Rome, the Prime Nagger of Westminster, the President of the Provincial Voyeurs and Eavesdroppers Association, the militant tendencies of either the extreme left or the extreme right, or anybody else, telling me how I've 'got' to live my private – or, for that matter, my public – life; what I mustn't feel, think, say, or do; what I may not watch on television, or whom not to have sex with.

Of course, any society has to have some laws. But these should be confined to what is essential for the smooth functioning of social life – 'rules of the road' type laws – and for the protection of individual citizens from unwanted harms such as physical assaults, slander, blackmail, theft, etc. The proper function of law is to protect everyone's privacies and freedoms: not to impose the moral, religious, or political opinions of one lot of people upon the rest.

This political philosophy was almost universally taken for granted thirty years ago when I was a student. It isn't any more. A spirit of vengeful intolerance and the will to persecute are once more abroad in the land, and Orwell's nightmare vision of 1984 looks disconcertingly more plausible than it did when he wrote it in 1948.

If some people choose to give away their own personal freedom and responsibility, allowing their life-choices to be made for them by some external authority, whether human or allegedly supernatural, that is their own business. But when they set out to extend their pet version of holy writ to the rest of us, it's time to call a halt to all their prattle of 'permissiveness'.

It's my conviction that each individual has not only the right, but the responsibility – and the duty as well – to make their own decisions for themselves about how they will live their lives; and that so long as these decisions do not interfere with the legitimate freedoms of others to do likewise, any person or institution which claims the right to 'permit' or to 'forbid' them to choose as they do is oppressive and should be resisted.

No, I don't want to live in a 'permissive society', thank you very much. Nor do I want to live in an inhumane, intolerantly inconsiderate 'grabbers take all' one. I intend to do my best to see that we all of us live in a self-responsibly free and creative society; and, so far as sexuality is concerned, a fear-free and uninhibitedly loving one.

Note

1. Action for Sexual Knowledge (ASK) was a sex education and information agency which I founded together with the late Bill Stewart (formerly of Sexual Problems of the Disabled – SPOD). After running some training workshops, and publishing one issue of the *Bulletin*, we unfortunately had to wind ASK up because of lack of funding.

Gay Fears and Anti-Gay Phobias

MAY 1987[1]

Whoever wins on 11 June, homosexuals are already losers in this general election. An always unpopular and misunderstood minority is under concerted attack from much of the press and some politicians as never before. Conservatives such as Norman Tebbit are busily whipping up prejudice and scoffing at any attempts to remedy anti-gay discrimination or to get more balanced discussion of the issue in sex education and elsewhere as 'loony Left barminess'. Neil Kinnock has relegated the Labour Party's conference commitment to gay rights to the 'fringe and tassel' wastebin for the duration of the election campaign. The Liberal/Social Democrat Alliance is keeping very quiet about its anti-discrimination policies. The drive towards a better-informed and fairer society is low on the political agenda.

Yet the scapegoating of homosexuals in conjunction with the inexorably developing AIDS crisis of which they have so far borne the main brunt is perhaps the most sensitive barometer to the sort of society we shall have in the 1990s. Understandably, there was something of a siege atmosphere at the recent Organisation for Lesbian and Gay Rights Campaign's conference. Some speakers declared feelings akin to those which must have gripped German Jews during the latter days of the Weimar Republic: a growing sense of vulnerability and powerlessness in face of the virulent hostility that is being whipped up against gays by some right-wing politicians and most of Fleet Street.

If such apprehensions contain a grain of paranoia, this is surely not surprising. There is far more paranoia about homosexuality amongst the heterosexual public, and far more phobic thinking about AIDS – verging, in some quarters, on hysteria – than there are groundless fears amongst homosexuals about their potential scapegoating and social victimization.

I believe this is a matter which should be addressed now, and without equivocation, by all those who are seeking election to Parliament. The issues are simple, and concern our basic freedoms. Do we want Britain to remain a society which makes at least some effort to understand the different and tolerates diversity in sexual preference as well as in other areas of life, or are we to become a more authoritarian country with strands of clerical and moral dictatorship which we have hitherto looked upon as unBritish?

There is a disturbing chasm between political rhetoric and practice. While these are in no sense 'party political' matters, the contradiction is currently most pronounced in the Conservative party. The Prime Minister[2] is fond of proclaiming that freedom of choice is the basis of morality; she has said that unless tolerance is applied to everybody, it is good for nobody. I agree with her. If I thought that she and her supporters understood the implications of this philosophy, I would be far happier. But what we are in fact now seeing is repeated and strident attacks by prominent Conservatives upon any notion that homosexual men and women are not obnoxious, degenerate, dirty-minded, and a menace to the young.

The latest example is the innocuously named 'Local Government Act 1986 (Amendment) Bill',[3] which has the objective of making it illegal for local authorities ('loony Left' ones, needless to say!) to spend ratepayers' money on 'promoting' homosexuality – by which the Bill's supporters appear to mean any policies intended to be supportive of homosexuals' equal rights as citizens and to foster more balanced views about them. The Bill, introduced by Lord Halsbury and passed by the House of Lords, was recently debated in the Commons. Its sponsor, Dame Jill Knight, spoke of 'evidence in shocking abundance' (which needless to say she did not produce) 'that young children in our schools, some as young as five years, are frequently being encouraged into homosexuality and lesbianism', and that some of what was being taught 'would undoubtedly lead to a great spread of AIDS'. The Local Government Minister, Dr Rhodes Boyson, expressing the Government's support for the Bill's aims, asserted that 'undermining the common standards of society, flaunting behaviour that the overwhelming majority of those brought up in this country and its traditions find revolting, unsettling the minds of the coming generation is one way – a subtle way – of changing the society in which we live'. He added that 'the positive promotion of the images of lesbianism and male homosexuality as though they are equivalent to family life could bring death in one generation . . . there is no future in it – it is the end of creation'.

For a Government minister – let alone one who is a former headmaster – not only to be unaware that there is widespread primitive prejudice against, and even hatred of, hundreds of thousands of our fellow-citizens simply because they are emotionally and physically attracted to members of their own sex, but also to fuel such ignorant prejudice with inflammatory statements of his own is a most serious matter. Dr Boyson, Dame Jill, Lord Halsbury, and their like, can accurately be described as homophobic – a clinical term coined by the American psychiatrist Dr George Weinberg to identify an irrational fear of and prejudice against homosexuals, justifying antagonism towards and mistreatment of them.[4] Dr Weinberg identifies the characteristics of homophobia as bigotry, sexual insecurity, envy (a dislike of others being happy), an urge to compel social conformity and – significantly in Dr Boyson's case – extreme dislike of those who reject the option of vicarious immortality through parenthood. 'Our great glorification of reproduction', he says, 'serves in part as a ceremony to circumvent death as if by magic.' It jars on homophobes to think that homosexuals may not be bothered about leaving offspring behind them when they die.

The phobic fears of death and dying which characterize our twentieth century Western culture are of course heightened by the advent of AIDS, so that it is all too easy to project these fears onto homosexual AIDS sufferers as the 'wrath of God' for their way of life. Yet the challenge which AIDS presents is not only to our compassion: it is also to our understanding. For the sake of public health, as well as from simple natural justice, we simply cannot afford to discriminate against homosexuals and exclude them from the mainstream of our society.

I am thankful that this simple truth has been accepted by the all-party House of Commons Select Committee on the Social Services in their recently published report on *Problems Associated with AIDS*.[5] The Committee – in contrast to Dr Boyson – recognized that in health education 'a balance has to be struck between further alienating a group which regards itself as outside society and drawing them in to the point where they are treated in the same way as that part of society they do not identify with'. Dutch AIDS literature for the gay community, the Committee said (para 63), 'is carefully worded so as not to appear to be imposing heterosexual norms or values upon them. . . . *The alienation of any sub-group from the rest of society, whether by their own intent or through the attitudes of others, will undermine the public health, since they may not then feel any responsibility to act for the general good.*'

These are wise words, and we can only hope that the next Government (whoever they are[6]) pay careful heed to them when presented in the new Parliament with demands for a fairer deal for the homosexual minority and effective action to curb irrational bias, bigotry, prejudice, and the verbally or physically violent expression of homophobic hatred.

Notes

1. I include this previously unpublished article because it articulates my concerns about the increasingly strident homophobia which culminated in Section 28.
2. Margaret Thatcher.
3. The forerunner of Section 28 of the Local Government Act 1988.
4. In *Society and the Healthy Homosexual* (Colin Smythe, 1975).
5. Third Report from the Social Services Committee, Session 1986/7.
6. They were Conservative yet again!

Ungay Tories

OPEN MIND, MAY 1987

I grew up during the war, when the Conservative Party was at first grudgingly, then thankfully, and finally wholeheartedly Churchillian, infused with his breadth of vision, magnanimity, generous compassion and humour. Like almost everyone else in the Party, I was stunned by the 1945 Labour landslide, and went up to Cambridge when the gladiatorial front bench combats of that Parliament were being echoed in the Union. It was an exciting time politically.

The mendacities of the Suez crisis jolted me out of the Conservative Party, and I have sat loose to any party allegiance ever since. But the concerns which made me a Conservative during my early life remain the same. They are the historic British commitment to individual liberty: freedom of speech, the right to personal choice in private tastes and behaviour (so long as others are not damaged or imposed upon), a healthy tolerance of the different and even of the eccentric, and that robust independence of mind and action that for the past three centuries has been the unquestioned birthright of John Bull.

Because I am gay, civil liberties and the rights of minorities have undoubtedly mattered more to me than they would have done if I had been heterosexual. The temptation to count one's bourgeois blessings and to look after No.1 is always strong, and too many comfortably off gay folk still succumb to it, keeping their heads well down in a variety of political and professional closets. For me, however, the imperative need to change the abominably repressive and unjust pre-Wolfenden law was a dominating force in my life ever since I first realized, as a teenager, that my attraction to other men was not just a 'passing phase'. As Ralph says in Mary Renault's novel *The Charioteer*, 'You can't make good wine in a bath-tub in the cellar, you need sun and rain and fresh air, you need a pride in the job you can tell the world about. Only you can live without drink if you have to, but you can't live without love.' This belief in my own and other gay people's entitlement to freedom and justice under the law motivated my decade of active involvement in the campaign for reform from the time the Wolfenden Report appeared.

Throughout the parliamentary battles to enact Wolfenden, homosexuality was never treated as a party political issue, or used by politicians to attack their opponents. There were authentically free votes in all the debates, and the Labour Government, with Roy Jenkins as an actively helpful Home Secretary, made extra time available for the Bill to complete its final passage onto the Statute Book because it was supported by cross-party majorities in both Houses. Not all the support, or all the opposition, was from the same side: some of the most vehement critics of reform were old-fashioned Labour MPs, who quaintly regarded sodomy as the vice of the idle, degenerate rich; while a solid phalanx of some 60 Tories, including Margaret Thatcher, voted for the Bill, even if not all of them care to remember that now. (Though why not?) In the Lords – scarcely a hangout of the Loony Left – opponents of the late Lord Arran's brave and persistent campaign were in a dwindling minority.

What a contrast to today, when in the run-up to a general election gay rights are being shrugged off by the Labour leadership, because it sees them as an electoral liability only a few months after they were voted into the Party's manifesto by a two-thirds conference majority; and any sympathetic Tories are silent while Norman Tebbit jeers at any notion that there is unfair prejudice or discrimination against gays as 'an Ealing comedy joke'.

This menacing change cannot be entirely ascribed to the onset of AIDS. Nor can it be blamed on the naïve conflation of gay rights with the snark-like chimera of 'socialism' by the surviving rump of Gay Liberation Front jargonists. If today's Conservatives wish to espouse the cause of justice for homosexuals – or for any other underprivileged and vilified minority – they will surely do so, regardless of what the Left has to say on the issue.

It is unfortunately the case that the Conservative Party of the 1980s has become a very different animal from the one I belonged to in the 1940s and 1950s. It is not one that I could feel at all at home in – and I must admit to considerable surprise that there are still some homosexuals who do.

What has changed in the Party, and why do I dislike so many of its vocal members so heartily now?

While I do not deny the Prime Minister's[1] virtues of purposeful determination, her utter conviction of her own rectitude and the impatient scorn with which she is apt to sweep aside anyone who dares to differ have seeped down into the Party's guts with pretty disastrous results for its claim to be any longer a 'broad church' or to represent British fair play. It is nowadays much more akin to a sect – or even a cult, displaying the same blinkered self-righteousness and arrogant intolerance of dissent that one finds in 'born-again' religious freaks. Most alarming, to me, is the growing divergence between the rhetoric of freedom and individual choice still employed in Tory sloganizing and the increasingly authoritarian measures employed to crush and discredit opposition both outside the Party and within it. Even more sinister is the concerted move to delegitimize and brand as 'subversive' viewpoints, attitudes and lifestyles which surely have a right to exist and to be heard and seen in a genuinely democratic society.

Today's Tory Party strikes me as a factional tail hellbent on wagging the national dog. And the Party dog itself is nowadays being wagged by a powerful, cliqueish and unrepresentative tail of New Right MPs and ideologues – Boysons, Worsthornes, Scrutons, Digby Andersons and Lady

Coxes – whose stock-in-trade is unbridled bigotry and vituperation against everyone they dislike – with homosexuals high on the list.

While one may fault the style of the Left's gay rights campaigning, there is no denying that they have highlighted the anti-gay discrimination that is rife in our society – and now so much more serious and urgent because of the AIDS crisis. They have achieved a political impact in the Labour Party which gay Tories have not matched in theirs. Surely it is ostrich-like to attack them for fighting *our* battles, however clumsily: it is high time for each of us to take up the cudgels in our own political patch.

In my view, things are going to get worse for gay people in the immediate future, whoever wins the general election on 11 June. There will only be an improvement when the tone and temper of society as a whole moves back towards the former, more tolerant, inclusive attitudes making for social cohesion – attitudes which are, I believe, the stuff of a more authentic Conservatism than the current fashions.

To put a polite gloss on a crude saying attributed to President Lyndon Johnson, you can either stay in and pitch out or get out and pitch in. Having got out of the Tory Party half a lifetime ago, and still retaining some shreds of nostalgic feeling for it, I pitch in this squib to all my fellow homosexuals who still think – incomprehensibly to me – that the Conservatives are a worthwhile political home for gay people. Do not rest until that is true. Speak out loudly in vigorous protest whenever a national or local Conservative insults and denigrates homosexuals and tells untruths about homosexuality. Write to your parliamentary candidates and new MPs and use the media to tell the people of this country that the millions-strong homosexual and bisexual minority are a responsible, decent and valuable group of men and women who deserve long overdue recognition of their true nature and disadvantaged situation and are entitled to be treated properly. And don't settle for second-rate citizenship – inside the Conservative Party or outside it.

Note

1. Margaret Thatcher.

Calling All Yukkers!

Following an article I wrote for The Freethinker *in 1992 on the silver jubilee of the 1967 Sexual Offences Act, a woman reader wrote to me asserting that most people are intolerant of male homosexuals mainly 'because of shit', since gay men do not share the majority's instinctive disgust at buggery. She challenged me to 'stop preaching' and 'get down to basics'. The following hitherto unpublished open letter is an attempt to do so.*

Dear Mrs Yuk,

You tell me that, in order to be accepted, gay men must 'explain to heterosexuals why they are not put off by the contact with faeces'.

This, you surely realize, is an impossible task. No one can explain 'why' they have certain tastes and certain aversions, or why they lack them. I say 'yuk' at the notion of having any form of sexual intercourse with a woman, while you say 'yuk' at two men (or a man and a woman) having anal intercourse.

If I were to tell you that buggery doesn't turn me on either, would that really make me more acceptable to you as a gay man? I doubt it – you would probably then wax eloquent over the iniquities of cocksucking. If not, why not? Just a matter of preference, I suppose.

You see, I really don't believe that the intimate details of my sexual desires and diversions (or yours, or anyone else's) are any business whatsoever of anybody except ourselves and our willing sexual partners. If you cannot agree with me that this level of toleration for practices and beliefs (sexual or other) which we may ourselves abhor is an essential component of a decent, civilized society, you and I have very different notions of what such a society is.

You tell me that 'the likes of [me]' blur the issues. I consider that it is the likes of you who will not face up to the consequences of allowing irrational prejudices to dictate social policy. For everyone is in some respects a Yukker. The list of my own personal yuk targets is quite lengthy. Among the major items are: ill-mannered small children and their feckless parents; the practice of abortion, and its false presentation as a fail-safe for birth control; tobacco smokers of any kind and pipe smokers in particular; pickled onion eaters; people of a good many political and religious persuasions (better unspecified, for I have some of them as neighbours); and bigots of every hue.

I say 'Yuk' to them all. I won't have them in my house if I can jolly well help it. But they are free, so far as I am concerned, to pursue their malodorous behaviour and to peddle their daft ideas consentingly and in private: whatever they do is *none of my business*, unless they intrude upon my or your privacy and freedom. It is at that point that their obnoxious personal preferences become of legitimate public interest; and determining where that point lies is the most crucial and delicate decision of social politics. It's no wonder that society so often gets it wrong. One reason I am a freethinker is that I believe that on many fundamentally important issues – buggery included – the non-religious have got it right more often than the God-botherers, of whose persistently malign influence you speak much too lightly.

Since you have pinpointed and personalized the issue, I shall do the same. Why are the likes of you so obsessed with, and revolted by, shit? Freud, I suppose, would put it down to over-strict potty training; and I must say I think it is unhealthy to be either nauseated or fascinated by a substance which is a normal, healthy waste product of normal, healthy human bodies. Of course, if shit is not dealt with hygienically it becomes a source of dirt and disease. During the 1960s [homosexual law reform] debates, one of your fellow Yukkers considerately sent some shit by post to Lord Arran, whose stalwart secretary sensibly threw it away on arrival because she decided it wouldn't keep until her employer returned to his office.

I think, you see, that this constant harping on homosexuals' attitudes to shit (or piss, or cum, or whatever) is just naïve rationalization of *dislike of the different*: the basic reason why the majority dislike gay people is simply that we are different, and won't conform, and the 'yuk factor' conveniently bolsters this prejudice and intolerance. Insecure 'male chauvinist pigs' – who still, alas, constitute the great majority of the male population – feel their fragile 'masculinity' is threatened by gay men, while some women resent being rejected or ignored by them. Reasons why lesbians are less bothersome to most are that they are seen as less powerful, not so threatening to macho notions of maleness, and more appealing to male prurience – and, perhaps, sheer lack of imagination about what *they* get up to in (or out of) bed.

Frankly, Mrs Yuk, I am utterly choked off with your sort – constantly invoking your yukkiness as an excuse to abuse those you happen to dislike and to condone inhumane treatment of them, while at the same time parading a phony tolerance. I too say 'yuk' quite a lot; but thank goodness I am not (as you appear to be) a paid-up member of the loud-mouthed tribe of censorious Yukkers.

Ever so sincerely yours (yuk!),
    ANTONY GREY

Towards Homosexual Emancipation

THE ETHICAL RECORD, DECEMBER 1992[1]

In writing *Quest for Justice: Towards Homosexual Emancipation* I wanted the book to be authoritative and comprehensive, but inevitably a lot had to be left out. I hope the result will not strike you as too bland. For homosexual law reform and gay rights are not bland topics.

At the outset, the issue seemed simple. The criminal law, which since 1885 had prohibited all physical sexual contacts between men, however willing their consent and however private the circumstances, was abominably unjust. Those of us who were homosexual knew its dire cost, not only in stress and personal unhappiness, but also in lives wrecked by blackmail, imprisonment, and suicide. The Wolfenden Report of 1958 vouchsafed an opportunity to end this state of affairs, and this was the goal of the Homosexual Law Reform Society. We simply wanted to get the law out of the private lives of consenting adults. We had no thoughts of a crusade for homosexual respectability or acceptance: 'Gay Rights' was in those days an unheard-of concept.

While the law change of 1967 was a culmination, it was also a prelude. The rise in the 1970s of a visible and vocal Gay Rights movement produced a series of ongoing clashes in some ways more bitter than the pre-1967 debates. While the harsh injustice of the old law was plain to all except the most blinkered of bigots, the far-reaching and in some respects socially subversive claims of Gay Liberation were much more contentious and were perceived as intolerably threatening by the 'Moral Majority' defenders of religious and social orthodoxy.

In my view, the shrill articulation by some gay liberationists of extreme demands for total sexual freedoms perceived by their critics as unbridled license, coupled with intemperate attacks by both gays and feminists on the family as an institution, have done considerable damage by polarizing attitudes to an extent where it has become much more controversial for sympathetically concerned people of most political persuasions except the extreme Left to support Gay Rights. My head often deplored the political ineptitude of the radicals while my heart endorsed much of their anger and impatience. They were fighting real oppression and entrenched bigotry, and still are.

The recent fiascos over alleged 'Satanic child abuse', and the mayhem perpetrated by some doctors and social workers in Cleveland, Rochdale, Orkney and elsewhere, are a direct spin-off from the hysterical hullabaloo with which Mary Whitehouse and her allies greeted the Albany Trust's modest efforts in the 1970s to put the vexed topic of paedophilia onto the social work agenda and to provide responsible counselling for paedophiles. The term 'paedophile' is not synonymous with 'child molester', but in fact denotes the unfortunate condition of an adult who is emotionally and sexually attracted to pre-pubertal children without necessarily physically molesting or sexually abusing them or even desiring to. (For the record, my personal preference is to avoid the company of children below the ages of reason and puberty whenever possible!)

All that I and my colleagues at the Albany Trust in fact did was to sponsor a few private talks between professionally interested therapists, social workers, and some paedophiles, to explore what kind of counselling and support systems might be set up to help some lonely, emotionally isolated, and often very frightened, people. For our pains, we were vociferously lambasted by all those good Christians in the Festival of Light, National Viewers' and Listeners' Association, and their assorted allies for allegedly using public money to 'normalize sexual attraction and activity between adult males and little girls' – and we ultimately forfeited our meagre Government funding because of the parliamentary rumpus kicked up over a period of months with this bizarre charge. You will not be surprised that, ever since, I have regarded these people's pretensions to be regarded as vessels of moral purity and truthfulness in public life with a large pinch of incredulity.

Humanism is of course a prime scapegoat of 'moral pollution' in the eyes of these people, who firmly link it to what they regard as its inseparable Siamese twin, Communism. They see those of us who are engaged in social reform campaigns of which they disapprove as forming a sinister and deliberately concerted conspiracy to subvert the nation's moral fibre. My own lifetime's observation of people's ethics and behaviour leads me to conclude that, at the very least, the morality and conduct of professedly religious people often does not measure up to that of non-believers in terms of sheer human decency. Humanists are faced with an ingrained social hypocrisy where the evils of malicious slander and deliberate misrepresentation masquerade as 'godly' and are accepted as such by far too many bemused bystanders.

There is much about gay life, and gay attitudes, that I do not admire. But as a democrat, I believe that self-government is better than good government. The snag with this is that nowadays too few people have any notion of what good self-government – which requires self-discipline – involves. Those of us who have spent much of our lives struggling to get oppressive and inhumane laws off people's backs have had far too little time and energy left to do nearly enough about helping people to use their new-found freedom wisely.

I am not convinced that today's gay rights campaigners are on the right tracks, or are likely to make effective political progress with the draft reform bills and other strategies they are at present following. I believe that what is needed is a complete overhaul of the legal and social frameworks dealing with all aspects of sexuality. One's sexual attitudes, desires and relationships are each individual's most intimate and personal possession, and should only be interfered with by the law or social agencies on the clearest possible evidence of direct harm to others. It is time to do away with 'victimless crimes' by redefining the age or ages of consent so that it will no longer be possible to criminalize willing participants in either heterosexual or homosexual behaviour, whatever their ages, although they may be subject to civil protective procedures in appropriate circumstances

Above all, we must move towards what Francis Bennion[2] calls a 'sex-positive society', in which notions of sin, guilt and dirt are no longer inculcated into our young people, who instead must be taught how to achieve self-respect, encouraged to show a caring concern for others, and helped to make responsible choices. In this sphere no one will ever convince me that the old religious shibboleths are superior to a rational humanist ethic which has due regard for oneself and for others. Ultimately, this is what I mean by a 'quest for justice'.

Notes

1. Summary of a lecture given to the Ethical Society on 8 November 1992.
2. In *The Sex Code: Morals for Moderns* (Weidenfeld and Nicolson, 1991).

Society Bordering on Sexual Paranoia

THE SCOTSMAN, 5 MARCH 1993

In August 1992 I was interviewed by a woman journalist from The Scotsman, *supposedly about my recently published book,* Quest for Justice. *It quickly became apparent that this lady's main interest was to enquire whether or not I believed children should be 'protected' from sexuality. When I told her that they should be equipped with the facts they needed to make their own choices sensibly, she published an article depicting me as having a 'phobia' about value judgements and 'heading for the lunatic fringe': according to her, I was someone to whom 'responsibility is anathema' and (she implied) who believed that 'sending for a snap of a naked eight-year-old is no more a crime than stamp collecting'. Naturally, I was extremely annoyed at this blatant misrepresentation of my actual beliefs and attitudes. It took several months of persistence on my part before the editor offered me an opportunity to contribute the following article. Even then, he chose to omit the passages enclosed in square brackets, on the ground that he felt 'a little uneasy' about them. I wonder why?*

Fettesgate;[1] President Clinton's skirmish with his Colonel Blimps over gay soldiers; weird tales of 'Satanic child abuse'; outrage at the notion of parents presuming to choose a child's sex: why, I ask myself, are sexual issues generating so much more heat than light these days?

The sheer bigoted prejudice and ignorance about homosexuality displayed by so many in the British police forces, and by the military on both sides of the Atlantic, provide a sad commentary on the lack of impact of a quarter-century's efforts at public education since I helped Leo Abse and the late Lord Arran to pilot the 1967 Sexual Offences Act onto the Statute Book for England and Wales. That law – belatedly extended to Scotland, with all its blemishes, in 1980 – is now ripe for revision.

I vividly recall the scene in the House of Lords when the status of members of the armed forces under the new homosexuality law was debated in 1965. The victor of Alamein, Field Marshal Viscount Montgomery, having unavailingly (and only half humorously) proposed that the age of consent in the Bill should be raised from 21 to 80, countered the reminder that other NATO armies accepted homosexuals into their ranks without discipline crumbling with the choleric cry: 'We are not French, and we are not other nationals. We are BRITISH, thank God!' Today, on the other side of the duck pond, General Colin Powell (seemingly forgetful of his own minority's fight for acceptance) holds similarly prejudiced gut-feelings which he rationalizes by protesting that having open gays in the US army will destroy the mental peace of their straight colleagues. I am mystified as to why all these robustly heterosexual senior warriors go completely to pieces at the merest whiff of same-sex affection, like Victorian virgins with the vapours.[2]

All this is the stuff of fantasy bordering on paranoia [as, apparently, are the grotesque allegations by presumably sane social workers of obscene Satanic sex rituals in Orkney quarries presided over by elderly Christian ministers]. While not going all the way with Freudian theories of projection, I am increasingly dismayed that, in these days of ceaseless and largely mindless sex chatter, such bizarre notions meet with so much instant and widespread credulity.

This febrile atmosphere makes it much harder for those who bear the personal burdens involved in belonging to socially stigmatized sexual minorities to concentrate upon the main business of their lives – which is, like that of everyone else, earning a living (if they are fortunate enough to be employed), making their way in the world, and forming constructive personal relationships.

Surely it is time that gay men and lesbian women – who are no longer regarded by most of the medical profession as being sick – ceased to be socially stigmatized and looked down upon with such fear, loathing, and ridicule. In Scotland, there is more widespread good sense, and less prurient humbug, than south of the Border. I hope the day will soon come when the mere fact of being known to have homosexual relationships is no longer regarded as making a judge (or anyone else) unfit for professional and public service. Meanwhile, homosexual people will continue to be in the absurd Catch-22 position of risking their careers by being openly gay, and losing them (for alleged 'hypocrisy') if they conceal their sexual preference.

I believe, both as a private individual and as a counsellor, that shouldering personal responsibility is the essential linchpin of a civilized society. This must necessarily include showing understanding, tolerance, and respect towards those who differ from ourselves sexually, as well as racially, religiously, and politically.

The stupid public attitudes towards homosexuality fostered by some sections of the media and a few politicians place great burdens of unnecessary unhappiness upon very many individuals – not least adolescents, who still have to face the hostility and ridicule of their schoolmates as they struggle to understand and come to terms with their own sexual natures in the culpable absence of a balanced national sex education programme.

On the overheated question of children and sex, I believe that the sexuality of children has to be acknowledged and welcomed as a fact of life by adults. I do not believe that childhood 'innocence' can be bolstered or prolonged by keeping children in ignorance, or by denying the existence of their sexual interests and desires, whatever these may be. To do so is an abdication of adult responsibility.

As far as the law is concerned, while sexual assaults should of course be punished, I do not believe that there is any justification for criminalizing private sexual activities (whether heterosexual or homosexual) between partners who have freely consented to what they do. An *age of protection*, providing for appropriate civil (as opposed to criminal) proceedings where young people under the age of majority (18) are deemed to be at risk (or a risk to others) because of their sexual behaviour, would be a more effective way of safeguarding adolescents than is the current legal fiction of an 'age of consent' below which a sexual act is a crime however eagerly each of the participants has in fact engaged in it.

The validity of 'consent', however, has to be defined and tested; and, because of their lack of awareness of many aspects of adult society, children who have not reached the ages of puberty, or of discretion, are not in a position to give consent which is as meaningful as that of an adult.

[I earnestly hope we shall soon begin to take a more realistic and discerning attitude towards paedophiles – that is, adults who are affectionately and sexually drawn towards children. At present, there is almost total confusion between paedophiles and child-molesters – yet the distinction between them is similar to that between lovers and rapists. Paedophiles who genuinely love children do not physically harm or sexually abuse them: they are often gentle and unhappy people who suffer from a severe emotional and social handicap. To lump such folk together with the conscienceless and utterly irresponsible abusers of children (who are not infrequently members of the abusers' families) is not only totally unjust but crassly ignorant. Nor is it by any means the case that those children who are involved in relationships with paedophiles are always ignorantly innocent, or unwilling – indeed, the child is sometimes the instigator of the affair. And imprisonment is not always the most socially useful way of dealing with even the offenders who do abuse; it may satisfy primitive urges for revenge, but can sometimes make the family situation even more fraught and hopeless.]

While I have sympathy with the human predicament in which paedophiles (i.e. lovers of children, as distinct from child abusers) find themselves, I do not believe that their dream of a boundary-free sexual state of affairs between adults and children is socially acceptable – or desirable. But as a democrat, and a firm upholder of free discussion, I do believe that their opinions, however wrongheaded most of us consider them to be, should be given a fair hearing and not garbled out of all recognition. [To stereotype and demonize a category of people who are in fact widely dissimilar as individuals merely makes an already vexed problem even more intractable.]

Sadly, the current climate of unreasoning hostility to the mere mention of the subject obliges me to state categorically that, far from being a paedophile myself, I find the company of young children tiresome, and have no personal interest in, or sympathy for, paedophile relationships. I do, however, believe that all aspects of sex involving children and adults require far more sensible and clear-headed discussion than they are currently getting. So do all the other contentious issues surrounding sexuality in the 1990s.

Notes

1. A break-in at Lothian police headquarters, with the alleged involvement of gay criminal elements.
2. This scenario keeps running as long as *The Mousetrap*.

Pornography and Free Speech

Freedom of expression being the essential bedrock of democratic liberty which underpins all other freedoms, anti-censorship has always been one of my central preoccupations. In 1966 I was asked by the publishers John Calder and Marion Boyars to help prepare the defence for an American novel, Last Exit to Brooklyn, *which faced an obscenity prosecution that proved to be a landmark in British literary history. This led John and Marion to form the Defence of Literature and the Arts Society, which for more than a decade became the most influential advocate of free speech and publication and played a leading role in defending a series of notable cases. I was a member of the DLAS executive committee for several years, and in 1982 I contributed the following chapter to a book called* The Influence of Pornography on Behaviour.[1] *I include it here because it remains my considered view on censors and censorship.*

That virtue . . . which is but a youngling in the
contemplation of evil, and knows not the utmost
that vice promises to her followers, and rejects it, is
but a blank virtue, not a pure; her whiteness is but
an excremental whiteness.

John Milton, *Areopagitica*, 1644

The Unloved Censor

Censorship has a bad name. It is associated – and rightly – with totalitarian
regimes and the circumscribing of individual freedom. It is curious how
even its enthusiastic advocates seek more palatable euphemisms (e.g.
'quality control') with which to commend it.

This essay is concerned primarily with the censorship of obscenity and
pornography: although, as will be seen, I regard this as being just as
political as other forms of censorship. I start from the premise that *all*
censorship is evil, because it diminishes human freedom and interferes
with the spontaneity of communication. In an ideal world there would
be no censorship, but the world we live in is far from ideal; and for the
foreseeable future there will be some censorship. What there is should be
as limited as possible, and should be kept under constant and vigilant
scrutiny. The burden of proving that censorship is the lesser evil in any
given instance should always lie upon those (be they the representatives
of the State or private bodies or persons) who seek to impose it. And such
proof should include solid evidence of demonstrable harm, greater than
the harm wrought by the proposed censorship, to an individual, to a
group, or to society as a whole, if the article or information in question
remained uncensored.

Such harm can usually be proved in cases of legitimate restriction of
information on grounds of State security or libel upon an individual (even
though the law on these matters is widely acknowledged to be defective
and awaits legislative improvement). In matters of public taste and morals,
however, to which censorship of obscenity and pornography relates,
tangible evidence of harm or damage is much more elusive. These
questions are essentially subjective – and it is for this reason above all that
I believe the less the law intrudes into the realm of public and private
morality, the better.

What Is Pornography?

The 1959 Obscene Publications Act, which is the main plank of the existing law of England relating to obscene material, is entitled 'An Act to amend the law relating to the publication of obscene matter; to provide for the protection of literature; and to strengthen the law concerning pornography'. It is thus clear that the Act – while it is designed to permit something which is obscene to be published legally if it is found by a court to be for the public good because it is 'in the interests of science, literature, art or learning', or of 'other objects of general concern' – is intended to give no quarter to pornographic matter devoid of redeeming qualities.

And of course, we all know what smut is when we see it. Or do we? Like the traveller who, when asked by the customs officer 'is that book pornographic?' growled, 'How do I know? I haven't got a pornograph!', one may well think at times that dirt lies in the eye of the beholder. Courts and juries have grappled inconclusively with this problem for over 200 years.

The *Oxford Concise Dictionary* unhelpfully sends us round in circles:

> *Pornography* – description of manners etc. of harlots; treatment of obscene subjects in literature.
>
> *Obscene* – repulsive, filthy, loathsome, lewd.
>
> *Lewd* – lascivious, unchaste, indecent.
>
> *Indecent* – unbecoming, immodest, obscene.

D. H. Lawrence – himself a prime sufferer from the obscenity laws – is more explicit. In his essay *Pornography and Obscenity* (1929) he writes:

> Genuine pornography . . . is almost always underworld, it doesn't come out into the open . . . you can recognise it by the insult it offers, invariably, to sex, and to the human spirit. Pornography is the attempt to insult sex, to do dirt on it. This is unpardonable.

Yet pornography, he goes on to claim, is itself created by our society's prudish sexual furtiveness. 'Without secrecy there would be no pornography. . . . No other civilization has driven sex into the underworld, and nudity to the W.C.' Poor Lawrence! What would he have said about Soho today, I wonder? There are, it would seem, ways of doing dirt on sex quite openly.

A number of more recent definitions of pornography, cited by Francis Bennion,[2] collectively indicate that pornographic material has one or more of the following characteristics:

> It causes offence or outrage (usually, but not necessarily, sexual).
>
> It stimulates sexual excitement without engaging the emotions (i.e., it promotes lust but not love).

It dehumanizes sex.

It exploits sex for commercial gain.

It harms those who read, see or hear it or who participate in its production.

Most people would agree that debasing or doing dirt on sex is not desirable, either for individuals or for society as a whole. Lasting harm to individuals or to society is even less desirable – if it can be proved. Is censorship, then, the answer, or does it simply make forbidden fruit seem sweeter? One of the most immediately apparent drawbacks to censorship as it has been operated by prosecuting counsel and judges in our courts, even in recent years, is its assumption that *all* sex – and not just pornographic sex – is dirty: surely a most unhealthy attitude. Indeed, one might almost conclude that prurience appears to be a characteristic sexual stance of lawyers. In the mid-1960s, for instance, a former Lord Chief Justice (Lord Parker) made it quite clear that the naked human body was, so far as the law was concerned, 'indecent' in judicial eyes:

> 'Indecent' means unbecoming and immodest . . . something that offends the ordinary modesty of the average man. . . . If you are on the beach with your children and a woman takes off her clothes, that is indecent. We just don't do that sort of thing in this country. Or let us say you were attending an athletic or sporting event and the athletes, beautiful physiques though they may have, have not got clothing which fits properly, and as they perform you see their private parts. This is indecent. (*R. v. Stanley*, 1965)

What would Lawrence have thought of that? And in 1981, when the Indecent Displays (Control) Act was enacted by Parliament, its sponsors – and the Government – resisted the inclusion of a statutory definition of 'indecency' on the ground that any definition which could be devised would prove unworkable. We are therefore saddled with Lord Parker's views, quoted above, until such time as the House of Lords is asked by the courts to redefine and clarify what 'indecency' means in law.

Such legal attitudes may well contribute to the trivialization of sexual feelings and to their becoming imbued with unhealthy guilt on the one hand, and to their commercial exploitation by bootleg purveyors of pornography and prostitution on the other. It is notable that the more censorious a society's prevailing attitudes towards the acting out of mutually desired sexual contacts, the more furtive, sordid, drab and corrupt is its sexual underworld – and the more widespread and acute are its psychological, moral and emotional disorders.

Capricious Law

It is not the task of this essay to describe all the complexities of the laws relating to obscenity, indecency and pornography. I do wish, however, to point out that these laws are almost certainly the most subjective and capricious area of the entire criminal law, because the matters with which they deal are so much ones of taste and opinion. As the Arts Council's Working Party on the Obscenity Laws (1969) succinctly put it, no one who publishes a book or other material can know for certain in advance whether he has committed a criminal offence by doing so, because the only issue at his trial will be whether the jury or the court agrees that what he has produced is not indecent or obscene. Furthermore, to punish someone for producing something which, in the court's opinion, has a tendency to deprave and corrupt is to punish them for being an unwitting accessory before the fact to a crime that may never be committed: 'A man can at least know in his heart whether he is guilty of embezzling; he cannot possibly know whether he is guilty of depraving or corrupting.'

It is fallaciously assumed, by those who wish to ban pornography, that no well-intentioned person would disagree with them once it has been demonstrated, or even shown as likely, that some pornography causes harm to individuals or to society. Consequently, much of the banners' energy is spent on quoting researches which have been carried out in various parts of the world with results tending to show that a positive relationship exists between exposure to pornographic material and the commission of crimes of sex and violence. No such studies, however, have yet established, so far as I am aware, a clear correlation between the availability of pornography and the incidence of sexual crimes or of violence. But far from it being the case that opposition to censorship depends upon an erroneous belief that all pornography is harmless, such opposition can be more convincingly grounded upon the contention that the operation of censorship is at least as harmful to society as the ready availability of pornography; and indeed that it is almost certainly more harmful.

Censorship Distorts Communication

For all censorship is a hindrance to the free flow of facts, of opinions and of ideas; and therefore, regardless of the motive with which it is imposed, censorship constitutes a distortion of spontaneous communication between human beings. I would not wish to argue that communication should never be restricted by convention or even sometimes by law; but I do maintain that every instance of such restriction ought to be scrutinized vigilantly in a democratic society, and that the onus of justifying it should be upon those authorities or individuals seeking to impose it. The only possible guiding principle for a society that is tolerably free in fact as well as in name has to be that enunciated by John Stuart Mill in his essay *On Liberty* (1859) that

> if all mankind minus one were of the opinion, and only one person were of the contrary opinion, mankind would be no more justified in silencing that one person than he, if he had the power, would be justified in silencing mankind.

Censorship is the intervention of a third mind between the communicator and those to whom the communication is addressed. The censor says: 'For a reason which seems good to me, I must stop this information reaching you.' 'You' may be either a specific individual, a class of individuals, or the public at large.

What is censored may be a *fact*, an *opinion* or a *scene*. A censored fact may be true or untrue. A censored opinion may be well-founded or ill-founded. A censored scene may be real or imaginary. As Mill points out, society can be harmed just as much by the censoring of falsehoods and errors as by the suppression of truth – not least because the truth or falsehood of information and opinions can be established only by free discussion and full examination of all the available evidence.

The censor's 'good reason' for censoring a *fact* is usually that a person learning it would be harmed (this argument is frequently advanced as a 'reason' for not giving sex education to adolescents); or that a third party would be damaged by it (the basis on which the laws of libel are founded and on which legal measures to protect privacy are advocated by some people); or that the community or the State would be harmed (the *raison d'être* of the Official Secrets Acts). The 'good reason' for censoring an *opinion about society* is usually that it would undermine the established order (i.e. it is seditious) or that it is highly offensive to the feelings of certain groups in society (e.g. the Race Relations Acts, blasphemy). The 'good reason' for censoring an *opinion about an individual or a group* is usually that the person or the group would be harmed or offended by its publication. The censor's 'good reason' for censoring a *scene* is usually that it will harm the people seeing it or that some of them are outraged by it: this is the common justification for censorship of pornography. In other situations, censorship may simply be used as a repressive weapon by the State or other authority without being directly related to the content of the material which is being censored.

Are the censor's 'good reasons' really good? The answers must depend not only on whether the harm he fears is real, but also on whether it outweighs the counter-harm which censorship does to freedom of speech. *Any* act of censorship, whatever its pretext, is by its very nature a *political* action: it is the exercise of power by one group over another. In a democratic society the presumption must always be in favour of free speech. If any other presumption prevails, the society is no longer free and open, but will – albeit gradually – become closed and authoritarian.

Pornography and Politics

Where pornography is concerned, its would-be prohibitors strenuously seek to demonstrate its individual and social harmfulness. David Holbrook[3] asserts that all pornography is a manifestation of hate. Hard pornography, says the Longford Report,[4] appeals 'quite unashamedly to various groups of inadequate or sexually maladjusted people'. Mary Whitehouse[5] comments, somewhat evasively, 'One is frequently challenged to define pornography, though why one should, when it is so obviously what it is, I sometimes wonder!' She contents herself by endorsing Lawrence's statement that 'pornography does dirt on sex', adding: 'it does violence to it, too'.

John Court,[6] National Chairman of the Australian Festival of Light, accepts the Kronhausens' definition[7] of material that is erotically stimulating in a context which lacks 'reality constraints'. He also cites with approval Schaeffer's view[8] that some contemporary pornography achieves the sophisticated status of 'a philosophy of life which closely associates pornography with atheism'. And he links it with perversion, drug-taking, extreme radicalism and moral anarchy. Here, he is clearly advocating its suppression for blatantly political reasons.

Of course, all censorship is inevitably conservative with a small 'c', in the sense of upholding a *status quo*, whether it is practised in the Soviet Union, South Africa, Sydney or Soho. The distinction between 'moral' and 'political' censorship is ultimately spurious.

Pornography itself may be deliberately political, and its use as a weapon against traditional values has been a recurrent feature of recent years. As Bennion says,

> Typically, the things attacked are established, conservative and elderly while the things promoted are underprivileged, radical and young. . . . Since suppression of sexuality forms a central feature of establishment attitudes the sexual attack liberates explosive forces.

The trials of *Oz* in 1971 and of *International Times* in 1972 were outstanding examples of the use of 'morals' offences to strike at politico-social attitudes. Ostensibly accused of conspiring to corrupt public morals by publishing obscene material, it was in reality the defendants' 'alternative' lifestyle (associated with anarchistically-flavoured left-wing politics) which was in the dock. These were effectively 'show trials' which did much to end the prevalence of the carefree 'flower power' era of the 1960s, with its emphasis on rock music, drug-taking and sexual freedom. After *Oz* and *IT* bit the dust freaks and hippies remained, but increasingly as a hangover. An ironical consequence was that the student generations of the mid- and later 1970s became much more directly political in their radicalism. According to one's point of view this may or may not be a good thing. What is indubitably neither good nor healthy is the use of obscenity laws as a political weapon, even against 'political' pornography. As John Trevelyan, the former film censor, has said:[9]

In a free society we must defend the freedom to express ideas, even if they are minority ideas, and we should therefore closely watch for any possibility of there being an 'unrevealed purpose' behind the use of the chaotic and confused obscenity laws.

Just as some pornography may be deliberately and overtly political, and opposition to it is frequently based on attitudes which are as much political as moral, so my opposition to censorship is grounded in an explicitly political viewpoint – namely, that it is in the end safer to run the risks involved in a free and open society where views, attitudes and opinions are expressed which one does not necessarily approve of, than to live under a regime where free enquiry and expression are stifled and suppressed. Censorship is a habit of mind which, once it gains a foothold, spreads like a cancer. Whatever its starting point, the end of the censor's road is likely to be the same: repression of 'dangerous' ideas, not only about sex but about morals, politics, art and life.

What the Law's Role Should Be

It is because this danger is a very real one – in Britain, now – and not because I am especially enamoured of pornography (much of which strikes me as crude, tasteless and boring), that I am vehemently opposed to the use of the criminal law to enforce standards of morality in sexual behaviour or attitudes . Sex is a peculiarly personal area of life, and I agree that there should be some protection, for those who wish it, from having what they regard as distasteful aspects of sexuality thrust upon them or flaunted in the streets. But that is an entirely separate issue from the right of all citizens – at any rate adult ones – to behave as they wish sexually, provided that they do not infringe others' rights and freedoms, and to have unrestricted access to pornographic or erotic material if they wish.

As the Sexual Law Reform Society stated in its evidence to the Criminal Law Revision Committee, which has recently studied the law relating to sexual offences, there are only three sets of circumstances in which the law should intervene to limit the citizen's sexual freedom. These are: where there is not true consent; where there is not full responsibility (by reason of age or other circumstances) on the part of all those engaging in the behaviour in question; and where offence is caused to others who are unwillingly involved in or unintentional witnesses to the behaviour. Where pornography is concerned, similar principles should apply and the SLRS report recommended that there should be freedom legitimately to obtain, in circumstances which are not obtrusive upon the public at large, pornographic material of an explicitly sexual nature for private use by consenting persons. Also, the law should protect those who, by reason of age or other incapacity, are incapable of giving fully responsible consent, from involvement in the production of pornography, and should control the display of sexually explicit material. Beyond this, the law has no legitimate role in this area of conduct in a free society: 'victimless crimes' should be decriminalized.

This standpoint will, I am aware, be vigorously contested by the advocates of censorship. Using the spurious argument that, when liberty is allowed to degenerate into licence, true freedom is lost, they aspire to control the tastes, to shape the thoughts, and to dictate the values of other adults. Their own values may possibly be superior to those of the millions who purchase *Playboy, Penthouse, Forum* and the rest – but they should nevertheless not be permitted to impose them by invoking the heavy artillery of the criminal law: education and persuasion are the only proper means for them to use. Otherwise they become potential tyrants, albeit virtuous ones. The famous declaration attributed to Voltaire: 'I loathe what you say but will defend to the death your right to say it' carries more hope for the future of mankind than the grotesque attempts by puritans down the ages to suppress a catalogue of works which range from high art to tawdry vulgarity – almost always with the result of increasing the popular awareness of, and demand for, the item in question. As a former chairman of the Defence of Literature and the Arts Society, the late William Hamling MP, once said: 'A piece of low-grade rubbish must be as important to us as *Ulysses*, even though that principle may lose us both sympathy and battles.'

The Harm Censors Do

I detest censorship and would-be censors because they attack *my* freedom – and *yours* – to read, see, hear and do what I – and you – choose. While not having the slightest desire to read most of the books and magazines, or to see most of the films, which the bluenose brigade seek to suppress, I feel personally violated by their insidious activities – 'Never send to know for whom the bell tolls; it tolls for thee.'[10]

The attempt to preserve people from harm by keeping them in ignorance of whatever may 'morally pollute' them strikes me as not only misconceived and futile, but as positively evil in its consequences, because it treats grown adults as if they were children. Living is, by its very nature, a dangerous process; and it is only by being conscious of the depths, as well as of the heights, of human imagination that we can make meaningful choices and accept full moral responsibility for ourselves. As Walker and Fletcher[11] point out:

> Sooner or later then, willingly or perforce, we must meet life face to face and take the inescapable risk of being what we are, doing what we do in our own freedom and on our own responsibility. Sooner or later we must make the discovery that the only security is the acceptance of insecurity, the only strength the acknowledgement of weakness. What must be done had better be done now. Until it is done we shall not enter into possession of ourselves.

It was not licentiousness, but Government licensing (i.e. censorship) that John Milton saw as the negation of liberty. Would I, then, defend the availability (to those who wish to have access to it) of smut? Of the portrayal of sexual violence and torture (as in Pasolini's film *Salo*)? Yes, I would – *because these things happen in the world whether we are allowed to know it or not: and because we shall never overcome evil by being kept in ignorance of its existence.*

Notwithstanding the oft-cited 'Moors murders', it would seem incontrovertible that a great many more people find the graphic description or depiction of torture and violence sickeningly aversive than are attracted by it, and that those few who are impelled to imitate it are psychopaths. Are we seriously being asked to limit what *everybody* is allowed to read or see because something or other might trigger off a psychopath? Although it is monotonously reiterated by the advocates of censorship that *aficionados* of pornography progress inevitably from 'soft' to 'hard' and then on to the perpetration of violent sex crimes, it is much more likely that 'hard core' pornography is far more aversive to people with a reasonably healthy psyche than it is addictive. When juries find that an allegedly obscene item has a tendency to deprave and corrupt, what they usually seem to mean is that they are disgusted by it – not that they find it dangerously attractive.

Irrational Opponents

And this, surely, is what a few minutes' reflection would lead us to expect. Former President Nixon's celebrated riposte to the 1970 US Commission on Pornography which reported that pornography had no lasting harmful effect: 'Centuries of civilization and ten minutes of common sense will tell us otherwise', merely demonstrates that one man's common sense is another's *non sequitur*.

That pornography does have a disturbing effect upon the rationality of at any rate some of its opponents is clear from the extreme claims of those who, like Ronald Butt[12] and David Holbrook,[13] maintain that it is so dangerous that it is likely to incite its participants and consumers to acts of brutal viciousness, rape and even murder. It is, incidentally, noteworthy that those, such as Lord Longford and Mary Whitehouse, who because they are its enemies must surely be numbered among the most continuous and assiduous students of pornography, find it highly aversive and a potent stimulus to extreme and sustained moral indignation.

Books in the dock – even hard-core pornographic books – are ideas in the dock. And ideas in the dock – even ideas which may deprave and corrupt – are the hallmark of the totalitarian State. I make no apology for returning to this point. There is fundamental difference between merely stating a point of view and exhorting your audience to violate the legitimate freedoms of others. This, of course, is as crucial a distinction in the political sphere (and one which is not always clearly enough perceived) as it is in the sexual sphere. There is all the difference in the world between depicting a ritualistic sado-masochistic scene involving consenting partners and inciting someone to go out and commit a brutal rape: such incitement would itself be a serious criminal offence, anyway.

Sexuality is fundamental to our lives; because of its central place in our physical and psychical make-up, it exerts a perennial fascination. By rights it should be a prime source of human liberation, inspiration and happiness: yet so often, it tragically becomes the opposite. In my experience, inhibitions and hang-ups concerning sex are far more damaging and disabling than an accepting attitude to one's own and others' sexuality. As Haynes and Pasle-Green have written:[14]

> Making love is one way to bridge language, cultural, racial, religious, political, and class barriers. In this violent, divided, confused, and intolerant world of ours it is one common denominator. Making love brings people together. Anything that increases our prurient interest, anything that encourages us to touch one another, is a step forward. At least when we are making love, when we are reading about it, when we are watching it, when we are thinking about it, we are not killing or hurting one another.

Misguided Concerns

While I am implacably opposed to the philosophy and the activities of the would-be sexual censors and suppressors, I yet recognize that their concern, however misguided, springs – at any rate in some instances – from a desire to increase human happiness. Yet I hold that because their ideas are mistaken they constitute – whether intentionally or not – a serious threat to the freedom, health, and happiness of humanity. It will indeed be a black day if they are enabled to enforce their views through the extended machinery of the law.

Their attitude to sex is, I believe, fallacious; and they draw a number of erroneous deductions from false premises. These, so far as I understand them, are:

> (1) Because sex is God-given, and at its best can impart emotions and sensations that are as near to the Divine as anything that human beings are capable of experiencing, therefore it should be treated as 'sacramental' and only approved of when it is hallowed by love and a lasting – preferably lifelong – relationship between the partners concerned.

Leaving aside theology, and the debatable question of whether sex is any more 'God-given' than Mount Everest, baked beans or washing machines, the 'sacramental' attitude to sex falls into the classic pit of making the best the enemy of the good. While it may well be that some sexual episodes are the purest and most blissful experiences that we shall know on this earth, that is no reason for writing off the second-best, either in relationships or orgasms. While we can all aspire to the peaks, and hope to avoid sinking too deeply into the troughs, most of us are very content to remain in the foothills for most of the time – and to obtain a great deal of worthwhile pleasure and fulfilment there.

(2) To be morally and socially acceptable, sexual activity should only take place when the parties concerned are (a) married, (b) in love, (c) of opposite sexes.

It is doubtful if as many as 10 per cent of all the human orgasms which occur conform with all of these criteria. Sometimes, it would appear, the formal correctness of a relationship is regarded as rendering it valid even though there is no mutual love between the partners (a view which was pushed to its sexist extreme by Galsworthy's Soames Forsyte in *The Man of Property* – the 'property' in question being his sexually alienated wife, Irene, over whom he forcibly asserted his marital rights). In all other cases, however, love is obligatory – whatever is meant by 'love'. In traditionally 'romantic' terms, it implies an exclusive possessiveness between the couple who are 'in love', with an inevitable overinvestment of excessive emotional expectations in their relationship and a corresponding disillusionment when their 'love' falls short of idealized requirements or even turns sour. While pair-bonding and the nuclear family will probably remain the chosen path of the majority for the foreseeable future (I see no necessity to brainwash most people in that direction), love – including sexual love – can take other, less constricting, forms. There are those who believe that the essence of love is sharing: that love is an attitude, how you feel about yourself and others. When people who are not monogamous talk about 'making love', it can be more than a euphemism for their sexual encounters.

Love can also exist, of course, in homosexual relationships as well as in heterosexual ones: but this simple and obvious fact is usually denied by puritanical people (especially evangelically religious ones, many of whom seem to be both excessively obsessed by homosexuality and exceptionally ignorant about it). The idea that homosexuality is 'unnatural' still persists, although it is self-evidently meaningless. Indeed, in a prize example of censorious megalomania, the Nationwide Festival of Light in 1977 considered calling for legislation to make it an offence to maintain that homosexuality was natural! With commendable prudence, this zany proposal was shelved as being 'unrealistic'. The notion that people of the same sex can actually experience deep emotional feelings of love for one another in the same way that heterosexuals do appears to be profoundly shocking to some folk. They react with incredulity and disdain, preferring to view all manifestations of homosexuality as lustful depravity which must always be immoral and, in the legal phrase, 'grossly indecent'. No doubt it is a simpler world when you can manage to avoid having to come to terms with the reality of how other people, who are differently constituted from you, actually feel – but the importance of having to do so is a prime reason why such ill-informed and narrow-minded censors must not be permitted to enforce their bigoted and ignorant views of sexuality upon the rest of us. Public education, and a more balanced appreciation of the real-life complexity of homosexuality and many other facets of sexuality, will only come about if there is the fullest possible freedom for different viewpoints to be expressed and exchanged.

Threat to Free Discussion

The next proposition of the censorious crew is a direct threat to free discussion which follows inevitably from points (1) and (2):

> (3) It is not in the best interests of society to permit free discussion of all aspects of sexuality, and especially not of viewpoints or categories of behaviour which do not conform with (1) and (2) above.

This constitutes a challenge to the whole concept of a democratic and tolerant open society. If one subject (sex) is to be excepted from the general rule that all matters of public interest are freely debatable within the broad boundaries set by the libel laws, what will follow next? Religious beliefs? Politics? Science? To quote from Mill's essay *On Liberty* once more:

> The peculiar evil of silencing the expression of an opinion is that it is robbing the human race; posterity as well as the existing generation; those who dissent from the opinion even more than those who hold it. If the opinion is right, they are deprived of the opportunity of exchanging error for truth; if wrong, they lose, what is almost as great a benefit, the clearer perception and livelier impression of truth, produced by its collision with error.

If it is the whole concept of 'sexual politics' which frightens the upholders of conventional morality into wanting to restrict or ban the expression of unorthodox sexual attitudes, whether or not these are expressed pornographically, this is surely a striking exhibition of fear and moral weakness. In any event, sexual politics is here to stay; and those of us who find its jargon unfamiliar and sometimes distasteful must perforce come to terms with the fact that its proponents are saying things which have an intense meaning for them and have a message for us.

Sex Education Controversy

> (4) Sex education should be postponed as long as possible, and when given should be designed to encourage young people to conform to the ideals of virginity before marriage and lifelong mutual faithfulness within it, rather than to encourage awareness

that there is a variety of possible sexual attitudes and lifestyles to choose from.

At first sight it may be thought that there is at least a plausible case for censoring, or at least filtering, the sexual information that is made available to adolescents and children; but on closer examination this argument too is seen to be highly questionable and indeed I would say positively specious.

Pro-censorship bodies . . . are currently mounting a sustained and vociferous campaign, not only to put forward their own views on sex education . . . as they are of course perfectly entitled to do, but also to attack and denigrate the sex education and teacher/youth worker training activities of bodies such as the Family Planning Association and the Albany Trust whose approach to the topic is too 'liberal' for their taste. What they apparently object to is the philosophy that *all* aspects of sexuality should be openly talked about and calmly discussed at some stage of the sex education process; and still more that it should be intimated to young people that it is possible, and perhaps reasonable, that more than one point of view is held on these matters.

But surely what is needed, here even more than elsewhere, is a clear grasp of the fundamental distinction between education and indoctrination. As the great *Manchester Guardian* editor, C. P. Scott, once said: 'Comment is free – facts are sacred.' At least they should be. And as regards sex, just as in any other area of knowledge, there are facts and there are opinions. Opinions may be either true or fallacious: facts can only be correct – otherwise they are not facts, but fallacies. There are bound to be clashes of opinions. But it is possible, by the usual processes of investigation, to ascertain what the correct facts are, in sexual matters as in others; and everybody – including children – should be entitled to know the correct facts when they wish to do so. To maintain otherwise is a gross infringement of human rights. Whenever it is sought to restrict access to factual information, it is incumbent upon those doing so to make out a cast-iron case. Where sex education is concerned, this has not been done.

The thorny question of what sort of sex education should be given, where, when, and by whom, will not easily be resolved. The principle that there is a body of factually correct information about sexuality which young people have the right to know before their educational process is adequately completed is, however, not negotiable. And some of this information may be pornographic. As the late Dorothy Dallas wrote in her book *Sex Education in School and Society* (1972):

A variety of teachers, young and old, mature and immature, demonstrating a variety of attitudes, methods and roles, both communicative, informative and authoritative, provides the ideal situation for sex education in its widest sense rather than searching for any one ideal teacher.

I believe that it is vital for the future health of our society that the channels of communication for imparting to young people the widest spectrum of facts, ideas and opinions about sex and its vital role in all our lives should be kept open, free and unfettered. Sexual innocence can no more be equated with ignorance than sexual knowledge necessarily implies guilt. It is only those who morbidly regard sex as a 'dirty secret' who can possibly hold such perverse views as to the wholly dire effects of sound sex education.

Dangers of Lust

(5) Any idea, book, magazine, film or other article which incites lust is self-evidently harmful and dangerous, and should be severely restricted if not totally prohibited.

Here, we are back to the 'pornography is harmful' thesis which, as I have already shown, is unproven. Far from being self-evident, it is an assertion for which surprisingly little solid supporting evidence has been adduced – despite all the ideologically committed work which has been put into the search for conclusive data. All Mary Whitehouse can produce is a reference to some research carried out for the 1970 US Commission on Obscenity and Pornography. Yet that commission itself reported that:

> Empirical research designed to clarify the question has found no reliable evidence to date that exposure to explicit sexual materials plays a significant role in the causation of delinquent or criminal sexual behaviour among youth and adults. The Commission cannot conclude that exposure to erotic materials is a factor in the causation of sex crime or sexual delinquency. . . . In general, established patterns of sexual behaviour were found to be very stable and not altered substantially by exposure to erotica.

And John Court, the pro-censorship psychologist so favoured by Mary Whitehouse, admits that such studies as have been undertaken are 'painfully inconclusive'. He simply reiterates that 'pornography is hate' and that it 'brings perversion'; and takes refuge in the not very scientific assertion that *because* there is no such thing as objective impartiality, even in scientific investigation, 'when the question of possible harm is involved, there is a strong ethical case for taking more note of those [studies] which indicate harm than those which fail to find it'. He also asserts[15] that

> The harmful effects of salacious material, suggestive advertising, and the like, are therefore best defined in moral terms of incitement to lust. . . . We must conclude that the Christian will take a distinctive position about the significance of erotica; *without in any way prejudging the scientific evidence* [my emphasis], he or she can

come to a resolute condemnation of its inherent harm and to firm opposition to its indiscriminate availability.

Any reader who did not accept Court's value-systems to start with, but was willing to be convinced, will probably smell a fairly large rat at this point, and it emerges into full view when Court attempts to dispose of the 'censorship is undemocratic' and 'free speech is valuable to democracy' arguments. He does so by calmly asserting that the committed Christian, because of his superior system of moral values derived from God's revelation, has a responsibility to prevent what he considers to be harmful; and that this is not paternalism, or busybodying in the affairs of others, but 'a high sense of social responsibility'! After this, it seems scarcely necessary to afford Court the courtesy of treating the remainder of his 'arguments' as calling for reasoned refutation.

Principle at Stake

Not the least interesting and remarkable aspect of the influence of pornography on behaviour is the effect that it has on the behaviour of would-be censors. In their anxiety to suppress the transmission of unwelcome sexual facts and fantasies, they altogether lose sight of, or dismiss as irrelevant, the fundamental issues of human liberty which are involved.

I have attempted here to state the case for freedom of expression, and against censorship, on general grounds, and have not confined my exposition to the censorship of pornography, because the case for free speech must stand or fall on principle: once the thin end of the wedge is inserted at any particular point, all freedom is obviously in jeopardy.

The impossibility of defining pornography in a way which would command general assent, and the difficulties attached to producing a workable legal definition of what is obscene, simply demonstrate the unwisdom of attempting to exercise censorship which lays any claim to be impartial over what are essentially matters of subjective taste. Few people nowadays would be happy with a censorship law explicitly grounded in feelings of disgust or revulsion, although these are the implicit criteria of our existing law. The test of 'tending to deprave and corrupt' is, as has been seen, extremely difficult to prove to the satisfaction of present-day juries (although magistrates seem readier to contemplate the possibility), while scientific evidence that pornography has harmful effects upon the morals or the behaviour of most of those who use it is still inconclusive.

Influential groups in this country and in the United States have concluded that the laws on this subject should either be liberalized or dismantled altogether. Most of those who press for them to be extended or strengthened do so from a standpoint of religious commitment which precludes rational argument. In the end, the crucial questions are not 'Is pornography harmful?' or 'Should pornography be banned?', but 'How much moral responsibility should each citizen carry for her- or himself?' and 'Do we want the Nanny State?' I don't! Do you?

Notes

1. Ed. Maurice Yaffé and Edward C. Nelson (Academic Press, 1982).
2. In an unpublished paper from which I am grateful to have his permission to quote.
3. *Sex and Dehumanization* and *The Case Against Pornography* (1972).
4. Longford *et al.*, *Pornography* (1972).
5. *Whatever Happened to Sex?* (1977).
6. *Law, Light and Liberty* (1975).
7. *Pornography and the Law* (1959).
8. *Escape from Reason* (1968).
9. *What the Censor Saw* (1973).
10. John Donne, *Devotions Upon Emergent Occasions* (1624).
11. Kenneth Walker and Peter Fletcher, *Sex and Society* (1955).
12. In *The Times*, 5 February 1976.
13. In *The Times*, 6 February 1976.
14. *Hello I Love You!* (1974).
15. *Law, Light and Liberty* (1975).

PART THREE

RELIGION

Christian Society and the Homosexual

Throughout the law reform campaign, we were in constant touch with leading members of various churches, and the support of the then Archbishop of Canterbury, Michael Ramsey, and several of his colleagues was crucial in the House of Lords debates. I was also asked to talk to a number of Christian audiences. The following extracts from an address which I gave to the clergy of the Rural Deanery of Westminster on 19 October 1965[1] illustrate the general line that I took on the theme of religious attitudes to homosexuality.

It is generally accepted that there are at least half a million – and probably more than twice that number – of male homosexuals in Britain. Homosexuality is thus a widespread social problem. But most of all it is a *personal* problem, involving for many thousands of people much human misery and heartbreak, a great deal of which can and must be mitigated for them and avoided for future generations. Like the poor, homosexuality is likely to be with us for as long as we can foresee. . . . Homosexuals can be helped towards a greater peace of mind, if not always to a greater degree of heterosexuality. . . . What can we, as a Christian society, offer them?

First of all, understanding. It is hard to be objective, but we must all make the effort. In this sphere, *empathy* is all-important; not mere sympathy, but the imaginative breakthrough needed to enter into another person's own view of his dilemma. Not merely do we have to comprehend the homosexual's feelings, desires and affections; we also must sense the fear and hopelessness which at times inevitably come to every homosexual (and the more intelligent and responsible he is, the more often will he feel this fear and hopelessness) while he knows that because of his innermost emotional nature not only is he regarded with scorn and derision by many of his fellow-men but he will also be treated as a criminal by the law for any relationship into which he may enter, even if it is one based upon deep and mutual love. (The homosexual *woman* does not have this legal problem to contend with; but her emotional difficulties over social hostility and personal relationships call for the same understanding and help.)

An effort at *objectivity* is essential here if any useful pastoral function is to be performed. As the authors of *Towards a Quaker View of Sex*[2] have said, all attitudes to sexuality are conditioned by the individual's own upbringing, experience and desires, and it is difficult to be objective. 'The attitudes of professed Christians tend to have a definite bias – not necessarily good.'

The distinguished German Protestant theologian, Dr Helmut Thielicke, in his recent important book *The Ethics of Sex*,[3] speaks of the 'unexamined rejective instinct' towards the homosexual on the part of many Christians which

> must be, if not eliminated, then certainly brought under control and regarded in the epistemological sense as a discriminatory prejudice, not only in the name of the demands of scientific objectivity, but also in the name of pastoral ministry. The person who has to deal with such cases as a pastor or even as a physician will find that a real personal encounter with this threatened and often unhappy neighbour will help him to get beyond this instinctual inhibition that blocks his judgement.

An examination of the Old Testament and Pauline texts which refer to homosexuality leads Dr Thielicke to the conclusion that 'the predisposition itself, the homosexual potential as such, dare not be any more strongly deprecated than the status of existence which we *all* share as men in the disordered creation that exists since the Fall'. Consequently there is not the slightest excuse for maligning the constitutional homosexual, morally or theologically. For his part, the homosexual is called upon not to affirm his status *a priori* or to idealize it, but rather to regard and recognize his condition as something that is questionable – though this 'does not rule out the possibility that it can become the vehicle of a blessing and a creative challenge'.

If the homosexual is willing to structure the man–man relationship in an ethically responsible way (Dr Thielicke continues), he can realize his optimal ethical potentialities on the basis of his irreversible situation. One must seriously ask whether the same norms do not apply here as in heterosexual relationships. Celibacy cannot be used as a counter-argument, because 'celibacy is based upon a special calling, and, moreover, is an act of free will'. While Christian pastoral care will have to be concerned principally with helping the person to *sublimate* his homosexual urge, this cannot be done by exposing the homosexual to defamation of his urge.

The British authors of *Towards a Quaker View of Sex* emphasize, rightly, that the study of homosexuality cannot be divorced from a survey of the whole field of sexual activity. 'The kind of morality that includes a vehement and categorical condemnation of the homosexual is not Christian, for it lacks compassion for the individual person and it lacks understanding of the human problem.' Homosexual affection, they point out, can be as selfless as heterosexual affection, 'and therefore we cannot see that it is in some way morally worse'.

> Neither are we happy with the thought that all homosexual behaviour is sinful; motive and circumstances degrade or ennoble

any act . . . [and] we see no reason why the physical nature of a sexual act should be the criterion by which the question whether or not it is moral should be decided. . . . The authors of this essay have been depressed quite as much by the utter abandon of many homosexuals . . . as by the absurdity of the condemnation rained down upon the well-behaved. . . . Society has not said 'if you do that, that is all right, but as to the other, we cannot approve of that'. It has said 'whatever you do must be wrong; indeed you *are* wrong'.

Similar viewpoints to those of Dr Thielicke and the Quaker group have recently been expressed by a Catholic priest, Father William Dempsey, in the *Dublin Review*.[4] And a Dutch Catholic priest, Fr Dr J. Gottschalk of the Amsterdam Pastoral Bureau, takes a favourable view of ongoing homosexual friendships as an antidote to the destructive loneliness of so many homosexuals which 'weighs heavily upon their mental development, and consequently upon their moral and religious development'. Such friendships should be viewed not merely as a 'lesser evil', but as an actual source for good. They should be encouraged to become permanent and steady relationships, with the emphasis on that fidelity and self-discipline which are inherent in any successful relationship.

Christians have an obligation to inform themselves accurately about the homosexual situation, and to review their own feelings and prejudices in the light of the Gospel ethic. There is a need to encourage a more enlightened, charitable and humane view of the subject amongst Christian congregations and all people of good will, in order that the present social isolation of the homosexual man and woman may be progressively reduced.

There is an urgent need in our contemporary life for a much more comprehensive social attack upon the miseries and difficulties of the countless people, young and old, who are facing life burdened with a sexual problem. Such problems are not, of course, confined to homosexuals. Skilled help is not nearly as widely available as it should be. Rather than allow people to struggle on unaided until they become full-scale casualties, we should be helping them to cope with their difficulties at a much earlier stage. This is not merely a task for the doctor and the social worker. It is a challenge to the individual citizen, and especially to the individual Christian.

For what are the root causes of these human problems? They are the old, old human failings: ignorance, fear, hatred and, above all, selfishness. And the cure? In human terms, better education, more diffused goodwill in society, more tolerance. Above all these things, for the Christian, is God's grace. Our Lord's injunction to love one another – how simple it sounds, how difficult it is. But if we are to help not only the homosexual, but all those with sexual problems, we must endeavour to follow it; for (to quote *Towards a Quaker View of Sex* once again), 'it is surprising how much the unrelenting hatred of society may eat into the soul'. As Dr David Stafford-Clark has said, to make someone feel unwanted and unloved is 'the most destructive wrong which can be inflicted upon a human being'. Let us not, ourselves, be guilty of committing this wrong.

Notes

1. Reprinted in *Faith and Freedom*, Vol. 19, No. 56, Spring 1966 (Manchester College, Oxford).
2. An essay by a group of Friends (Friends Home Service Committee, revised edition, 1964).
3 James Clarke & Co. Ltd, 1964.
4. No. 504, Summer 1965.

There Must Be Dialogues

ADDRESS TO THE ANGLO-AMERICAN CONSULTATION ON THE
CHURCH, SOCIETY AND THE HOMOSEXUAL
LONDON, AUGUST 1966

In the summer of 1966, the Rev. Ted McIlvenna, director of the San Francisco Young Adult Project and first president of the Council on Religion and the Homosexual (which had grown out of a weekend conference between homosexual men and women and church people held in California in 1964), asked the Albany Trust to organize a consultation on Christianity and homosexuality – the first, to my knowledge, ever to be held in Britain. The three-day gathering, which took place on 9–11 August 1966, with about 60 British and American participants who listened to prepared papers and took part in group discussions, was a memorable event – especially for me, as I was its chairman. It is indicative of the prevailing climate that in opening the proceedings, Ted McIlvenna felt it necessary to make it clear that those participants who were homosexually orientated should not feel obliged to say so, because 'that would be too difficult'. His own inspirational approach was apparent in his opening exhortation to 'Forget who you represent. We represent the human race. Let's start there'; and in his closing declaration that: 'I happen to believe that the only thing Christian faith has to say that is significant and distinctive is an unqualified "yes" to man. Forgiveness is continuous, and does not depend upon our state of righteousness at the moment.' The general tone of the papers was robustly modern, and they still read freshly today. An edited version of my own closing contribution follows:

Time and Tide recently published a letter which said: 'It would be very interesting to learn how, when and where our high-ranking ecclesiastics gained the extensive knowledge of homosexuality and other sexual perversions which enables them to speak with authority in the House of Lords and elsewhere and be accepted as experts.' The writer should have been here at our Consultation. Though we may not be high-ranking ecclesiastics or bishops, I hope we will go away and begin to spread the gospel in the sense of beginning to tell people where the knowledge is to be found.

If I had to take a text, it would be 'By their fruits ye shall know them'. I think this applies not only to the Church in the world and its ministry; it also indicates that society gets the homosexuals it deserves. Because society creates its homosexuals and its homosexuals react to society. Some of them are a pretty poor lot, but what else does society make it possible for them to be?

There has been a great deal of virulent correspondence in the press since Lord Arran introduced his Sexual Offences Bill, and it may distress you that so much of this comes from professed and professing Christians. One example which sticks in my mind was from an Anglican clergyman who wrote to his local paper recently saying that we really should not be surprised if a hydrogen bomb was dropped on Britain any day now, because we were about to tolerate the abomination of sodomy for which the Lord destroyed Sodom and Gomorrah – and we had no right to be more compassionate than God! That told me a great deal about his God, but it did not tell me anything about the problem of homosexuality. And it shocked me to hear Lord Ferrier say in the House of Lords that this is a very limited problem, and that no decent person comes across it very much in the course of their ordinary lives.

Most of the constructive and forward-looking social work which is being done in this country today is being done by Christians and by the Churches. In the field of homosexuality, of course, the whole process of re-evaluation which has ultimately led to the introduction of Lord Arran's Bill, and the powerful support which it has received from the Archbishops and the Bishops, was very largely started by the Churches – and most notably by the Church of England Moral Welfare Council way back in the early 1950s. No one considering the ethics of homosexuality should omit to pay tribute to the late Canon Hugh Warner's sterling pioneer work on the topic when he was Secretary of that Council.

Having started a dialogue, we must continue. There must be wider dialogues within the Churches and outside them; dialogues between the Churches, the community in general, and homosexuals. We should initiate a dialogue between those of us who feel that conceptions of ethics and morality and theology need re-examining and perhaps radically revising and those who are 'traditionalists' in the sense that they are broadly satisfied with the way things are and always have been. Such conservatism is not necessarily the result of evil or sloth or even lack of imagination: it is a very deeply ingrained tradition or condition of the

British race – this habitual tendency to reject novel concepts which has very deep philosophical as well as theological roots, but which I believe must be increasingly questioned in many areas of our national life.

We have got to increase the depth of understanding about homosexuality and about sexuality generally. We must do this not only in our own personal thinking, but also through promoting much deeper levels of education and fundamental research in the social sciences, in human behaviour, and in attitudinal psychology. I go round talking to many and varied groups of people – Church people, political groups, Rotary Clubs, Mothers' Unions, students – about homosexuality, which would have been largely unmentionable up to five or six years ago and I find a common desire first of all to *learn*: people who are prepared to come to such meetings are not primarily shocked any longer at the phenomenon of homosexuality; they want information, with a desire to understand before they can help.

We have got to do all that we possibly can to increase *empathy* on this question; and surely, if the Christian Church is about anything it is about empathy, because what the Church should be trying to do is to create a society of more warmly imaginative people – people who not only sympathize from the point of view of the fortunate person helping the down and out, but people who actually try to put themselves inside the other person's skin and experience what he is feeling before they are able to do something useful about it.

We have got to be aware of and to become more able to cope with the homosexual's life problems. Besides the crisis of growing up, the crisis of living in a rather socially disorientated way all one's life, and the crisis of old age, homosexual people need to attain fulfilment. A good deal has been said here about the contribution which the homosexual can and should make to society, and I entirely agree with this. But the only useful contribution that the homosexual will be able to make to society has to be a contribution which he makes as a fulfilled person. For those homosexual people who are not called to celibacy, this must necessarily mean as a sexually fulfilled person, either in a relationship which is meaningful and loving, or else in other ways which, if they do not entirely assuage loneliness, at any rate prevent sexuality from being the all-consuming problem of frustrated desire which it is for all too many people today.

We have grappled here with some very fundamental issues. First, we have grappled with the ethics of sexuality, and I myself feel that I have clarified a good many of my own concepts. One of the things which we have possibly shirked a little is the validity of guilt. I think one has to avoid the danger of denigrating guilt. Guilt can often be a healthy force in a person's life as long as it is guilt kept within proper and realistic proportions, and not an overwhelming guilt which makes it impossible for the person to do anything at all constructive for himself because he has lost all his self-respect.

We have at times found ourselves confused about the relationship between love and lust, and as to whether the 'New Morality' is anything more than the old immorality writ large. I personally do not believe that adherence to the 'New Morality' or to situational ethics means that one is saying 'anything goes'. But that point has got to be made a lot more explicit, and put over very clearly to the traditionalists, if the new insights which we are seeking are to gain acceptance within the Church as a whole.

Homosexuals, I think most of us are agreed, are not necessarily sinners just because they are homosexuals. Of course, some of them *are* sinners, but they are sinners because of what they do and the motives with which they do it rather than because of their being homosexual.

The question of counselling has loomed very large in our discussions, and most of us agreed that we have got to give bread and not stones when we are asked for help by people with homosexual problems. It is my own view – and I want to say this very clearly to those people who are troubled by this question of orgasms – that a lot of the immediate and most pressing problems of homosexual people who seek counselling arise from psychological and other blockages to sex, rather than from sexual overindulgence or promiscuity. The sort of sex they are having (if they are having any) is unsatisfactory, or else they are not having any at all and do not know what on earth to do about it. Because we must face the fact that most human beings desire and will attempt to have sexual experiences which are satisfying, both physically and emotionally. This is something which all counsellors have got to be honest about if they wish to perform a useful role.

Lines of action which I would hope might result from our gathering include further steps towards a comprehensive Christian re-examination of ethics; more adequate preparation and training for counselling, and the development of pastoral and clinical psychology teaching; the broad question of sex education; the need for more research; and last, but perhaps most important, the need for some positive social action.

I would like to end by reading some quotations which I think throw some light on our dilemmas. First of all, there are the traditionalist views from which many of us started out, which are basically sympathetic but which do not now seem adequate. One such statement was made by Mr (now Lord) Butler, speaking as Home Secretary in the 1960 Commons debate on the Wolfenden Report. He said: 'Those who speak of these matters should acknowledge the difference between sin and crime and . . . should freely acknowledge that homosexuality is, in general, an undesirable practice', going on to quote with approval a *Times* leader of the same morning which had said that the fight for reform 'would not be won by the presentation of homosexuality as something to be regarded otherwise than as unnatural, sinful and to be resisted wherever possible'.

Now this obviously is an attempt at a sympathetic approach, but I do not believe that most people with counselling or research experience would regard it as an adequate statement in relation to the homosexual condition.

How do homosexuals regard their own situation? I could give you many examples of this. But I would very much like to read you part of a letter which I recently received from a gentleman aged 86, and which I found most moving both for its humour and its frankness. He says:

> It may be that homosexuality has become in general as bad as Viscount Dilhorne[1] declared it in the House of Lords; it was in my glowing time of spring accompanied by an affectionate decency far greater than might be expected from many female prostitutes. . . .
>
> Looking back, I never regarded myself with pity at all. Had I been asked, I would have made no excuse for myself, except that it was as natural for me to be homosexual as for others to be normal. The normal was quite impossible to me; repugnant in every way. . . . What I did was to do as most careful young men do – exercise control, and never pick up a male prostitute or, in fact, any male that I did not know intimately already. . . . I would say to any homosexual (if I knew any now) 'Be true to yourself. Why should you be more ashamed of your homosexual inclinations than your sisters? But – only among friends for your safety, not so much of the male pickups. . . . My effort started when I was about sixteen. With variations. Both the efforts and the variations did me good. Be strong; be men. It is not going with women that makes one a man. It is a certain inner integrity. Sometimes forgotten; always gone back to. No hypocrisy at all. Doing one's best. Slipping up occasionally.'

A much younger generation's view appeared a year or two back in *Another Kind of Loving* by 'Anthony Rowley'. He says – and I think this is an important point to bear in mind when one is criticizing homosexuals and homosexual attitudes:

> Years spent lying to his normal acquaintances lead a homosexual constantly to suspect similar deceit in others, even someone with whom he is in love; so it is often difficult for him to establish any relationship based on mutual trust.
>
> [He concludes:] The generation of homosexuals who have grown up since the war are much less scared of their predicament than their predecessors were, and their fear of isolation is less. . . . When satisfactorily in love, they cannot conceive of a different or greater happiness. . . . The young homosexual's feeling is basically one of extreme irritation at the constant need for evasion and disguise, and the never absent possibility of his arrest for something that he KNOWS, as well as he can know anything, ought not to be considered a crime. . . . There is a creative urge common to all degrees and kinds of love, the feeling that out of a relationship *something* good must come.

Note

1. A former Conservative Lord Chancellor, and a leading opponent of Lord Arran's Sexual Offences Bill.

Squaring the Circle – Anglican Attitudes to Homosexuality

Since the 1950s, the Church of England has engaged in interminable, often anguished, debate over homosexuality. The conflict between 'traditionalists' incapable of modifying scriptural condemnations of same-sex genital activity as 'abominations', and 'liberals' who wish to accept gay men and lesbians into Church fellowship provided they confine their sexuality to 'committed' relationships, has led to much heart searching and several inconclusive reports. I have been involved in the consultative processes leading to some of these, and my mounting exasperation at what I came to regard as pusillanimous pussyfooting (some of it based on poor research and bad scholarship) found expression in my comments on the 1979 'Contribution to Discussion', entitled Homosexual Relationships. *What follows is condensed from two articles I wrote, for (a)* New Humanist *and (b)* Forum.

(a) New Humanist

Christians have always made heavy weather about sex; many religious people regard the means by which the human race is perpetuated, interpersonal love expressed, and a great deal of innocent pleasure obtained to be a Cosmic Mistake in the worst possible taste. When they have such difficulty in accepting the mainstream of heterosexuality, it is not really surprising that most Christians find same-sex affection and physical attraction an even greater stumbling block.

It is accordingly to their credit that some Christians have played an honourable part in helping to humanize barbaric legal and social attitudes. The appearance in 1963 of the essay *Towards a Quaker View of Sex*, with its striking observation that 'homosexual affection can be as selfless as heterosexual affection, and therefore we cannot see that it is in some way morally worse' was a breakthrough. This line of thinking was developed by the 'South Bank' theologians whose 'New Morality', though derided by traditionalists as 'nothing but the old immorality writ large', made it possible for many people (including myself) to believe for a time that some Christians might have useful contributions to make to the ongoing debate about social ethics.

In the 1950s, the Church of England's Moral Welfare Council produced some impressively thoughtful reports on homosexuality. During the law reform debates, both Archbishops and other senior Bishops spoke out courageously for reform. The distinction between sin and crime, which Wolfenden had emphasized, was maintained throughout: I recall remarking to the Archbishop of Canterbury's Lay Secretary that this was a case where the doctrine of the lesser evil could be applied, and being told: 'I can assure you it has been – copiously!' It was not until Dr Norman Pittenger published *Time for Consent*,[1] after the law had been reformed, that a senior Anglican theologian suggested that homosexual behaviour which was an expression of mutual love need not be regarded as sinful.

In 1970, a working party of the Board for Social Responsibility produced a report on homosexuality which was never published, because its members were irreconcilably divided as to whether physical homosexual relationships between committed partners were always wrong, or whether – though they could never be as 'fully human' or 'satisfactory' as heterosexual relationships – they were the best of which those involved were capable, and therefore not 'sinful'. As Archbishop Michael Ramsey said to me, 'We couldn't have published that – it was neither one thing nor the other!'

This new [1979] report is unanimous – but it is still 'neither one thing nor the other'. And though the working party managed to reach agreed conclusions, it ran into heavy pre-publication squalls with its own Board [for Social Responsibility], which contributed a tailpiece of highly 'critical observations'; while the Board's Chairman, the Bishop of Truro [the Rt Rev. Graham Leonard], added a sniffy foreword, making it clear that the Board would have preferred not to publish the report because many readers will find its questioning of received truths disturbing, but reluctantly felt obliged to do so to avoid incurring the odium of censorship. In a passage of gnomic casuistry, Dr Leonard observes: 'Many homosexuals have in the past and today given up opportunities for sexual relationships in obedience to Christian teaching: the Church must avoid any possibility of the deduction being drawn, from a reassessment of homosexuality, that they have made an unnecessary sacrifice.'

The report, according to its chairman, the Bishop of Gloucester [the Rt Rev. John Yates], sought to consider homosexuality in a contemporary social setting. Its assumptions about this were surprising, to say the least:

> We live at a time in which people's interest in sexuality is not only intense but also explicit and overt. A symptom of this state of affairs is the popular assumption that more or less everybody is sexually active. It is widely assumed, for example, that any two people living together will inevitably engage in genital activity.

Since 1967, the report says, attitudes have become more polarized: homosexuality is discussed more openly (if not always more sensibly) in the media, and both support for and hostility towards homosexual people is more stridently articulated. Many people confuse all homosexuality with paedophilia, so that 'homosexuals are believed to be men who corrupt little boys' – a definition of paedophilia which piles confusion upon confusion! But the report does not suggest (as one might expect it to) what the Church should be doing to educate the bemused public, or to combat what it admits is an irrational weight of anti-homosexual hostility.

Indeed, the working party is reluctant to use the term 'prejudice' because 'in popular usage [it] has come to possess an emotive and derogatory meaning'. They also sidestep the need to analyse the nature and origins of the hostility, or to accept the large measure of responsibility which Christians must undoubtedly bear for its existence. 'To be a victim of prejudice needs to be distinguished from the experience of alienation and rejection which may come to any member of a minority living in a society which does not cater for his needs.' So if the closeted homosexual feels out of place in a society in which 'the heterosexual married couple is seen as the basic and most important unit', he should not forget that he shares this experience with others, such as widows (who, however, are not so far as I am aware scripturally referred to as 'unnatural' or an 'abomination'). While claiming to sympathize with the concept of homosexual 'oppression', the working party say they must also 'recognise and take measure of the antipathy and revulsion which so many in the community feel towards homosexual practices, and even towards the homosexual condition itself'. Because they believe that such feelings express 'a basic conviction about the proper use of sex which is, in general, well-founded', they regard 'attempts to dismiss this conviction as unreasoning prejudice as misplaced and unlikely to succeed'. As they are 'uncertain' about the possible consequences of a more tolerant social attitude towards homosexuality, they stop short of advocating one.

Their medical, biological and psychological chapters are muddled and reach no clear conclusions. Their assertion that biblical condemnation refers to 'misuse' of sex by those who were not exclusively homosexual (a concept unknown in those times) is smartly rebuffed in the Board's appendix; nevertheless, it provides the foundation of their theological and ethical discussion. As against what they term the 'libertarian' approach (which they admit is tolerant and realistic), they prefer the 'personalist' view which maintains that what matters in a sexual relationship is the quality of personal relationship that it serves to express and confirm. Ideally, this should be lifelong and exclusive as a condition of genuine love. The working party reaffirm the Christian view of 'sacramental' marriage as 'the norm'.

For 'the homosexual predicament' the working party propose a modification in traditional Christian attitudes to allow for the fact that homosexual people also have a need to 'mirror the divine love'. The 'predicament' is in fact the working party's, rather than that of most homosexuals; and they steer a characteristically lukewarm middle course between total prohibition and recognition of homosexual relationships:

> We do not think it possible to deny that there are circumstances in which individuals may justifiably choose to enter into a homosexual relationship with the hope of enjoying a companionship and physical expression of sexual love similar to that which is to be found in marriage.

But such relationships cannot be regarded as the moral or social equivalent of marriage, because they 'would be bound to have a private and experimental character which marriage cannot and should not have'.

On legal issues, the working party display no burning desire to improve the homosexual's lot. As with 'prejudice', they baulk at the notion that anti-homosexual 'discrimination' is manifestly improper – because they cannot accept that 'homosexuality, despite being the sexuality of a minority, is entitled to full equality in social, educational and theological terms'. They raise the question of 'unfair' dismissal from employment, but give no clear opinion of what they consider to be unfair. They fudge the 'acute difficulties' faced by homosexual parents in obtaining custody of their children; they hedge their bets on the age of consent. While proposing some minor improvements – redefinition of 'in private', and abolition of common law 'conspiracy to corrupt public morals' – they are actually in favour of continuing discrimination against public expressions of same-sex affection, because they think that to allow them might operate to give homosexuals 'a specially protected status, not merely equality'. Their 'reasoning' – if it can be called that – is that because homosexuality has a deviant minority status, public displays of affection are more likely to create public offence than equivalent heterosexual behaviour is: homosexuals should therefore 'exercise greater restraint than others in ordinary public places and situations'.

In their final chapter, the working party teeter between recognition that homosexuals are the victims of social injustice and apprehension at the effects of treating them better. They appear to believe that, even with generally greater understanding and goodwill, the suspicion of homosexuality will debase friendship. It would be unfortunate [they say] if more liberal attitudes to homosexuality resulted in all close friendships being automatically assumed to include genital expression – 'if . . . it ever came to be assumed that every Sherlock Holmes and Dr Watson, or even Starsky and Hutch, were homosexually related, the value of friendship would be greatly threatened' – a curious assumption!

The working party encountered a great deal of age-old bigotry – such as that homosexuality, if given a toehold of respectability, will sweep through society like a prairie fire – in 'a surprising number of people': yet their only antidote is a string of platitudes. They seem to think that it is worse to be wrongly accused of being a homosexual than having to put up with being one, and that those who are gay should do their utmost to avoid 'scandalising' their fellow-Christians. Within the Christian community (they say), no one should deliberately cause another to stumble. The mere fact of being homosexual should not be regarded as any hindrance to Church membership or communion. 'We are dismayed by the evidence submitted to us by homosexual men and women who have experienced nothing but suspicion, or even outright rejection.' At the same time, Christian homosexuals should realize 'the stresses and strains which the Church fellowship may be called to accept on their behalf'.

And what of the homosexual clergy (who, one suspects, are the real cause of much of the working party's tortuous agonizing)? The clergy as a body should be able to expect reasonable privacy in their domestic lives, and a 'presumption of innocence' (tell-tale phrase!) in all matters concerning their personal behaviour. 'The simple fact that two priests live together in the same house should not, in our opinion, entail a presumption that they are living in a homosexual union.' (Whenever did it?) But a homosexual priest who has 'come out' and openly acknowledges that he is living in a sexual union with another man should not expect the Church to accept him on the same conditions as if he were married. He should feel morally obliged to offer his resignation to his Bishop.

After once more revealing its inbuilt bias by declaring that 'so far as ambisexual persons have a choice, they should seek to restrain their homosexual inclinations and develop a heterosexual orientation', the report concludes that no one knows 'the whole truth' about homosexuality. (Do they know it about anything?) 'We are still emerging, half-dazzled, from a long period of darkness in which the whole subject was regarded as shameful and unmentionable.' Christians have a responsibility in society 'to soften and reconcile, wherever they can, those who may be tempted to aggressiveness, provocation, scornfulness or malice'.

A vain hope, to judge from the ecclesiastical skulduggery which occurred even before the working party's report was published, let alone the almost universal chorus of disapproval which greeted it. Homosexuals are enraged that it denies the cogency of their claims to legal and social equality of treatment, while playing down the ugly nature of the discrimination to which they are subjected. Traditionalist Christians are enraged at its undermining of the fundamental concept that all sexual contacts outside marriage are 'sinful', and homosexual ones especially so. Clearly, the 'problem' the report fails to resolve arises from Christian beliefs about sex – not just from homosexuality.

Not merely do the working party deny the right of homosexual men and women to equal treatment with heterosexuals as human beings; by justifying some forms of discrimination on the dubious ground that, because homosexuals are an unpopular minority and the victims of ignorance and prejudice, therefore to treat them equally would cause offence, they lend spurious respectability to the rabid homophobes who infest the evangelical wing of the Church of England and who seek to impose their pale versions of theocracy upon us. The moral turpitude of these sections of the report is reprehensible and unforgivable.

(b) *Forum*

The report has already been assailed on the one hand by Christian traditionalists as a betrayal of the faith and on the other by the Campaign for Homosexual Equality as 'appalling', 'patronising', and a 'disgrace', and by the Gay Christian Movement as 'woolly-minded and pusil-lanimous'. It is sandwiched between a frosty introduction by the Bishop of Truro, who explains why it took the Board for Social Responsibility (of which he is chairman) a year to steel themselves to publish it ('many readers will find it disturbing' and 'we do not think the Church of England is yet ready to declare its mind'), and a stinging tailpiece from the Board itself castigating its own working party's level of biblical scholarship, the relevance of its arguments, and the validity of its conclusions. After all this, its authors must be feeling as if they had been bitten by a flock of sheep.

Forum has asked me how I feel about the report as a gay person and a longtime fighter for a better social deal not just for homosexuals but for all human sexuals.

Quite simply, reading it made me feel really mad. And a bit sad as well.

SAD – because the Church of England has in the past played an honourable part in ending the worst legal discriminations and social injustices against homosexuals. While we were getting the 'consenting adult' Bill through Parliament, they said that what was sinful shouldn't necessarily be criminal.

MAD – because this working party now says that even if homosexual relationships aren't always sinful (just *nearly* always!), homosexuals still shouldn't have equal social or legal rights in such innocent matters as public displays of affection. And why? Just *because* they are widely held to be 'deviants' – so that the spectacle of two people of the same sex kissing and holding hands in the street is more likely to cause public offence than two people of opposite sexes doing exactly the same thing! This sort of zany reasoning could be used to justify discriminating against *any* perfectly harmless but allegedly unpopular minority (blacks? Jews? Christians?), and it strikes me as shockingly craven codswallop.

Both MAD and SAD – because for all its 'white liberal', skin-deep tolerance, this report shows no recognition of the fact that the people it's talking about, who probably number about 5 million in this country, might reasonably have expected to be given an open and acknowledged voice in the working party's discussions. If there *were* (as little birds have whispered) some gay or bisexual members of the working party – and a question to that effect was neatly sidestepped by its chairman, the Bishop of Gloucester, in a *Church Times* interview – I hope they feel thoroughly disgusted with themselves for being such frightful Uncle Toms as to sign such a patronizing document, and for acquiescing in some of its astonishingly naïve views and its (perhaps unconscious) put-downs of homosexual people.

MAD – because, after four years' work, the authors of this document still seem to be ignorant of most of the recent basic research which has been done on human sexuality and which makes their work look simplistic and ill-informed.

MAD – because, notwithstanding the tentative and tepid nature of the report, the Church of England hierarchy got its ecclesiastical knickers into such a preposterous twist about whether or not to publish it. The resulting revelation of official Christianity's inability to stomach what it finds distasteful because its antiquated preconceptions are threatened will no doubt hasten the exodus of modern-minded people from the Anglican faith.

MAD – because all the private assurances I and others received over a long period that *this* time the nettle of prejudice really would be grasped have proved false.

MAD – because I am sick of being 'talked about' like a laboratory specimen by persons who apparently believe that they are entitled and qualified to do so. (How about the gay community setting up a working party to look into and pronounce upon the morals, social relevance, acceptability, and claims to superiority of Christians?)

MAD – because, in order to write this, I had to read a document which proved to be the biggest let-down I've had in years.

MAD – because perhaps the most surprising – indeed, scandalous – omission from this mealy-mouthed report is its inexcusable silence over the indisputable fact that for centuries past the Christian churches have been foremost amongst the persecutors of homosexuals, and that today a crescendo of homophobic paranoia, prejudice, and bigotry is emanating from the crackpot 'Evangelical Christians' who believe that it is their God-given mission to scourge and oppress those of us who are gay.

In evidence which I gave to an earlier Church of England working party (whose report never saw the light of day) I said that the first thing Christians owed to homosexuals was atonement for all the evils and misery heaped upon those who love their own sex by self-proclaimed spokespeople of the 'God of Love'.

It was in 1963 that the eloquent and courageous pamphlet *Towards a Quaker View of Sex* denied that homosexual affection was in essence morally worse than heterosexual affection. The following year, a group of church people and homosexuals meeting together for the first time in California were greeted with the memorable words: 'Forget who you represent. We represent the human race. Let's start there.'

All these years later, in stark contrast, the Anglican church still affects the worn-out posture of 'us' talking about 'them', and cannot begin to come to terms with the sheer richness of human sexual diversity.

As a gay person, I don't want sympathy, compassion, condescension, or even concern from Christians or anybody else. I want simple justice and full acceptance on my individual merits as a human being.

Note

1. SCM Press, 1967, 1970.

Evangelical Evils –
An Ex-Christian's View

THE FREETHINKER, DECEMBER 1979

When I was a Christian, it was in spite of Evangelicals, who then struck me as cranky but harmless. I no longer see them as such, but as positively evil; and it is because of this that I have recently left the Church.

For I have become convinced that people who imagine themselves to be set apart from the rest of us frailer mortals because they believe they are 'born again', 'saved', or 'washed in the Blood of the Lamb', partake of the demonic for that very reason, and are as far from being 'of God' as it is possible to be. I can no longer share a faith which breeds such spiritual élitism.

Christ said: 'By their fruits ye shall know them.' What are the fruits of Evangelicalism? Some which I have personally experienced are: arrogance, bigotry, condescension, deviousness, fanaticism, humbuggery, ignorance, malice, unscrupulousness, and untruthfulness. If theirs is true spirituality, I want none of it.

I have spent more than twenty years dealing professionally, as a lawyer and a social worker, with people's difficulties connected with sexuality. I have observed how many of these difficulties are exacerbated, and some are initially caused, by traditional Christian attitudes to sex – which is still regarded by all too many Christians as a Cosmic Mistake. Evangelicals, in particular, whilst professing to 'hate the sin and love the sinner', frequently go out of their way to make life more difficult and unhappy than it already is for those who – even though they may never give way to the temptations of the flesh – have emotional preferences which diverge from the so-called 'norm'.

I think particularly of the Goebbels-like vilification of homosexual people which is constantly carried on by some Evangelical groups. Much of the 'information' they circulate is inaccurate; some of it is downright lies. I recall their recent endeavours to smear with the totally false tag of sympathy for 'child molesting' individuals and organizations – including myself and the Albany Trust, of which I was Director – who had courageously shown humane concern for the plight of that most demonized of all sexual minorities – paedophiles.

I am utterly shocked by the dishonest twaddle being dished out to confused young people under the banner of 'Christian counselling' – which seems to me to be neither Christian nor counselling as it is nowadays professionally understood. The amount of hysteria generated by Evangelicals is in fact making it extremely difficult to discuss the sexual and emotional development and needs of adolescents rationally and calmly.

So my mounting disgust with the obnoxious activities of these people has forced me to quit a religion which nurtures such deplorable adherents. Some of these blinkered worthies, indeed, seem to hanker for the biblical moral law (Old Testament style of 'an eye for an eye, a tooth for a tooth') to be written in its entirety into the criminal law, and for Britain in the 1980s to revert to a Cromwellian 'rule of the Saints' – or perhaps to a Khomeini-style theocracy.

When Jesus said: 'O generation of vipers, how can ye, being evil, speak good things?' was he addressing only the Pharisees of his own generation, I wonder?

How Moral Is the Backlash?

Late in 1976, the Albany Trust suffered a ferocious onslaught from the combined forces of the 'Moral Majority' (an alliance of mostly Christian groups who campaigned for 'family values' and against what they disapprovingly termed 'permissiveness'). For the next two years, the thankless task of denying the groundless accusations made by these unco' guid people absorbed enormous amounts of the Trust's energies and deflected it from its educational and counselling work. Partly because of the stresses generated by this artificially drummed-up battle, I finally left the Trust in April 1977. In 1981, I gave my assessment of the tactics of our assailants in a talk to Brighton and Hove Humanists with the above title. The following extracts (edited with a few later additions) convey some of the fraught atmosphere we were caught up in at that time.

My answer to the question posed in the title is 'Not at all'. I think that a great deal of the public behaviour of these new puritans is quite unethical and indeed unscrupulous – presumably because they believe that the 'Christian truth' which has been revealed to them absolves them from observing ordinary mundane standards of human truthfulness in their dealings with those whom they regard as fighting against God.

We are confronted, in these self-styled protagonists of 'absolute moral standards', with behaviour which belies their pretensions; behaviour which not infrequently is totally ruthless in its misrepresentation of other people's motives, views and actions and in the lengths to which it is taken in order to win battles. And make no mistake: these standard-bearers of 'Christian morality' are out to win their battles and – just as much as the most dyed-in-the-wool Stalinist – they believe that the end justifies the means. Of course it must – because their ends are God's ends and they are God's instruments.

[The bodies I referred to included the National Viewers' and Listeners' Association, the Nationwide Festival of Light, The Responsible Society (subsequently known as Family and Youth Concern), the Community Standards Association, the Order of Christian Unity, and the Church Society.]

The most striking characteristic of all these people and organizations is that they adopt a very lofty moral posture. They stand for righteousness and against sin. They all proclaim that there are God-given moral absolutes – and especially, in the case of Mary Whitehouse at least, they espouse the 'four absolutes' of Moral Rearmament: absolute honesty, absolute unselfishness, absolute purity, and absolute love. They are nearly all 'Born Again' people. (Indeed, they put one in mind of Katharine Whitehorn's immortal quip that 'the trouble with so many "born again" people is that one wishes they hadn't been born the first time'.) They have what Roy Hattersley once described (referring to Mr Gladstone) as 'that special sort of Christian humility which, in practice, is impossible to distinguish from arrogance'. They KNOW they are right.

o O o

Far from perceiving the modestly liberalizing reforms of what they scathingly term the 'permissive sixties' as an overdue acknowledgement of the valid role of personal choice and individual responsibility, most of these people regard the modernization of laws concerning capital punishment, abortion, homosexuality, and divorce as retrograde steps. Some of them repudiate the key 'Wolfenden' distinction between sin and crime and want the State to resume its historic task of punishing vice and immorality through the agency of the criminal law.

Furthermore, some of the leading 'anti-permissive' campaigners appear convinced of the existence of a worldwide conspiracy linking everything they most hate and fear, with 'subversion' (atheism and communism) deliberately fuelling 'perversion' (sexual immorality and deviation – especially homosexuality) through the spread of pornography.

In recent years, these groups have built up a vociferous lobby in Parliament for 'Family and Child Protection' under the Commons leadership of Mrs (later Dame) Jill Knight, Conservative MP for Edgbaston, and tirelessly promoted in the Lords by (among others) Lord Longford, the Earl of Halsbury, Viscount Ingleby and Lord Nugent of Guildford. They have notched up a good few scalps lately: the Whitehouse-inspired Protection of Children Act, resulting from an assiduously drummed-up scare about the 'menace' of kiddieporn; the 1980 campaign to force the Department of Health to revise its guidelines for doctors about prescribing contraceptives for under-16s; a concerted onslaught to get the Department of Education to allow parents to withdraw their children from school sex education lessons if the parents disapproved of what was being taught; and the recent triumphal progress through both Houses of Tim Sainsbury's hypocritical Indecent Displays (Control) Bill – hypocritical because, while presenting it as a 'clean up the streets but no censorship' measure, it was crystal clear from their speeches that the Sainsbury camp were itching to ban altogether material which they regarded as pornographic, and not merely to banish it into back rooms. Anyone who has read the Hansard reports will be left in no doubt that 'the *vice anglais* is not buggery but humbuggery'. To listen to the Bill's supporters, you would imagine that the chief threat to Britain's world prestige and economic stability today was the proliferation of sex shops throughout the land, and that the suppression of pornography should be the government's primary task.

[The Sainsbury Bill became law in 1981. Later successes included the Video Recordings Act of 1988, and Section 28 of the 1988 Local Government Act, which prohibited local councils from 'promoting' homosexuality as 'a pretended family relationship'.]

o O o

The increasingly open threat to freedom of expression, of speech, and ultimately of thought is no laughing matter. Nor is the undermining of honest, clear-thinking, common sense, the willingness to judge issues on their merits and – not least – decent standards of integrity in public life. All of these I lay at the Whitehouse/Festival of Light/Responsible Society circus's door.

In 1979 a book was published called *Respectable Rebels*, about various middle-class pressure groups. I was intrigued to read, in a chapter on 'Religion, Morality and the Middle Class' by Dallas Cliff, a Huddersfield Polytechnic lecturer in sociology, the following:

Other groups which are considered [by Whitehouse's NVALA] to come under the Communist umbrella include the National Council for Civil Liberties, the Albany Trust, the Campaign for Homosexual Equality and the Humanist Society (*sic*).

So I wrote to Mr Cliff and asked him for precise information as to the source and context of this – to me – astonishing allegation. Here is part of his reply:

> To the best of my knowledge no authoritative spokesman of any of the groups I researched has ever publicly accused the Albany Trust of being a Communist organisation. What I was trying to convey . . . was the way in which members of the 'moral right' misguidedly used the term 'communist' to refer to any vaguely liberal organisation. . . . The nearest thing to chapter and verse I can give you is that in my hearing the Trust, along with the other groups mentioned, has been referred to as an organisation infiltrated by 'pinkos and commies' by ignorant and ill-informed rank and file members. . . . I hope it was clear from my article that these allegations are absurd and spring from the hysterical and ill-informed ways in which 'communism' is used as a term of abuse and hurled at groups which are disagreed with, rather than as a precise political term, by these people.

This sort of thing is, of course, pure Humpty Dumpty:

> 'When *I* use a word', Humpty Dumpty said, in rather a scornful tone, 'it means just what I choose it to mean – neither more nor less.'
>
> 'The question is', said Alice, 'whether you *can* make words mean so many different things.'
>
> 'The question is', said Humpty Dumpty, 'which is to be master – that's all.'

In September 1975, when I was Director of the Albany Trust, I went with the Trust's then Chairman, Harold Haywood, to a seminar organized by MIND [The National Association for Mental Health] on sexual minorities and their problems. A young man spoke there very openly and courageously about his experiences, thoughts and feelings as a paedophile.[1] Afterwards, Mr Haywood said to me that this of all sexual minorities was the most execrated and doom-laden, and that the Trust had a moral duty to see whether anything could be done to help those who carried this heavy burden to live more at peace with themselves.

So I organized some private meetings at the Trust offices with a number of psychiatrists, psychologists and social workers who were professionally interested in paedophilia, and also invited some paedophiles, including the young man who had spoken at the MIND conference and other members of the Paedophile Information Exchange (PIE) and another group, PAL (Paedophile Action for Liberation). These meetings were in accord with the philosophy and policy of the Trust as an educating, training and helping agency. The fact that they were taking place was briefly mentioned in a list of the Trust's activities in the first edition of its new paper, *AT Work*, published in the autumn of 1976, their purpose being stated as 'to discuss possible ways of providing supportive help for paedophiles who feel themselves to be in need of it'. The 'supportive help' envisaged was individual counselling and possibly a supportive group run by professionals for lonely, isolated and frightened paedophiles – not any assistance to organizations such as PIE: though the failure to make this absolutely clear proved to be an ambiguity which had most unfortunate consequences for the Trust.

Another project discussed was the joint production by the group (including its professional members) of a 'Questions and Answers' booklet on paedophilia, to be published by the Albany Trust. A drafting committee (of which I was *not* a member) produced a text, but the Trustees could not agree on it, and so the project was dropped. The Trustees decided that, apart from some limited public educational work, any Albany Trust supportive help for paedophiles (including counselling) should be linked to the sex offenders' project which the Trust was involved in jointly with NACRO (the National Association for the Care and Resettlement of Offenders).

This was the actual extent of the Trust's interest in paedophilia. I never thought, and did not intend, that this topic should become a major focus of the Trust's work – though it seemed to me then, and still does, a legitimate area of potential counselling provision and social concern to explore. Years earlier, Tony Dyson (the Trust's founder) had remarked to me that paedophilia was still an issue which would not be sensibly and calmly confronted by society in the foreseeable future. I knew he was right – even so, I did not foresee what a minefield we were walking into. By following our own philosophy of bringing more light than heat to bear upon contentious aspects of sexuality, we exposed ourselves to ferocious attacks from the 'moral majority' against the Trust's hard-won public credibility.

Rashly, perhaps, the same issue of *AT Work* carried an editorial which I had written criticizing the Festival of Light-inspired 'PILOT' counselling service for homosexuals, which described itself as being run on 'similar lines to the Samaritans' but was in fact, from accounts we had received of it, a crudely evangelizing and guilt-inducing missionary operation which could well do considerable harm to anxious and unhappy youngsters and bore no relation to 'counselling' in the sense that term is used by the British Association for Counselling[2] and similar professional bodies.

I had also reviewed, in *AT Work*, a recently published book on paedophilia, *The Forbidden Love*; and although the authors (one of whom was a Jungian psychiatrist whom I knew personally and liked very much) took no exception, what I wrote greatly offended the Responsible Society and their allies. I commented that while in nineteenth-century Europe childhood and sexuality were regarded as mutually exclusive, this belief could no longer be maintained in the light of modern knowledge. But (I added) at a time when the propriety of adolescent sexuality is still a fierce battleground for conflicting adult attitudes, it is scarcely surprising that the inevitably harmful nature of paedophile relationships remains an almost unquestioned assumption.

Let me, at this point, make it crystal-clear that I am not myself personally inclined towards, or approving of, paedophile relations – but I passionately believe that even the most unpopular minorities, whether sexual, racial, religious or political, are entitled to a fair and patient hearing however incomprehensible or distasteful their viewpoint. Largely thanks to the hysterical hullabaloo kicked up by the 'moral majority', aided and abetted by the sensationalist press, paedophiles have been denied such a hearing and have been enabled to assume the role of martyrs more convincingly than would otherwise be the case.

Earlier that summer (1976) I had spoken, in my capacity as Secretary of the Sexual Law Reform Society, about the age of consent at a National Council of Social Service Women's Forum; and in October I addressed a meeting arranged by the National Council of Voluntary Youth Organisations on the same topic. One of those present at the latter meeting was the Secretary of The Responsible Society, Mrs Valerie Riches, who scolded me for 'getting at the children'. I endeavoured to explain to her that I was as anxious as she was to protect and guide young people during the formative process of growing up – though without making them or their consenting sexual partners into criminals; but she would not accept my assurances.

A few weeks later, in late November, Mary Whitehouse got shockwaves of national publicity for her strident claim – made at a 'Christian Lunch and Dinner Clubs'[3] meeting at Central Hall, Westminster – that the Albany Trust – 'the homosexual lobby front-runner', as she flatteringly though inaccurately called it – was using its public funds to 'support paedophile groups' so that *we are all subsidizing and supporting, at least indirectly, a cause which seeks to normalize sexual attraction and activity between adult males and little girls'*.[4] And she prefaced her reference to the Albany Trust's public funding with the curious remark: 'one constantly has to ask oneself – does the right hand of the Government know what the left hand is doing? And I MEAN the left hand!' A deft Red smear, indeed.

There wasn't a shred of truth in any of her innuendos. All that the Trust had done was to invite three or four paedophiles as a minority presence at exploratory talks with professionals who wished to know more about their problems and points of view. The extent of the 'public funding' which they had received amounted to a few cups of tea. PIE had purchased from the Trust for £1 a single copy of the translated Speijer Report – a Dutch Government document which recommended reducing the age of consent for male homosexual behaviour to 16 (soon afterwards implemented in Holland).[5] The translation into English of this important and useful document had been paid for by the Sexual Law Reform Society, although one or two explanatory footnotes had been added by the Albany Trust to the English text – all long before the Trust had obtained any public funding whatsoever.

My immediate (and, I now realize, extremely naïve) reaction was that the Whitehouse speech was either made recklessly or on the basis of misinformation. In either case, it was clearly and seriously libellous of the

Trust collectively and of each of the Trustees individually. I therefore advised them that, if she would not retract, we should sue her in order to protect the Trust's good name. It was agreed that, as a first step, a letter drafted by lawyers should be sent to Mary Whitehouse listing the numerous errors of fact in her speech and requesting her to withdraw.

The history of this letter became a miniature saga in itself. I posted it by recorded delivery, and as no reply had been received after several weeks, Mrs Whitehouse was telephoned and said she 'could not recollect' whether or not she had received the letter. So a copy of it was sent to her by ordinary post. She still did not reply. The Trust did not publicize the contents of the letter until the late Spring of 1977. But lo and behold! That May Mrs Whitehouse published a book, *Whatever Happened to Sex?* – and in it there appeared extracts from the Albany Trust's letter to her which she had never replied to and could not recall having received! (Nor could the Post Office confirm its delivery to her.)

Far from apologizing or retracting, Mrs Whitehouse simply sat back while her preposterous allegations were gleefully embroidered and spread widely around by the Festival of Light, the Responsible Society, and the rest, being repeatedly brought to the attention of Government Ministers through numerous parliamentary questions about the Albany Trust's alleged misuse of its (tiny) public funds. In the House of Commons, Sir Bernard Braine MP (later Lord Braine) alleged that the Trust was using public funds to support PIE. His 'reasons' were that PIE had sold photocopies of the Albany Trust-annotated translation of the Speijer Report for £1 each; and that under my Directorship the Trust had 'openly campaigned' for the reduction of the age of consent.

So I wrote to Sir Bernard Braine, telling him point-blank that what he had said was totally without foundation, and asking him to withdraw it. He sent me a long, rude, blustery letter full of underlined questions such as: '*May I ask if you are the Mr Grey who spoke at these meetings?*' – the effect was as if a bullying, red-faced man was shouting at me from two inches away at the top of his voice. I sent him a detailed, very polite and wholly factual reply, in the course of which I said:

> I do not approve of paedophile practices. I do not favour the social acceptance of paedophilia. I do not belong to or support PIE. I disagree with PIE's aims, pronouncements and activities. I would not advocate or support any changes in the law other than those proposed in the enclosed Sexual Law Reform Society's report. . . . [I added:] Just as I suppose you have done, I have participated in many hundreds of meetings during my working life where numerous bodies with whom I quite violently disagreed were represented – but nobody has ever before accused me of holding views which I in fact reprobate because I have sat round a table and engaged in dialogue.

I heard no more from Sir Bernard Braine.

The Festival of Light, in its Autumn 1977 Broadsheet, castigated PIE and added:

> A *sympathetic and related body* [my italics] is the Albany Trust – an organisation set up to provide counselling for homosexuals and receiving grants from Government funds. Until recently it circulated a Dutch report that recommended the abolition of 'the existing penal provision concerning homosexual offences with minors'. The Albany Trust took the initiative in translating the report.

The Trust's chairman, Rodney Bennett-England, who had been swamped with anxious enquiries from Government Ministers and funding bodies about the Trust's activities (and who incidentally is himself a devout Anglican) wrote to the Festival of Light's director, O. R. Johnston, pointing out that this paragraph contained no fewer than five serious errors, adding:

> Since all of these allegations have been answered by us through parliament, the press and elsewhere over a period of many months, it is surprising that you choose to continue ignoring the truth, preferring the less attractive and certainly unChristian alternative that if you sling enough mud some of it is bound to stick. We may well differ, and must agree to differ, in our respective panaceas for the treatment of people with sexual problems. That does not give any of us the right to debase the standards of public debate by spreading malicious and deliberate untruths. I would hope this is not your intention. . . .

Johnston replied, demurely, 'As you may imagine, we have always taken great care to avoid misrepresentation, and are always willing to make amplifications and corrections where it appears to us that these are needed'. He enclosed an extract from the Festival's latest Broadsheet stating that:

> Mr Bennett-England, Chairman of the Albany Trust, has given an assurance that the Albany Trust does not support and is not connected with PIE . . . Mr Bennett-England denies that the Albany Trust took the initiative in translating the [Speijer] Report, as PIE had claimed.

He did not, however, apologize for or withdraw the assertion that the Trust was 'an aggressive supporter of paedophilia'.

In December 1977 an evangelical monthly magazine, *Life of Faith*, carried an article on child pornography which included references to the Albany Trust as 'a sympathetic and related body' to PIE. It took protracted correspondence with the magazine's editor and business manager, and the threat of a libel action, to obtain a grudging correction. A letter which I wrote to the organizer of the 'Christian Lunch and Dinner Clubs' shortly after the Whitehouse speech, requesting an opportunity to address a similar meeting in order to acquaint the Christian eaters with accurate facts about the Albany Trust and its work – which, I pointed out, enjoyed widespread Church support – was not answered.

A letter from Rodney Bennett-England published in *The Times* in January 1978, stating that for some time the Albany Trust had been the victim of 'a particularly vicious campaign' and was 'completely powerless' to defend itself against a barrage of MPs' questions was answered by the Responsible Society's chairman, a Dr Ellison, who explained that what was alleged was that the Trust had given PIE 'encouragement and assistance' and that it was 'clearly linked' with the English translation of the Speijer Report – which he weirdly described as 'a document which seeks to justify adult sexual gratification with minors' (and which he admitted the Responsible Society had purchased from PIE for £1!) – and ending: 'The fact of the matter is that the Albany Trust has actively campaigned for the reduction of the age of consent.'

Bennett-England replied, pointing out that the Speijer Report's proposal was to reduce the Dutch homosexual age of consent to 16 – not to legalize paedophile relationships. *The Times* did not publish this letter, but in a subsequent private correspondence Dr Ellison (who curiously claimed that the Responsible Society was a primarily secular body without any religious bias) wrote to Bennett-England reiterating that my review of *Forbidden Love* was 'aggressive' and 'takes the authors to task for criticising the attitudes and activities of child-molesters'; asserting that the Trust was 'considering producing a leaflet explaining the point of view of child-molesters', and maintaining that PIE 'used evidence from the Speijer Report to support its case to the Home Office Criminal Law Revision Committee that the age of consent for adult sexual activity with children should be reduced to four years of age'.

Refuting the misinterpretations and twisted reasoning of Dr Ellison (who was apparently unable to imagine a paedophile who did not molest children), Mr Bennett-England was driven to conclude that 'you regard me as a liar and [I] must consequently warn you that if any of these quite unfounded allegations are repeated we are quite resolved to take appropriate legal action and seek substantial damages'. Ellison seized upon this 'threat' as a pretext to break off the correspondence.

A three-pronged ding-dong between Mrs Whitehouse, Bennett-England and myself in the correspondence columns of the *Guardian* in December 1977 and January 1978 climaxed with her impudent statement that 'for Rodney Bennett-England to deny an association between the Albany Trust and PIE is to move the debate into such a realm of unreality as to make rational argument impossible' – to which he retorted: 'it is she who makes rational argument impossible by refusing to accept the truth if it doesn't suit her purpose'; and I for once found myself at a loss for suitable adjectives to describe her (even under my breath).

All these quite empty charges which had been wantonly put into circulation by this most effective alliance of highly 'moral' worthies and their hangers-on continued to reverberate around the country for months, surfacing in a variety of parish magazines and local newspapers and causing the Albany Trust (from which I had departed in April 1977) an enormous amount of extra work and worry. Typical was an article called 'Gay Is Sad – and Bad' which appeared in a Swindon parish magazine in January 1978, in which the Vicar said:

> As a writer in a recent issue of the *Church Times* put it: 'All human society has its roots in the family, and of all the threats to the family today none is so direct and so powerful as militant homosexuality.' But few seem to be aware of the extent of that threat. Did you know, for example, that the Government has made available large sums of public money to organisations which exist to promote homosexuality and are sympathetic to paedophilia (sexual interference with children)?
>
> For example, the Albany Trust (which was formed out of the Homosexual Law Reform Society) has received £21,000 from the Department of Education and £22,000 from the Home Office. Yet the Albany Trust is aggressively sympathetic to paedophilia, has been actively campaigning for the reduction of the age of consent, and is spreading the message that homosexual activity is normal and natural and the equivalent of sexual intercourse. It labels adolescents as 'teenage gay people', long before they have the opportunity to develop fully, thereby possibly inhibiting the maturing process to heterosexuality.

Not surprisingly, this sensational piece was picked up and quoted by the local papers. Fortunately the Bishop of Malmesbury who – as he wrote to Mr Bennett-England – had always had a considerable regard for the Trust's work, and was concerned at the sudden spate of adverse publicity which it was attracting, sent the articles to the Trust which was able to send a letter to the Swindon papers setting the record straight. This produced a handsome apology from the Vicar. In a letter which was also published in the local press, he said:

> These allegations [against the Albany Trust] were not manufactured here at my desk. I took them, word for word, from a source which one would naturally have supposed to be entirely reliable and trustworthy. Nevertheless, I now contrast the fact that Rodney Bennett-England has set out the Albany Trust's position clearly and openly with the insistence of my own source that on no account must it be revealed. I must, therefore, prefer the former; and I do so readily and completely.

One can only speculate upon the consciences of people who send highly libellous – indeed, scurrilous – material around the country to unsuspecting clergymen, inciting them to disseminate it publicly, whilst stipulating that the source must 'on no account' be divulged. God made no bones about telling Moses who had written on the Tablets of Stone on the mountain!

I find not only striking, but positively sinister, the manner in which such a concerted attack was launched on the Albany Trust from such a flimsy basis of a farrago of quarter-truths, false inferences, sheer myths and blatant misrepresentations which, when refuted, were only grudgingly corrected under strong pressure by two of the worst culprits and stoutly maintained by their supporters. Public and private attempts to arrange face-to-face meetings at which the real opinions and activities of the Trust could be discussed and elucidated were stonily ignored. There was not the least genuine desire on the part of Mary Whitehouse, the Responsible Society, the Festival of Light or any of their parliamentary mouthpieces to hear and understand the Albany Trust's case. All they wanted was to inflict the maximum damage upon the Trust. Even a personal approach to Lord Longford, whom I had known for many years, and to whom I sent full details of the controversy with a request that he would see fair play, was met with an equivocal 'Well, it's very difficult. I like you very much, and I like Mary Whitehouse very much. She's *a Good Christian Woman.*' [My italics.] As I did not feel disposed to argue that toss with him, I departed in disgust and have never spoken to him since.

A concerted campaign of vilification such as I have described raises very serious issues for British public life. Are these 'Crusaders for Love', who claim to stand for 'essential Christian ethics', and quote St Luke chapter 18 ('You must not bring false witness') in their propaganda, sincere but genuinely confused? Or are they totally reckless as to the actual facts of a situation, just as long as they can successfully blackguard and discredit their targets? Was this campaign of sustained misrepresentation against the Albany Trust deliberate? And, if so, are all the many other campaigns from the same stables equally flawed?

I wish I knew. Indeed, I would dearly like to know – because the appropriate response to a systematic campaign of deliberate lies is obviously very different from the best way of dealing with sincere people who are simply muddled and confused, don't understand the facts clearly, and don't want to admit they could ever be wrong.

I am prepared to assume that my adversaries in public disputes are sincere until very positive and definite proof to the contrary is forthcoming. Possibly the questions raised in the above story relate less to sincerity than to sheer misunderstanding and blind persistence in believing what one wants to believe about other people. However this may be, mere sincerity is not sufficient in public debate if facts are habitually treated in such a slapdash way.

For example, Mary Whitehouse recently hit the headlines yet again with the claim that 'police around the world' now have 'proof' that 90 per cent of sex crimes are caused by pornography. Shortly afterwards, a newspaper cutting turned up on my desk attributing this piece of information to one police inspector in a small Danish town. Again, Polly Toynbee (who was a member of the Williams Committee on Obscenity and Film Censorship) has said in the *Guardian* that Mrs Whitehouse told the Williams Committee that she had received numerous letters from people who said that their lives had been ruined by pornography. But when the Committee begged Mrs Whitehouse for a sight of these letters, she said that they were stored away in a loft at her house, and she couldn't get at them easily.

Responding effectively to this sort of thing is like trying to swim through a sea of porridge. And it is increasingly all around us. The people and groups I have been describing constitute a vociferous network who assiduously aim at public influence and who have succeeded – through sheer persistence, rather than because of the solidity of their evidence or the quality of their arguments – in making some impact not only on public thinking but also on government policy.

They are strongly motivated and tirelessly active. They lobby politicians, press and public with great persistence and vigour. They plan. They organize. They write letters. They recruit. They publish. They raise funds. Incredibly (in the light of my own experience of them) they claim a moral monopoly of compassion and concern. They *know* they are right. They *know* that those who disagree with them are wrong. They attack 'evil' by proclaiming that they hate sin but love the sinner. (So did Torquemada, as he sniffed burning flesh.) They proclaim their allegiance to 'absolute truth' – but they recognize only the facts which fit their version of it. They oversimplify the complexities of life. They hound, denigrate and blackguard those who reject their naïve nostrums. They have a silly and sentimental view of childhood and adolescence which, if it ever gains a foothold in the educational system of this country, will make all the pitfalls which beset the hazardous and complex process of growing up even more treacherous than they are today.

Mary Whitehouse and her 'moral majority' allies claim the loftiest standards, and yet on several occasions within my own experience of them they have behaved like moral hooligans. Far from practising the high ideals of love and truth which they proclaim, they drag the levels of public debate down into the gutter. And, since they profess to be motivated by Christian principles, I am astonished and dismayed at the failure of the mainstream churches and their leaders to publicly condemn and rebuke these dubious tactics which are being employed in the name of Jesus Christ. The strenuous efforts which are being exerted to brand those of us who work for a balanced and mature approach to the subject of sexuality, so crucial for human happiness, as tools or dupes of the Communists surely merit public rebuke from the leaders of the Anglican and Nonconformist Churches and from public figures who are culpable in their failure to curb the rampant bigotry and intolerance, almost amounting to fanaticism, and containing within itself the seeds of a McCarthyite witchhunt, which is nowadays masquerading as 'Christian Truth'. Formerly, the Churches were much more aware of the inherent threat posed to traditional British decency and tolerance by the excesses and distortions of such sects as Moral Rearmament.

Although these people are no laughing matter, neither are they an inexorable, irresistible, invincibly all-conquering force. Most certainly, whatever they choose to believe, they do not have the moral edge on those of us who stand for honesty, truth, justice, and decent behaviour in the time-honoured sense that our forebears did and not in the Orwellian Newspeak fashion which they employ.

Looking back upon this sorry episode almost two decades later, I am still filled with distaste by the manner in which the Albany Trust was so recklessly assailed, and the attacks persisted in even when the falseness of the allegations was exposed and refuted. The chorus of half-truths and untruths inside and outside Parliament undoubtedly influenced the newly elected Thatcher government to cut off the Albany Trust's public funding abruptly at the end of 1979.

The protection of children concerns everyone of good will in our society. Children most certainly do need protecting – not only from physical abuse and emotional cruelty, but also from over-simple beliefs which ignore the complications of living and loving, and which see most of human sexuality through a glass, darkly. Those who seek to help the young effectively have a duty to offer them a compassionately balanced and mature approach to sex – a facet of life so crucial to human happiness.

Notes

1. A word which has succumbed hopelessly to Humpty-Dumptyism. Its accurate etymological meaning is 'a lover of children' – in psychosexual terms, an adult who is emotionally and also sexually attracted to children below the age of puberty. Nowadays, however, the word's only understood meaning seems to be 'child molester', making it synonymous with the sexual abuse of children. That this is an activity which fills many genuine paedophiles with horror – because their love for children makes the idea of sexually violating them abhorrent – cuts no ice with the political and journalistic hi-jackers of the term.
2. On whose executive committee I sat for some years.
3. I never heard of this prandial body before – or since.
4. My italics.
5. See pp. 176ff.

PART FOUR

YOUNG PEOPLE

Consenting but Illegal?

SCOTTISH MINORITIES GROUP, AUGUST 1971

The concept of an 'age of consent' below which a boy or girl is unable to have any lawful sexual contact however much he or she may desire it is widely held and largely unexamined. Indeed, it is enshrined in our law, and arguments about the age of consent are usually confined to whether it should be 16, 17, 18, 21, or some other age. Yet the very notion is question-begging and itself questionable, for it postulates a state of affairs that is remote from actuality. And lawyers, legislators and even doctors fall into this trap, generalizing from dubious assumptions about adolescence or human nature itself to lay down wrong-headed rules which not infrequently cause more social harm than good.

Recently I took part in a broadcast discussion with Baroness Summerskill, who professed herself shocked that the British Medical Association had urged a re-examination of the age of consent because so many girls under 16 were having abortions. Lady Summerskill's remedy was to enforce the law more rigorously against the erring young men who 'impregnated' these girls. When I demurred, pointing out that the intervention of the criminal law into people's freely chosen behaviour almost invariably did more harm than good, Lady Summerskill accused me of a 'primitive' attitude in wanting a 'free for all' which would deprive the girls in question of the benefits of a higher education.

In venturing to suggest that the notion of an 'age of consent' begs so many questions that it probably does more harm than good, I do not believe that I am in fact being primitive. There is obviously much confusion of thought here. While there may be something to be said for the view (held in extreme form by Lady Summerskill) that the immature need protecting from their own impulses, there is little that can sensibly be said in defence of the contention that young adults who in every other respect are treated by the law as fully responsible are incapable of choosing whom they wish to go to bed with. Even where there are grounds for regarding their choice as anti-social, let us at least stop logic-chopping as to their capacity to consent.

At the present time, in English law, girls under 16 are deemed to be incapable of consenting to sexual intercourse (whether with the opposite sex or their own). Youths aged under 21[1] cannot lawfully consent to homosexual intercourse, and those aged between 16 and 21 are liable to up to two years' imprisonment for having such intercourse, even with someone else in the same age group and even if they both eagerly sought the experience. Such a law seems manifestly unjust. Even more unjust are the still harsher penalties – up to five years' imprisonment – which can be imposed upon a man aged over 21 who has a homosexual relationship with a youth under that age. Yet, since 1969, young people have been regarded by the law as fully adult in almost every other respect when they reach their eighteenth birthday.

'Over himself, over his own body and mind, the individual is sovereign.' Thus wrote John Stuart Mill in his classic essay *On Liberty* more than 100 years ago. True, Mill himself excepted from this principle 'those below the age which the law may fix as that of manhood or womanhood' on the ground that 'those who are still in a state to require being taken care of by others must be protected against their own actions as well as against external injury'. It can scarcely be maintained that young men aged between 18 and 21 nowadays fall into this category. The Wolfenden Committee, in considering at what age a man should be regarded as 'adult' for the purposes of homosexual behaviour, distinguished four sets of considerations: the need to protect young and immature persons; the age at which the pattern of a man's sexual development could be said to be fixed; the age at which he could be held responsible for his own actions; and the consequences which would follow from the fixing of any particular age. On the analogy of heterosexual behaviour there was a case (the Committee felt) for making the age 16; the first two of its four guidelines also pointed to this age – the Committee significantly concluding both that a young man could reasonably be considered capable of 'standing on his own feet' at 16 and of having a psychologically fixed sexual pattern by that age.

But although the fourth set of considerations would have led them to prefer 18, they finally (and obviously with some reluctance) recommended 21 as the 'age of consent' on the strictly pragmatic and expedient ground that this coincided with the then existing legal age of majority. This is, of course, no longer so; and we are left with an anomaly which – as one of the reform's supporters (the Hon Nicholas Ridley, Conservative MP for Cirencester and Tewkesbury) pointed out during the debates on the 1967 Sexual Offences Act – can make no sense at all in the minds of those young men who will grow up having to observe it.

So there is little that can now be convincingly said in support of 21 as the age of consent. But the question which I set out to discuss is not what the best age of consent might be, but whether we ought to think or to legislate in terms of an 'age of consent' at all. And this question is far from academic. Personally I believe, with Mill, that my body is my own property, and that what I do with it from the age of puberty onwards is my business, not the State's; but I can appreciate that there are also those who genuinely believe that some people – and certainly young people – need to be protected from their own impulses not only for their own sake but for society's. However, if we *are* going to do this, for heaven's sake let us be frank and admit that we are behaving in an essentially paternalistic way; let us stop pretending that those in question are incapable of giving valid consent and tell them bluntly that we are denying their freedom by imposing protective restrictions upon them.

And if this concept of 'protection' is to be admitted at all, it must, surely, be limited as much as possible. For I do not believe that the vast majority of doctors, social workers, and other counsellors favour compulsion as a preferred method, or even as a last resort. Is it not in fact the doctrine of despair? We are witnessing its dire results in the field of drug addiction, and I am sure that any attempt to extend it to the treatment of venereal diseases would encounter united opposition from the professional people chiefly concerned.

But sex, unfortunately, is the traumatic Achilles Heel of our hyper-neurotic society. And so while we may with luck succeed fairly soon in banishing the fiction of 'ages of consent', it seems utopian to suggest that a protective age limit of up to at least 14, and possibly (for the time being, at any rate) 16, for both sexes can be abandoned altogether. Indeed, there are some young girls and boys (I agree with Lady Summerskill) who do need protecting – though not necessarily punishing. But so far as possible I should like to see them protected from sexual assaults by a general law which would punish these (whether heterosexual or homosexual) no more and no less severely than an equivalent non-sexual physical attack, and under which the degree of mutual willingness would be factually assessed and taken into account as a mitigating circumstance, or even as disproving the alleged assault, instead of arbitrarily being rendered irrelevant because of one or both parties' age. This would restore a good deal more realism into a law which, despite the Act of 1967, remains riddled with unrealities.

Note

1. For '21' in this and subsequent references, substitute 18 since 1994.

Paedophiles – Are We Dodging the Issues?

FREETHINKER, AUTUMN 1977

Neither the public nor the press should congratulate themselves over the hysterical hullabaloo which has recently been focused upon a tiny group calling itself the Paedophile Information Exchange. The idea of adults seeking sexual relations with children may well turn the stomachs of most of us – but must we really vomit so publicly and collectively as to sidestep the moral obligation to apply ourselves as rationally as we can to serious consideration of several important issues?

While I do not claim more self-control than most of my neighbours, I endeavoured, when I was Director of the Albany Trust, to listen over a period of several months to what PIE and other paedophiles (whom PIE does not necessarily represent) were saying, and to evaluate its validity. While not accepting all their assertions, I find myself still pondering over a good many questions which were raised during these discussions.

First, is the public's image of the paedophile as being always and without exception a 'dirty old man' who is a 'child molester' accurate? The answer is without doubt 'no'. While there are, of course, some sexual psychopaths who molest, assault, and sometimes murder, small children, the majority of paedophiles, whose characteristic feelings for children are gentle, feel as much if not more revulsion at such atrocities as the rest of us do.

If, then, the public is wrong in believing all paedophiles to be evil, malevolent people, should we not take a fresh and more critical look at what happens to those who are apprehended for having illegal sexual relationships with children? Anyone who is at all aware of what happens to alleged sexual offenders before, during and (most of all) after trial would almost certainly answer 'yes'. The treatment frequently meted out to imprisoned sex offenders, not least by their fellow-prisoners, is a national disgrace. Social ostracism and discrimination outside prison is also often cruelly inhumane.

But even if not all paedophiles are sinister and aggressive people, are they not, nevertheless, bound to endanger a child who becomes sexually involved with them? Here there is no simple or straightforward answer. Most members of the public, and nearly all parents, would probably instinctively say the answer must always be 'yes'. Paedophiles would maintain that it is usually 'no' – and that indeed such relationships can even be beneficial to the children in various ways. Psychiatrists, while having a much greater understanding of, and sympathy for, paedophiles than the average person does, would mostly maintain that such contacts are bound to have some damaging effects, given society's current attitudes, if only because of the furtive secrecy in which they must take place while undiscovered, and the trauma of discovery if unwanted discovery occurs.

My own view is that social attitudes towards children's sexuality would have to change so enormously before such relationships can cease to be perceived as damaging that the proposition that they *need* not be damaging will remain pie in the sky for the foreseeable future. However, some researches which have been published in various countries indicate that paedophile relationships are not inevitably or always damaging to the children involved.

The equation of childhood's innocence with sexual ignorance, and consequent attempts to prolong the latter, strike me as misconceived. I do not believe that we should flinch from attempts to become better informed about the facts, as opposed to the myths, about children's sexuality. It is, I hope, common ground that we are all sexual beings from birth, even though we do not usually become fully aware of our sexuality, or much preoccupied with it, until adolescence.

While some paedophiles would deny that puberty is a significant event, I cannot bring myself to believe this. Indeed, I think that it is crucial to an intelligent and responsible consideration of the subject to make a clear distinction between pre-pubertal childhood and post-pubertal adolescence; and paedophilia relates to the former, not to the latter. And, since it is possible to question the emotional and/or economic readiness for sexual relationships of at least some of those in their teens who have passed puberty, it is surely difficult to maintain convincingly the pre-pubertal child's readiness for sex – still more so his or her comprehension of what a sexual relationship with an adult involves for either of them.

I think we should, nevertheless, contemplate the possibility that it might on balance be healthy if society became more accepting of, and less alarmed by, children's explorative sexual curiosity at the onset of puberty, and certainly less vindictive towards those adults who may become involved with a child at this stage. For, as the Dutch Speijer Report[1] pointed out, 'a society which seeks to eliminate seductive situations will not encourage public moral welfare. . . . a normal development requires broad possibilities of introduction, experiment, contact and initiation.'

In his essay on *The Enforcement of Morals*, Lord Devlin discerned the obscure roots of the tangled relationship between morals and law in what I regard as a most unholy trio of emotions: intolerance, indignation and disgust. In urging that these are bad guides to either good law or good morals where sexual behaviour is concerned, I am not saying that there should be no moral standards or no laws whatever. But at least let us try and make those laws and standards which we do uphold as rational, humane and well calculated to attain commonly desired ends as possible. Above all, in discussing paedophilia and other emotionally loaded topics, let us consciously strive for more light and less heat in our debating.

Note

1. See below, pp. 176ff.

Men, Boys and Sex

REVIEW OF *SEXUAL EXPERIENCE BETWEEN MEN AND BOYS* BY THE
REV. PARKER ROSSMAN, APRIL 1979

The amount of emotional, moral and legal heat which some people focus on how other people obtain their orgasms has always bewildered and scandalized me. I believe that sex is a fundamentally personal and private matter, and that the choice of how people gratify their bodies with consenting others must be theirs, and theirs alone. The role of the law should be confined to protection from physical assault and unwilling involvement (including the preservation of public decency); that of morality to the inculcation of a responsible and considerate ethic of personal behaviour.

I should have thought that these simple principles would have been shared by everyone who cares about individual freedom and responsibility and about good morals. But this is unfortunately far from being the case. Christianity's sex-hating lunacies are all too familiar; and whoever first dreamed up the notion that the pleasurable exercise of natural bodily functions is sometimes 'dirty', 'wicked', and 'sinful' was one of humanity's greatest evil-doers. One can leave to their fellow-Christians the question of whether fundamentalist groups such as the Festival of Light and the Whitehousians are interpreting the Christian attitude to sex correctly, or distorting it; whatever the answer, they are undoubtedly doing great social damage by their indiscriminate attacks upon sexual enlightenment and their spreading of sexual furtiveness and guilt.

Nowhere has this been more the case than in respect of homosexuality – and especially over the vexed question of homosexual behaviour involving adolescents. Though the daft hullabaloo about paedophiles has died down (at least for the time being), it would be difficult to imagine a respected British churchman and educationalist bringing out a study of pederasty without a vociferous hue-and-cry from his fellow-Christians.[1] In the United States, things are evidently different. When Dr Parker Rossman, former Dean of the Ecumenical Continuing Education Centre and Associate Professor of Yale, published *Sexual Experience Between Men and Boys* in 1976, it was generally well received. It will be interesting to see what are the reactions to the British edition.[2]

Dr Rossman became involved in his researches as chairman of a study commission on revolutionary youth, looking at various 'undergrounds' – political, criminal, sexual, and religious. His concern for the boys who act as consenting sexual partners to adult males led him to a realization that this particular 'underground' was far more widespread than commonly thought; and that there is probably no other which is so enmeshed in a conspiracy of silence or represents such a potential for tragedy. Suicides and ruined lives are the price of a social hypocrisy and wilful ignorance which brands all the older partners in such liaisons as evil corrupters, and all the younger as irretrievably ruined. As Dr Rossman emphasizes, the impact of a particular sex experience depends to a great extent upon the way it is interpreted. Much adolescent sex play isn't interpreted by adults at all, but adult/adolescent sex play is widely regarded as calamitous – at any rate if it is homosexual.

Dr Rossman's data come from questionnaires answered by 215 pederasts and written material from 800 more. In addition, he interviewed 300 adolescent boys who had been sexually involved with older men. He defines a 'pederast' as a man aged over 18 who has had a sexual experience with, or is erotically attracted to, boys of between 12 and 16. That is to say, he is dealing with *post-pubertal* younger partners, and *not* with paedophilia (which is an erotic interest in children *below* the age of puberty). This is a crucial distinction: we shall make no headway towards clearer thinking, or better laws, until we acknowledge the real difference between the sexual behaviour of teenagers (whether with another teenager or an older person) and sexual activities which involve a child who has not reached puberty and who requires a greater degree of protection than a teenager does.

Our attitude to teenage sexual behaviour is, indeed, the crux of the debate about sex education, sex law, and personal responsibility. Far too many people still believe it shouldn't happen; a few even pretend that it doesn't. But, as Kinsey pointed out, their mid-teens are the peak of potency for most males, and these days an increasing number of teenage girls also expect to enjoy sexual experience. We have a clear choice between educating our teenagers for responsible freedom in their sexual behaviour (which of course includes the freedom to abstain from it), and continuing obviously futile efforts to ignore or repress their sexuality.

Where heterosexuality is concerned, many people accept that adolescents should be given adequate education about the biological, physical, and emotional aspects of sex, and information about contraception and venereal disease, as of right; and that they should then be allowed to choose for themselves in the light of their general moral beliefs. Where homosexuality is concerned, however, most are much more confused and unsure. The belief lingers on that, if homosexuals are 'made' rather than 'born', adolescent homosexual experience – especially if instigated by an older partner – will result in permanent 'deviation' from heterosexual normality.

There is, in fact, little evidence to support this fear and a good deal to show that it is unfounded. Most authorities now agree that a person's basic emotional pattern, which will determine the sex and characteristics of the persons he or she is attracted to, is formed very early in life – probably before the age of 6. Also, there is an increasing acknowledgement that heterosexuality, while the majority preference and the one which secures the continuation of the human race, is not more 'natural', in any meaningful sense, than homosexuality; and that bisexuality is probably the underlying core of sexuality in everyone and underpins a conscious preference for exclusive heterosexuality or homosexuality. A great many adolescents, who are not essentially homosexual, go through a temporary experimental phase which is far more likely to be blown up out of all proportion into a serious, ongoing element in their lives if it is treated with exaggerated parental and social fuss: the best way of ensuring the transience of adolescent homosexuality is to play it down.

Stereotypes always distort accurate perceptions, and sexual labelling is no exception. This is especially true of the hostile, negative descriptions of 'pervert', 'child molester', and 'sex offender' which are indiscriminately pinned onto anybody who is found out in what is really very common and widespread, and often quite trivial, activity. The purple press and the pious self-appointed 'protectors of innocent children' wax wrathful, judges pass swingeing sentences, and fellow-prisoners make life hell for the convicted delinquent. Where is our sense of proportion in all this? It is as if society is seeking a scapegoat for the collective sexual fantasies which it has repressed.

To read Dr Rossman's book is a useful antidote. His extensive quotations from many pederasts demonstrate convincingly that many of these men are not monsters – just quite ordinary, often highly moral and loving human beings who are frequently bewildered about their sexual feelings and are themselves the victims of society's irrational response to them. As one put it, they cannot see why they should be more seriously punished for giving a moment of sexual pleasure to a boy than for beating him savagely or for breaking his heart.

The main issues which Rossman clarifies are that – contrary to the mythical stereotype – most pederasts are not 'sex monsters'; they are not even emotionally disturbed; they don't 'molest' or 'interfere with' the adolescent boys with whom they are involved, who are as a rule willing (even eager) participants and most of whom do not become permanently or exclusively homosexual as a result. Large numbers of men and boys are involved. Why do the boys – who come from backgrounds right across the social spectrum – get into sex-play with older men? One reason, Rossman suggests, is that, paradoxically, current social attitudes make such activities easier for them than forming relationships with girls.

Such boys have positive attitudes towards sex; they cannot see why anything they choose to do with their bodies for pleasure or fun is 'wrong'. Most of them have already had some sexual experience with a friend or relative of near their own age before getting involved with older men. They need affection, and often receive it from their older partners – as Rossman observes, 'it is no coincidence that youngsters seek physical reassurance and affection when they are at a stage of life when no one is hugging them any more'. There is frequently a protective, tutoring aspect to the relationship which survives the sexual episodes to become lasting friendship. Boy-lovers sometimes have a very positive effect on young delinquents, some of whom become much more stable and less antisocial as a result of their older friends' attentions. On the other hand, 'it may well be that many criminals are created by society's tendency to teach adolescents that they are criminals if they are sexually adventurous or deviant'.

By refusing to acknowledge that there may be at least some truth in these unorthodox views, we store up trouble for ourselves in a most sensitive area – that of adolescent rebellion. 'A boy's breach with the morality of his parents and society, and their authority, begins when he finds that the "dirty old man" he was warned against is in fact the understanding and trusted friend he desperately needs.' Such 'uncles' are often strongly heterosexual; many are married, and some regard it as an important part of the relationship to initiate the boy into the pleasures of lovemaking so that he can proceed to involvements with girls confidently and happily. One pederast said: 'Kids love sex and become joyous when they are sexually happy. I'm not just rationalizing when I say that 90 per cent of the trouble we have with teenagers is the result of sexual frustrations.'

This is a view which I think makes a lot of sense. In contrast to those who hold that violence and sexual 'permissiveness' advance hand in hand, I agree with Rossman that there is a lot of evidence to show that as either violence or sexual pleasure goes up, the other goes down. Indeed, much violence is almost certainly due to the repression of sexuality. Ours is a curious society. We censor frank depictions of physical love, but not those of killings and other brutalities. Many families are far more tolerant of destructive substances such as alcohol, drugs and tobacco than of sexuality. Our values are topsy-turvy, and the young know it.

I am convinced, also, that repressive legal provisions accentuate the evils of the situation. They breed fear, hypocrisy, dishonesty, blackmail, theft, and sometimes death. As Rossman points out, 'adolescents are probably the least likely of anyone to tell the truth about sex, for they have everything to lose and little to gain by truth-telling – especially if they are involved with something taboo and illegal'. As for the men, 'once a man has engaged in a moment of mutual masturbation with a boy, he is vulnerable . . . as his moral restraints are eroded by the knowledge that he is now a criminal sex offender. . . . Pederasty thrives not because of "sexual freedom" and "moral laxity", but by quite the contrary because so many adolescents are pushed into rebellion and secrecy by their lack of freedom. . . . A majority of the adolescents of today are rebels against the sexual establishment as they understand it. They resent and reject the unwelcome repression of what they consider to be natural processes and feelings.'

Moralizing alienates youngsters – and crying 'wolf' is a silly remedy, as most boys who run away from home or get mixed up in pederastic activities do not, in fact, get murdered or even molested. But this does not mean that we should abandon our responsibility to commend sound standards and values to our young people; we should, however, take a very critical look at the appropriateness of what we do tell them and the treatment we mete out to them. Dr Rossman suggests that there are some sensible steps which can be taken, even if (and it remains a very big 'if') society gets around to re-evaluating its hitherto hysterical response to pederasty. We can condemn, and where possible punish, the use of force or violence in sexual situations. We can inculcate a positive approach to sexual health and hygiene and get rid of smutty furtiveness. We can encourage our teenagers to resist exploitation: 'Parents can shelter children up to a point, but finally neither society nor parents can protect them unless they are willing to be protected – which is what a lot of adolescent rebellion is all about.'

Above all, we should end the alienation of the young which is such a sickly symptom of our social ills: 'Youngsters not only need sex education, values, self-respect, and the right to sexual privacy but they also most of all need money and jobs in an urban society. . . . At present too many young boys from depressed sections of the community receive adult friendship, affection and life-enriching experiences only from pederasts.' Is it any wonder that kids reared in drab surroundings and failing schools suffer from both emotional and cultural starvation, and can get their only fun and adventure through furtive delinquency, drugs and sex?

Whatever our feelings about homosexuality in general, and pederasty in particular, Rossman's ground-breaking book provides new insights to what is obviously a widespread facet of human nature. Much of what he has to say should stir our consciences – for it is no longer sufficient to go on mouthing the old platitudes and anathemas. Can society dare to become more realistic about the facts? Can it afford not to?

Notes

1. Which was indeed the fate of John L. Randall, who was asked to resign from his post as a church organist, and from youth club work, in the Midlands after publishing his excellent study *Childhood and Sexuality: A Radical Christian Approach* (Pittsburgh, PA: Dorrance, 1992).
2. Published by Maurice Temple-Smith.

What Speijer Really Said

FEBRUARY 1979

The Dutch Speijer Report has been luridly described by that paragon of accuracy, Mrs Mary Whitehouse, as 'a campaigning document which seeks to justify the gratification of adult lust for children';[1] while the Chairman of the Responsible Society, Dr S. E. Ellison, has said that the Report is 'a document which seeks to justify adult sexual gratification with minors'.[2]

So what is this shocking report, and what does it in fact say? Not at all what you might gather from Whitehouse and Ellison.

Unlike the British, the Dutch have never had laws which criminalized all male homosexual behaviour, whether consenting or not (except under the Nazi wartime occupation). But in 1911 they did introduce, at the instigation of a puritanical Catholic Minister of Justice, a discriminatory age of consent of 21 for homosexual behaviour.

In 1967 – the year that the Wolfenden reforms became law in Britain – a Dutch woman MP proposed the repeal of this section of the criminal code, saying that a Catholic psychiatrist had recently expressed the opinion that an individual's sexual orientation was decided before the age of 6, and that it was 'out of the question that a person in his 16th year of life could be made into a homosexual by seduction'. The law also, she pointed out, gave rise to blackmail.

In his reply the Dutch Minister of Justice said that, at his request, the Minister for Social Affairs and Health had asked the Health Council to report on what consequences were likely to arise from repeal, with special emphasis on the dangers of homosexual seduction and of otherwise heterosexual adolescents being permanently deflected into a homosexual way of life. The Council's advice was to be limited to the medical and scientific aspects.

A committee was accordingly set up under the chairmanship of Professor Dr N. Speijer, Professor of Social Psychiatry at the State University of Leyden, with five other members, all but one of whom were eminent psychiatrists or neurologists. The sixth member was an Inspector for Public Moral Welfare. The committee met ten times, and received evidence from numerous medical colleagues (mostly professors of psychiatry) as well as from the police, public prosecutors, representatives of youth welfare and education services and the Dutch Association of Homosexuals (COC).

They consulted a lengthy bibliography of scientific works and set themselves to answer the following questions:

(1) What are the current medical and scientific views about homosexuality?

(2) Is there any danger of the seduction of minors above the age of 16 by homosexual adults?

(3) Does a homosexual experience turn minors aged over 16 permanently homosexual?

(4) Could a young person's heterosexual development be adversely affected by homosexual experiences between the ages of 16 and 21?

(5) Are there any other harmful consequences for young people's psychological development of a change in the law which need to be taken into account?

I already hear you saying: 'Hold! There must be some mistake – can this be the same committee which so deeply shocked Mrs Whitehouse and Dr Ellison?' Yes it is, and this is why: the answers which these learned mental health professors came up with to their five questions were:

(1) A homosexual orientation is fixed in most people long before they reach puberty and is perfectly compatible with mental and moral health.

(2) No, generally speaking.

(3) Again no.

(4) No.

(5) No.

– not at all pleasing news for the homophobic warriors of the 'moral majority'!

How did the Speijer Committee justify these conclusions? First, they reviewed the history of the law of 1911, and concluded that the main reason for its enactment was parliament's conviction at that time that homosexual seduction of over-16-year-olds was a real danger. Second, they comprehensively reviewed the current literature on homosexuality and found that the majority of researchers believed there was usually a congenital factor in sexual orientation but that environment – especially relationships with parents in early childhood – also played an important part. They agreed that a homosexual predisposition was usually determined long before puberty.

Next, the committee examined the concept of 'normality' in sexuality, and noted that this was determined according to the context in which it was being discussed – statistical, biological, ethical, sociological, or medical. The very act of making a certain category of people (homosexuals, women) into an 'object of study' is (they pointed out) of itself judgemental, and leads to alienation and to generalizations which are not always valid and which may create discrimination. The committee pertinently pointed out that 'if, for example, someone conceived the idea that we should no longer divide people according to the colour of their skin, but according to their height, the whole world would be different'. (And indeed, giants and dwarfs do experience discrimination because of their size.)

It was the Speijer Committee's considered opinion that homosexuality should not merely be tolerated as a 'deviation', but recognized as a distinct form of human love. In this way, the common attributes of homosexuals and of heterosexuals would be acknowledged.

In the current state of knowledge, it was only possible to give provisional and subjective answers to the question of whether homosexuals were both morally and emotionally healthy and mentally fit; but if the World Federation of Mental Health's 1948 definition of mental health as 'a condition permitting the optimum physical, intellectual and emotional development of the individual' was applied, homosexuals who were fully self-accepting and socially well-adjusted could not be regarded as 'sick' – although this did not exclude the desirability of a supportive therapeutic, psychological and pastoral environment.

Where homosexuals were not self-accepting, psychotherapy resulted in better adjustment to homosexuality more often than in transition to heterosexuality. It was usually not desirable to encourage a basically homosexual person to marry. To a great extent, the emotional conflicts and disturbances of homosexuals could be attributed to the prejudice and discrimination which society exercised against them. Many homosexuals lived in good harmony with themselves and their environment, and could be considered as healthy persons.

The Speijer Committee then proceeded to examine and discuss the concept of 'seduction'. In my view, their contribution on this issue is the most original and constructive section of their report – and the main reason why that document is so unpalatable to our made-to-measure moralists who so shamelessly misrepresent and denigrate it.

The concept of 'seduction', with its implication of leading astray to do wrong, assumes a morally disapproving judgement, the committee pointed out. They therefore preferred to use the more neutral term of 'initiation' in discussing the establishment of sexual contact (whether heterosexual or homosexual) between adults and younger people. Such situations, they emphasized, can be initiated by either the older or the younger person; and frequently they are mutually constructed. A large proportion of human behaviour – and, especially with young people, their appearance, mode of dress, and form of transport – involves the creation of 'seductive' situations and is comparable with the decoy, 'showing off' and sexually motivated behaviour observed in the animal world.

> A society which seeks to eliminate all seductive situations as much as possible will not encourage public moral welfare. On the contrary, it is desirable for young people of both sexes that they are able to meet and cope with such situations. A normal development requires broad possibilities of introduction, experiment, contact and initiation. Only the existence of such possibilities will enable the young person to choose independence and responsibility, to accept and to reject, to recognise and acknowledge himself and by so doing to realise himself. The risks and dangers of sexual maturing and self-realisation are part of life, and like other fields of exploration they belong to the growing-up process.

These are indeed wise words – but they are of course anathema to that vociferous school of moral and sexual stone-agers who want society to treat adults as children and teenagers as toddlers.

Bearing in mind that homosexuals experience the same need for contacts and relationships that heterosexuals do, is homosexual initiation (the Speijer Committee asked) likely to cause greater damage to an adolescent than heterosexual initiation? First and foremost, they endorsed the provisions of the Dutch penal code protecting minors below the age of 16 against sexual seduction in any circumstances (although if you took Mrs Whitehouse as a reliable guide to their report, you would never think so). But, they thought, a youngster of 16 and older is quite capable of forming his or her own opinion – not least concerning sexual activity – and by 16 a permanent propensity towards heterosexuality or homosexuality has been established in the great majority of cases; while many young people aged less than 16 were known to have taken the lead in seeking initiation. Numerous researches cited by the committee, supported by the committee members' own professional experience, showed that from the sixteenth year onwards the sexual propensity was sufficiently well developed to eliminate the possibility of a heterosexual youngster being diverted by 'seduction' into permanent homosexuality. It was therefore incorrect to speak of 'seduction' in the sense of 'leading to permanent homosexual behaviour'. If, after such an approach, the young person responded positively, 'it must be assumed that he or she was emotionally ready for this approach, and in a sense had been waiting for it'.

People who were hostile to homosexuality were easily inclined (the committee said) to advise the prohibition of homosexual behaviour. But such a prohibition could only rightfully be founded on the dangers which this conduct might cause to other people. And the dangers of sexual activity for children and young people were often overestimated. At the same time, youngsters properly needed, and were given, protection against abuse of authority by parents, teachers and others.

The Speijer Committee went on to remark that discrimination – legal or social – against young homosexuals created an obstacle to the provision of support and aid for them; and it agreed with the Dutch Federation for Mental Public Health that, far from being damaging to a young person who was homosexual, initiatory contacts could often be of positive help to them by reducing or eliminating the stress and frustration caused by isolation. The young homosexual, unsure of her- or himself in the formative stage of personality, urgently needs sympathetic and understanding support, for lack of which he may remain in an emotional vacuum for a long period. And not only will a greater amount of honesty about their situation, and appropriate possibilities of contact, assist young homosexuals in their maturing process: it may also have a positive aspect for heterosexual young people (who are often extremely ignorant of, and prejudiced against, homosexuality).

'Sexual dangers and the risk of seduction are greatly exaggerated amongst the other dangers to which a young person is exposed in life', the Speijer Committee sensibly concluded. It is heartening that within a few months of the publication of this eminently level-headed report, the

Dutch parliament approved, by a large majority, repeal of the discriminatory law of 1911.

Notes

1. The *Guardian*, 10 January 1979.
2. *The Times*, 21 January 1979.

Old Enough to Choose

INDEPENDENT, 24 JANUARY 1994

I welcome the prospect that Parliament will soon equalize the age of consent for heterosexual and homosexual behaviour. The law bears especially harshly upon young men who engage in homosexual lovemaking, since those under 21 are still frequently prosecuted for such activities, even though under-age girls commit no offence by consenting to sex with a man. Successful prosecutions for consenting homosexual behaviour which breached the 21 age limit averaged 280 over the six years to 1991, and resulting prison sentences averaged 28 a year, so there is significant hardship – and, I would maintain, injustice.

Equalizing the ages of consent must be the most immediate consideration. Ultimately, though, it would be desirable to rethink the whole legal concept of an age of consent to sexual activity and consider a completely new framework. This would give effective protection to those below the age of majority (18), without punishing them for behaviour to which – however unwisely – they have consented.

In 1974 the Sexual Law Reform Society's Working Party, of which I was Secretary, submitted a memorandum to the Criminal Law Revision Committee in which we endorsed the view of our then Chairman, the late Bishop John Robinson, that the law's proper function in relation to personal behaviour is 'not to prohibit but to protect, not to enforce morals but to safeguard persons, their privacies and freedoms'.

We argued that it would be in the public interest to abolish 'sexual offences' as a separate category – because all sexual behaviour which merited punishment could be classified as an assault, a breach of protective provisions for children or others in a state of dependence, or an offensive nuisance to third parties.

The Working Party – which included Church people, doctors, lawyers and politicians – concluded after extensive discussion that the traditional framework of an 'age of consent' was a hindrance, not a help, to the effective protection of young people. We reasoned that it is a legal fiction: either someone is in fact a willing partner to a sexual act, whatever their age, or they are not. If they have consented to what they were doing and understood the consequences of their consent, this could be proved in court if necessary; and for the law to treat them as being incapable of giving such consent introduces an element of unreality into the proceedings which is confusing, harmful and in no one's best interests.

We recognized, however, that as well as punishing those who interfere with or abuse young people sexually, the law may need to protect young people whose sexual behaviour is potentially damaging to themselves or to others. We recommended an 'age of protection' up to the legal age of majority (18), with appropriate civil and social – not criminal – sanctions. If the age of consent was not abolished, we urged that it should be fixed at 14 for both heterosexual and homosexual behaviour.

The CLRC responded to our challenge by asserting that it, too, saw the proper function of the law in sexual matters as protective rather than punitive, but opted to keep an age of consent on the grounds that it was necessary for legal certainty. It was also preoccupied by the 'psychological harm' it believed 'premature' sexual intercourse, heterosexual and homosexual, inflicts on youngsters.

I do not believe these arguments were convincing or conclusive; and I still think we must replace the whole concept of an age of consent with something more realistic, humane and useful for the twenty-first century.

Certainly there must first be a period of discussion to encourage public recognition of some obvious facts. First, 'ages of consent' do not provide effective protection to those who are sexually active below them; but they frequently bring great misery and disruption into the lives of such young people. Second, older men and women who sexually pressurize, interfere with or abuse youngsters can be adequately deterred and punished through other, mostly already existing, legal provisions.

Britain in the 1990s is still a very sex-negative society. The ceaseless media chatter (much of it prurient and intrusive) about people's sex lives may seem to contradict this. But many who work in the health education and counselling fields agree that there is an enormous amount of sexual unease and unwarranted guilt around sexuality, much of it resulting from social pressures that demand conformity to outdated 'norms'.

No society can do away with all standards and controls, and a total sexual free-for-all would probably produce even more unhappiness (a prime argument of those who oppose any relaxation of laws concerning sex). But good personal and ethical standards and considerate behaviour towards others are not as closely bound up with legal controls as traditional moralists would argue. As the Wolfenden Committee said in its 1957 report, such views exaggerate the effect of the law on human behaviour; the law itself, the committee said, probably makes little difference to the amount of [homo]sexual behaviour which actually occurs.

Personal standards of morality and behaviour are the outcome of a socializing process that begins at birth; they are the product of a lifetime's education in wise choice-making, rather than of legal finger-wagging. In a newspaper interview before she became prime minister, Margaret Thatcher wisely observed: 'Free choice is ultimately what life is about, what ethics is about. . . . Do away with choice and you do away with human dignity.'

That, in a nutshell, is the case for replacing the 'age of consent' with protective provisions that pay more respect to the personal choices (including those which others think are mistaken) of adolescents in their growing-up years. By regarding and treating adolescents too much as if they were overgrown children, rather than as young adults, society makes a rod for its back which manifests itself in juvenile delinquency and teenage tearaways.

If we don't take teenagers seriously, why should they take us seriously? In a recent survey of 146 English sixth-formers carried out by John Randall for his book *Childhood and Sexuality*,[1] the young people gave a massive thumbs-down to the notion of confiding their sexual problems to 'helping' adults: only 1.4 per cent of the sample said they would approach a social worker, 2 per cent a teacher, 3.4 per cent a doctor and 0.7 per cent a clergyman, although almost half felt able to talk with their parents.

There are lessons here for adults. An important one is that it is high time for us to start treating teenagers' sexual needs and experiences less dismissively and more sympathetically, and to replace the outdated and punitive legal fiction of an 'age of consent' with a benign and carefully thought-out framework of effective protection.

We British pride ourselves upon our devotion to individual freedom, yet in practice we still operate our social system on a basis of 'benevolent paternalism'. This is especially true where personal choices around sex, free expression, entertainment, drug use, and other aspects of personal life are concerned. Is it not time to enter the twenty-first century as a personal, as well as a political and social, democracy, and 'trust the people'?

Note

1. J. L. Randall, *Childhood and Sexuality: A Radical Christian Approach* (Pittsburgh, PA: Dorrance, 1992).

PART FIVE

SEX EDUCATION

In the 1970s, sex education became, as it still remains, a prime battleground between 'traditionalists' who believe that the subject should be taught – if at all – in the context of Christian morality and preparation for marriage, and those who have sought to apply the insights of modern biology, psychology and sociology to help young people prepare themselves for life's complexities. Unfortunately, the self-righteousness of those who identify their views with the mind of God has created a scenario where there has been little constructive debate, and all too often the two sides shout past each other in a fog of mutual suspicion and hostility. This has made the task of those responsible for the National Curriculum an unenviable one. The following are a selection from my own numerous contributions to the ongoing argument.

Hot Potato

NEW HUMANIST, WINTER 1977/78

Sex education remains the Cinderella of the curriculum, an arena where common sense is the casualty of contending battle cries. Efforts to impart factual knowledge are as hazardous as attempts at rational discussion of values. It is no wonder that teachers are timorous and parents puzzled when it comes to presenting the young with the 'facts of life'.

Yet can sex education realistically be split off from education for living? Are we not all continuously giving one another informal sex education through the sheer fact of human interaction? And is not the complexity of human sexuality one of the most wonderful things about *homo sapiens*? Above all, is not basic information about sex a human right?

To read some of the recent outpourings of 'the less we tell the children the better they will behave' brigade, one would not think so. 'Many parents would rather that their children had no explicit teaching of contraceptive methods, usually because they believe in the basic principle of chastity before marriage, and contraceptive teaching to children appears to condone the opposite view' [*Sound Sex Education*, Order of Christian Unity]. Teachers who show youngsters books which describe sexual intercourse in detail 'are taking part in a conspiracy to destroy the family' [*Tomorrow's Parents*, Grosvenor Books]. 'There is not a shred of evidence that sex instruction reduces the number of unwanted pregnancies among teenagers, nor the number of abortions, nor the spread of disease, nor the willingness to risk illness through early promiscuity' [*Sex Education: Its Uses and Abuses*, The Responsible Society]. 'Zealous sex education . . . such as some schools give, can seriously disturb the natural maturation process' [*The Truth in Love*, Nationwide Festival of Light].

Faced with such rip-roaring obscurantism, mostly emanating from purportedly 'Christian' sources, it is scarcely surprising that any teacher embarking upon sex instruction feels beleaguered from the outset. Are all attempts to put into rational perspective for nubile adolescents what is currently known about the development of sexual identity, the physiology of intercourse and childbirth, the statistics about venereal disease and abortion, and the existence and viewpoints of sexual minorities, really so retrograde and antisocial? Or is it those who decry such efforts, unless they are laced with strong doses of moralistic indoctrination lauding the 'traditional' virtues of celibacy before marriage and faithfulness within it, and denigrating all extramarital and 'perverse' sexuality, who are the real flat-earthers of our time? Do they not throw out the baby of a sensitive approach to other people's sexual natures with the bathwater of depersonalized promiscuity, and make the 'best' – their sentimentalized, candy-floss vision of love – the enemy of a less exalted but much more solid 'good' which is to be found in a considerate responsiveness to the varying natures, needs and difficulties of a wide range of human beings?

True sexual morality surely begins with the comprehension of human variation, and a respect for others' uniqueness – it does not reside in authoritarian demands for conformity to one's own beliefs and standards. Yet, not content with making such a moral hullabaloo about sex education, the neo-Puritans are using every political and legal lever at their disposal to decry and denigrate the work of bodies such as the Family Planning Association and the Health Education Council, who may not be perfect in every respect but who at least do have their feet firmly on the ground about where most young people are at with their sexuality, and the sort of questions which call for honest answers.

A recent conference on sex education sponsored by the Family Planning Association, the Albany Trust, the National Youth Bureau, and the Campaign for Homosexual Equality was attended by about fifty people and generated much useful discussion and exchange of information. It was apparent that a great deal of careful thought and effort is going into the preparation of basic syllabuses, although these are not always adequate. For instance, a representative of the Schools Council felt they were being brave by daring to mention the existence of homosexuality to young men and women in their middle and upper teens – yet many homosexuals experience an early puberty, and are often fully aware of, and deeply confused by, their emotional responses at as early an age as 10 or 11. Certainly, if Freud's theories and Kinsey's data about sexual development are remotely correct, it is far too late usefully to tell 16- and 17-year-olds about homosexuality, for by that age they are imbued with the still flourishing ancient myths and stereotypes.

Virtually every one of the several hundred people with whom I have discussed the sex education they received has said that it was inadequate and several years too late. Yet the anti-sex educators cry in the name of 'chastity' that it is better for girls and boys to marry as sexual illiterates than to be given the facts they need (and are surely entitled to) in order to become considerate lovers and caring parents.

Of course, there is a real danger that children may be given inaccurate or inadequate information in the wrong way, and by the wrong people: there is an urgent need for many more teachers of sex education to receive the training they need in order to carry out this delicate task well. What should such training consist of? Essentially, it needs to be approached from at least three distinct, though interrelated, angles.

First, factual information. Facts are either correct or incorrect – and this is as true of facts relating to sex and sexual behaviour as of any other facts. An honest teacher has a responsibility to make sure to the best of his or her ability that the facts about sex which are imparted are as accurate as possible, regardless of the teacher's own personal likes or dislikes. Some of the facts about sex – such as the high incidence of certain types of venereal disease, or the number of early teenage unwanted pregnancies – may be unpleasant and dismaying, but their impartial presentation *as facts* must be kept apart from one's personal reaction to them.

The second major theme of good sex education is an exploration of attitudes – one's own and other people's – towards sex, and requires the inculcation of an awareness that there are various possible moral and emotional responses to sexual behaviour. Attitudes and tastes, which may well differ, are one aspect; the question of a personal ethic which is good for the individual and for society as a whole is a distinct topic for consideration and debate. Contentious matters such as abortion and homosexuality need presenting and discussing so as to enable young people to reach their own conclusions through an awareness of the existence of a variety of sincerely held viewpoints.

The last, and perhaps the most important, element in sex education is the contribution which it can make, if well taught, to the growth of self-knowledge. Every adolescent grapples with an identity crisis which, if he or she is unfortunate, may not be resolved until middle life, if then. In asking 'Who am I?', questions about sexuality inevitably loom large. It is the sex educator's task and responsibility (and, I would add, privilege) to help young people towards a meaningful answer. If we are to do so, the crucial distinction between education and indoctrination must never be lost sight of. For if sex education becomes the stamping ground of blinkered bigots of whatever hue, then our last state will be even worse than our first.

Sex Education in Danger

NEW HUMANIST, JANUARY 1981

A friend with professional contacts in the Department of Education tells me he is appalled at the recent shift in attitudes there concerning sex education, and is convinced that a carefully devised plan is now operating in Britain aimed at cutting away all the ground which has been gained during the past decade in the presentation of fuller, more accurate and balanced facts about sexuality to young people.

I have no doubt that he is right, and that it is high time for everyone who believes that this topic should be taught with modern insights, realism, and sensitive concern for individuals' needs to organize in defence of these values against the obscurantist bigots who bray, bluster and bully to achieve their morbid aims of perpetuating ignorance and spreading dis-ease.

What evidence is there for such an alarmist view? Here is some of it:

SCENE 1: The Chapter House, Truro. In the chair for a meeting organized by the Community Standards Association, the Rt Rev. Graham Leonard, Bishop of Truro,[1] who is also chairman of the Church of England's Board for Social Responsibility. Enter Mrs Valerie Riches of The Responsible Society to deliver an oration entitled 'Has the Family a Future?' In this discourse, Mrs Riches (according to the Community Standards Association's Winter 1979/80 newsletter)

> lucidly explained the present policies and practices of the Family Planning Association and Brook Advisory Centres, which assume that young people will have sexual intercourse as soon as they are physically old enough to do so and that education in contraception is the only answer. There were many who were astonished to hear the [FPA] described in such a sinister role, and Mrs Riches had to make it clear that the former activities of the organisation, that is, helping women with very large families, have now been taken over by the Health Service and another role had been found by the FPA, namely, the encouragement of children not in chastity, but in promiscuity.

Following this and other West Country meetings, local press and radio publicity led to pressure from CSA supporters and others on local MPs to press the Department of Health to withdraw Section G of their 1974 memorandum on family planning which had advised doctors that they would not normally be at risk of prosecution if they acted with good faith in prescribing contraceptives for under-age girls without their parents' consent. The circular has since been revised so as to draw doctors' attention to the desirability of consulting parents wherever practicable.

SCENE 2: An amendment to the Government's Education Bill tabled in February 1980 by George Gardiner, Conservative MP for Reigate, sought to provide parents with the right to withdraw their children from sex education lessons if they disapproved of what was being taught or of the teaching materials used.

SCENE 3: The Times, St Valentine's Day. In an article remarkable for its hysterical venom, Ronald Butt supported Mr Gardiner's amendment and lambasted what he termed 'sex education missionaries' who, he claimed, spare no effort in instructing the young in every sort of activity, however perverse. ('Or, as Mr Gardiner put it to me: the success of sex education seems to be measured by the number of girls on the Pill and the number of boys buying sheaths.') Butt and Gardiner singled out a best-selling sex education manual for teenagers, *Make It Happy* by Jane Cousins, which Butt described as 'quite the filthiest book of its kind that I have encountered because, directing itself at the most vulnerable age group, it drains sexual activity of every meaning except what purports to be pleasure, diminishes the subject by its flippancy and vulgarity, and instructs its young readers in degrading concepts that would naturally never occur to them'.

In fact, Ms Cousins – who is a friend of mine, and a highly competent and responsible teacher and writer – wrote her book in response to questions about sex she was asked by a class of teenagers to whom she was teaching other subjects. It has proved a best-seller, and won the *Times Educational Supplement* Information Book Award for 1979. Worst of all (for Butt), it has been endorsed by a National Council member of the FPA, which 'continues its indefatigable effort to get into the schools' where (Butt speculated) 'how far morally down-market are all the children driven to accommodate the FPA's idea of the standards of the lowest common denominator?'

Notwithstanding these strictures, *Make It Happy* has been reprinted in a new edition by Penguin Books; but as a result of the attacks on it, it is viewed with disfavour by the Departments of Health and of Education, and at their 'request' it has been withdrawn from the FPA bookshop.

Such correspondence as *The Times* deigned to publish after Butt's diatribe was (unsurprisingly, to those familiar with its editorial bias in these matters) mostly sympathetic to his fevered fantasies. The existence of the conscienceless 'sex missionaries' was almost universally taken for granted – they have now become part of our national folklore, like the Russian soldiers with snow on their boots who were widely reported as having been seen in various parts of Britain in the autumn of 1914.

A pungent letter from Ms Cousins' publisher was, however, printed, likening Butt to 'a fearful witchdoctor, jealously guarding the tribe's taboos and outraged at the thought that control may be slipping from his grasp'. There was also a more restrained rebuttal from the FPA chairman, who made the telling point that individuals can only reach their full potential if they are able to choose how life is best lived in freedom and with responsibility on the basis of full knowledge. Unrepentant, armchair warrior Butt returned to the charge – and the chairman of the Responsible Society joined in the letters column attack, as did the Order of Christian Unity.

SCENE 4: The House of Lords, 14 and 24 March 1980. The Gardiner amendment resurfaced, supported by a predictable posse of Peers (Ingleby, Halsbury, Nugent of Guildford) who have been active on the obscurantist side of 'morality' debates in recent years. The debates merit reading in full: what is highly intriguing and significant is the vague yet repetitious nature of the 'evidence' adduced by these noble Lords, and its quite obvious emergence from the same stable as the Riches/Butt assertions. The 'obscene' *Make It Happy* was again in the pillory. A group identified as 'Gay Teachers' was alleged by Viscount Ingleby to be working its way into sex education in schools 'in order to promote their teaching that homosexuality is both natural and normal'. According to the Earl of Halsbury,

> those engaged in sex education are a mixed bag. Some of them are highly responsible, dedicated people, but, alas, infiltrated from time to time by highly unpleasant types. We know what infiltration can do. From time to time the repercussions of a scandal, like a jumping cracker, will explode in the public domain starting with permissiveness at Oxbridge and softness at the Foreign Office, and ending with treason-based sodomy. We know the whole unfortunate history of it, and that is what comes of soft attitudes in Ministries towards undesirable people. . . . There are people who get a sexual kick in talking about sex to young people and adolescents, and one needs some sort of an assurance that these people are not enfranchised to enjoy their perversion in the context of the schools where we send our children. Of course they never tell the children the whole truth of the matter. They never tell them that sex is part of an enduring relationship, but only part, between two people. They use the deterioration of our language to talk of it in terms of 'having sex' as if it were something that you had like a bun or an ice cream, or drink of beer. They begin and they end with the mechanics of orgasm, no matter how procured. They never tell their clientele what being jilted means to a teenage girl; what being deserted when pregnant means to a teenage girl; what are the psychological as opposed to the clinical concomitants of abortion; what infection by VD, which is on the increase, means to a teenager.

Anyone who reads this effusion for what it is worth will no doubt be unsurprised to learn that polite private letters to Lord Halsbury requesting the names and addresses of these antisocial people, and a list of the occasions he is aware of on which they behaved as he alleged, remain unanswered.

The debate rumbled on along well-set lines. Lord Monson said that, although he was not one of 'those surprisingly numerous people who contend that family planning clinics . . . are clandestine agents of Soviet subversion, whose aim is the undermining of the moral fabric of our society', nevertheless there was no doubt that 'there does exist within the realm of sex education a small clique who seem to have a crusading zeal to encourage young children to start sexual experimentation at a younger and younger age'. There was, the Bishop of Norwich maintained, all the difference in the world between telling children the 'facts' of violin playing (which he quaintly claimed to be 'the drawing of the hairs of a horse across the entrails of a pig') and leading them to appreciate Yehudi Menuhin playing Mozart. (How does he think Menuhin learned to play the violin?) The Earl of Lauderdale deplored the erosion of 'nature's built-in sense of shame; the shame that separates us from the animals'.

By the Bill's report stage, a deal had been struck. Baroness Young (Minister of State at the Department of Education) said that if the amendment were withdrawn (which it was), her Department would look at ways of ensuring that under the Bill's proposed regulations headmasters would be required to publish, and to draw to the attention of parents, the arrangements existing within individual schools for the provision of sex education; they would also give further thought as to whether any fresh guidance from the Department to its inspectors on the treatment of sex education within the curriculum would be helpful – and they would discuss the content of such regulations and guidance with the amendment's sponsors.

SCENE 5: The House of Commons, 14 May 1980. John Stokes, Conservative MP for Halesowen, attacked the FPA and Brook Advisory Centres as prime movers in the 'enormous' growth of the 'sex education industry':

> The whole of their theme is not the need for self-control in sexual relationships but the necessity at once, and at the earliest possible age, for girls to take precautions against having a baby. This is a positive encouragement to indulge in sexual intercourse from an early age, coupled with the sinister suggestion that everyone is having sexual intercourse with everyone else all the time and that is the most normal and natural thing in the world.

He called upon the Government to withdraw its grants from these bodies, and to 'insist that no teaching about sexual behaviour can be given in the classroom without the fullest consultation with parents'. In a letter to the *Guardian* (17 May), Alastair Service of the FPA wrily commented that 'the many thousands of responsible people who find the FPA a source of sympathetic and accurate information' would hardly recognize it as described by Mr Stokes. But the latter has not, of course, withdrawn his offensive allegations, made under cover of parliamentary privilege. Nor are he and Lord Halsbury and their obnoxious kind likely to. Truth is a major casualty when hysterical blimpery, fuelled by backstage bigots, struts across the parliamentary stage.

SCENE 6: In an article on sex education published in *Now!* in June 1980, Mrs Riches is cited as 'believing most sincerely and in common with fellow [Responsible Society] members such as Sir John Peel, Lord Shawcross and Pamela Hansford Johnson, that the trend away from the more traditional forms of sex education is part and parcel of a grand conspiracy to exploit the young commercially and to corrupt family life'. Some of the alleged members of the 'tremendously powerful British network' of over thirty organizations set up by 'all the same people' that Mrs Riches conjures up as providing funds and staffing government research bodies to promote this 'absolutely devilish ideology' are eyebrow-raising: her list kicks off with the Department of Health, Inner London Education Authority, Health Education Council, Department of Education and Home Office, and includes the Family Planning Association, Birth Control Trust, London Rubber Industries, Campaign for Homosexual Equality, Sexual Law

Reform Association (sic) and National Association for Mental Health, as well as the British Humanist Association, National Council for Civil Liberties, and Communist Party of Great Britain. . . .

'I don't really know what it is', Mrs Riches is reported as saying in her artlessly vague way: 'communism, humanism, world domination, I don't know. But I do know it's happening. And it's terribly clever.' So is Mrs Riches, if she can discern such concerted plotting between such different bodies.

SCENE 7: The House of Commons, 4 August 1980. Yet another debate attacking family planning groups, initiated by Mrs Jill Knight[2] (Conservative MP for Edgbaston, who is chairman of the all-party parliamentary Family and Child Protection Group – which has close links with the Responsible Society/Festival of Light/Mary Whitehouse axis, and is intensively briefed by them). 'When little children, far under the age of consent, are encouraged to go on the Pill, told that ideals are outdated, given contraceptives of all kinds . . . the time has come for the strongest complaints to be made', declaimed Mrs Knight in her best 'have you stopped beating your wife?' manner. FPA workers visiting a West Country school recently had, she claimed, 'sneered at ideals and almost said that ideals were things that one could not possibly live up to and should not try'. Such activities ought not to be funded with public money. The Health Education Council had 'done some extremely dubious things and backed some quite disgraceful publications'.

But Mrs Knight did not get it all her own way, being rebuffed by William Hamilton (Labour MP for Fife, Central) who spoke of 'a concerted attack on the principal family planning charities' and by Charles Morrison (Conservative, Devizes) who said it was not the family planning movement which had changed the standards of sexual morality, but wider social pressures, particularly on the young; and that if these charities did not exist, the situation would be far worse and there would be many more unwanted pregnancies. And the Minister of Health, Dr Gerard Vaughan, reaffirmed the Government's support for 'reputable voluntary organisa-tions' working in the family planning and sex education sphere (he didn't say how reputable or otherwise the Government thought The Responsible Society to be).

SCENE 8: The House of Commons, 8 August 1980. Neil Macfarlane, Under-Secretary of State at the Department of Education, announced that his Department was about to consult 'interested parties' about proposed draft regulations under the Education Act 1980 requiring local education authorities to publish information about the ways and contexts in which sex education is provided in their schools, 'including the question of excusing attendance for those pupils whose parents object'.

In the light of this hue and cry, it is clearly now the time for all 'interested parties' to jump on to this lopsided bandwagon and inject some much-needed common sense into the sex education debate.

Notes

1. And later Bishop of London, who converted to Roman Catholicism because of his opposition to the Church of England's decision to ordain women priests.
2. As Dame Jill Knight, she was the parliamentary spearhead of the infamous 'Section 28' a few years later.

Family Furore

FREETHINKER, MARCH 1981

The tiny, loud-mouthed clique of fundamentalist evangelical Christians who constitute the core of the morally self-righteous Moral Right in this country cannot be lightly brushed aside. Bullfrog-like though they are, they pose a serious threat not only to free thought but also to our society's basic shared values of democratic free speech and tolerance. In recent years they have spawned a coterie of campaigning pressure groups, nominally distinct and independent but all emitting that peculiarly distinctive odour of rancorous, persecutory pharisaism which was formerly confined to the nowadays low-profile, but by no means defunct, Moral Rearmament.

One of the totem poles to which this lot nail their dubious colours is the sanctity of family life. They seem to hanker after the revival of the Victorian-style 'nuclear' family unit where wives and children are reduced to the status of unquestioning chattels of a lordly paterfamilias. But since the subjection of women is no longer feasible to that extent, they campaign vigorously to assert and uphold parental authority, indignantly denying that children (including teenagers) should have any rights, or even any opinions which conflict with their parents' views and wishes. The parents, of course, are visualized as being of a certain sort: properly married and monogamous; morally sound (i.e. practising Christians); and, above all, implacably opposed to daughters on the Pill.

An undercurrent of concern – some of it justified – about slipping social standards and the decay of community life led, a few years ago, to senior politicians of both major parties flirting with the notion of a government department being set up with responsibility for the family. How the idea would have worked out was never clear; and not altogether surprisingly, it came to nothing. What *has* emerged, however, is an agency called Family Forum, set up last year under the wing of the National Council for Voluntary Organisations to act as a central consultative body 'in matters of public interest concerning families', and currently bringing together some seventy member-organizations. Conspicuous amongst these – need I say – are our old friends the Nationwide Festival of Light, the Responsible Society, the Community Standards Association, the Order of Christian Unity and similar national and local groups. Their first ploy was to nominate a high proportion of the candidates for election to Family Forum's executive committee. Nothing wrong with that, of course; but it was what followed after only two or three of their nominees were elected that gives yet another interesting sidelight on how these folk strive to discredit everyone and everything they cannot dominate.

On 21 January [1981] their tame *Times* fugleman, Ronald Butt, wrote one of his characteristic 'vials of wrath' diatribes pitching into Family Forum and all its works, and bellyaching about its £30,000 government funding. According to Butt, Family Forum's birth was the outcome of a sinister conspiracy masterminded by Alastair Service of the Family Planning Association ('and formerly lobbyist of the Abortion Law Reform Association') – who, needless to say, is one of the Moral Right's most unfavourite persons – 'to tap public resources by brandishing a word that (in its common meaning) has everybody's approval, and then to promote social change by re-defining the word's meaning'. Service (according to Butt) had been 'most active' since Family Forum's inception in opposing a close definition of the family, and in supporting the inclusion of such maverick groups as single-parent families and – horror of horrors! – homosexuals.

Worst of all, the dire question of contraception for the under-16s had promptly reared its ugly head; not really surprisingly, Butt insinuated, since Alastair Service had actually told the *Sunday Times* in 1976 that his own children thought they would want their first sexual relationship at 'around 16'. And the slimy Service had even had the gall to express his disquiet – in private correspondence to Family Forum's chairman, Peter Bottomley MP, which somehow found its way to hawkeye Butt – at the 'plethora of nominations from small local pressure groups' of the 'Parents and Children Concern' type which he believed were offshoots of the Responsible Society, and had proposed that Family Forum membership should be restricted to national organizations. 'I don't think he has much to worry about', sneered Butt; Family Forum, he predicted, was all set to emulate American experience in which the word 'family' has been taken over by the social engineers and applied to communes, group marriage, and homosexual liaisons. A proper family, Butt stoutly maintained, is linked only by marriage, blood, or formal adoption.

The stage was now all set for the concerted assault which was promptly mounted in *The Times'* letter columns. A ritual reply by Family Forum's chairman, Peter Bottomley MP, whose view was that 'it is neither Christian nor sensible only to regard families as containing two parents and their children', and who bravely hoped that Family Forum would be a meeting place rather than a battleground – went virtually unheeded. All the angry correspondents (nearly all female) who piled into Family Forum were really interested in was to get across loud and clear the single message: 'Don't put our daughters on the Pill.'

The President of the Mothers' Union – attacked by Butt for endorsing the hated DHSS memorandum which (according to him) virtually licensed doctors to prescribe the Pill to girls below the age of consent without telling their parents – protested that at no time had they ever agreed to the indiscriminate prescription of contraceptives to the under-aged; but the alternative to the policy laid down in the memorandum was to deny such girls any form of counselling or contraception, however much they might need it. 'We have however never ceased to urge that the proper course of behaviour for all is chastity before marriage and fidelity within it.' So presumably, chimed in Lady Grantchester, the Mothers' Union expects the proposed counselling to be given along these lines? But 'permissive counselling' may accompany contraception and encourage rather than inhibit promiscuity. No advice had been offered by the Minister as to who precisely is to counsel, or what their professional standards should be. 'Parents should not be deprived of their legal right and moral obligation to counsel and protect their children.'

Dr Adrian Rogers – chairman of Responsibility in Welfare,[1] a Devon-based group which has been spearheading the campaign to get the DHSS memorandum withdrawn – wrote: 'If the nation's teenagers are entitled to run into Brook Advisory Centres or Family Planning Clinics and obtain contraception, albeit in "exceptional circumstances", exceptions will become – and are quickly becoming – the rule and the whole principle of protecting children within a family will have been thwarted and irreparably damaged.' Dr Margaret White JP – a leading light of the Order of Christian Unity – followed on with her reminiscences of a 'government-funded course' on counselling which she had attended and had been shocked to be told that 'counselling means helping the "client" to discover what she wants, and when she has done so, to provide it for her'. Dr White claimed that she had been informed that it was 'wrong' to give clients relevant information, such as that sex with under-16-year-old girls is illegal, or that there are medical and psychological risks attached to 'premature' sexual intercourse, because that would be 'moralising'.

I have an interest here, as I am an active member of several British Association for Counselling committees, and I know full well that no reputable counsellor thinks that to impart necessary factual information to a client is 'wrong'. On the contrary, all the counsellors I know would regard it as totally unethical *not* to give a client every fact that is relevant for making responsible decisions. I also happen to know which course it was that Dr White attended, and I have the strongest doubts that whatever took place there could credibly bear the interpretation she has placed upon it. I wrote a letter to *The Times* to this effect, and to my knowledge several other people involved in the counselling movement, and concerned to protect its good name, did so too. But none of our letters was published; and so readers of *The Times* were left with the impression that Dr White's account was unchallenged.

For the 'defence', the chairman of Brook Advisory Centres, Caroline Woodroffe, wondered whether Dr Adrian Rogers would prefer to see a girl under 16 suffer an abortion or childbirth rather than allow her doctor to protect her from pregnancy, and asked: 'Can moral outrage really be so cruel?' (The answer has to be 'Yes'.) Lady Brook herself wrote that 'a doctor who moralises and scaremongers instead of listening may simply be writing a prescription for pregnancy', and explained that counselling at Brook involved a full and careful exploration of all aspects of each client's situation.

Back on the attack, Responsible Society warhorse Valerie Riches maintained that 'the more contraception has been made available to under-age children, the more recruits have been drawn in, resulting in more sexual activity', and asked what is obviously for her the sixty-four-thousand-dollar question: have we, as a nation, lost control of our children to the extent that the only care and help we offer them is the provision of 'protectives' behind the backs of their parents? True courage and foresight, announced a Mrs Beasley, are shown by those girls who risk the mockery of their peers by using the simple device of saying 'No' to sex before marriage.

This peculiar correspondence, which although it bore throughout the heading 'Family Matters' was conducted on the assumption that all that mattered was whether or not under-age girls were to be allowed access to contraception if they desired it, ended after a weighty and thoughtful letter from Dr Michael Thomas, chairman of the BMA's Central Ethical Committee. Dr Rogers, he said, failed to appreciate that 'medicine is best practised when a doctor acts in the best interest of an individual rather than a group'. Would Dr Rogers prevent a doctor from supporting a 15-year-old girl in continuing her pregnancy in the face of her parents' demands that she should be aborted? Since Dr Rogers' massive publicity campaign started, there had been an unprecedented upsurge in calls to 'agony aunts' from young girls stating that they were now frightened to visit their doctors for fear of their parents being told. How sad it was that parents and doctors were being set at odds in this way when both seek the same end – the best for the child.

Sad, too, isn't it, that those of us who seek what is best for society and *all* its members – the irreligious as well as the religious, and the unconventional as well as the conventional – are set at odds by the crude over-simplifications and the moral humbuggery of the Butts and the Beasleys, the Riches and the Rogers, the Whites and the Whitehouses. Family Forum, if it survives, looks like having quite a bumpy ride.

Note

1. And later of the Conservative Family Campaign.

The Changing Social Climate in Sex Education

ADDRESS TO THE BRITISH SOCIETY FOR RESEARCH INTO SEX EDUCATION, 30 MARCH 1981

Discussing human sexuality, let alone teaching about it, is a high-risk occupation. Whatever one says is likely to make someone else angry – either because they disagree with what is said, or think that it oughtn't to be said at all. The most matter-of-fact statement about any aspect of sexual knowledge is liable to arouse shrill trumpetings of outrage from several different directions.

I used to think that, if the facts about sex were brought out more into the open, nearly everyone would then become more balanced and reasonable about it. What a hope! Looking back over the past thirty years, which is about the span of time that I have been embroiling myself in the endeavour to educate people about the sexual spectrum, I see now how naïve I was. It's true that considerable progress has been made towards more openness and honesty. A great many people have taken big personal risks in saying what they knew to be true, even when such facts were violently unpopular. Some (though I am not among them) would say that the media are so saturated with sex penny plain, twopence coloured and downright kinky nowadays, that the love that dare not speak its name would do us all a favour by shutting up for a while.

The trouble is that, by and large, greater openness has not brought deeper understanding or cooler reasoning to most of those who shout the loudest. The popular press manages to sensationalize sex and to trivialize it at the same time – just as they have always done, but with even greater lack of taste. I believe that most people would welcome a more balanced approach, even to such touchy topics as paedophilia and incest.

In the course of my own work I have become convinced that three fundamental requirements must be met if sex education, and not least the work of British ROSE, is to succeed.

First, sex education must be accepted as not just a basic need, but also a basic right, of all our citizens. It is not simply a matter of deciding what shall be taught about sex at school, when, and by whom; it has to be an ongoing task in and for the community as a whole. Any sex therapist will tell you that sexual ignorance is at the root of so many of their clients' difficulties. And sound sex education is one of the most potent tools for reducing unnecessary misery and increasing the sum of human happiness.

Second, human sexuality is a subject requiring academic study and research in all its aspects of an importance that is second to none. Yet there is still no major academic centre existing in Britain specifically for the study of human sexuality, or any body of source material which can make available to serious students a tithe of what the Kinsey Institute has amassed at Bloomington during the past forty years. Nobody who has read Wardell Pomeroy's sobering account of Kinsey's epic struggles to keep his project in existence – struggles which hastened his sudden and untimely death – or who has had the privilege, as I have, to talk with Paul Gebhard, John Gagnon, and others of Kinsey's former associates, will underestimate the difficulties (not least, political) of establishing and maintaining such an archive.[1] But to see one coming into existence in the United Kingdom with adequate academic, financial and public support is a long-cherished hope of mine.

Third, it must be realized that the battle for sensible sex education is essentially an aspect – and a crucial one – of the larger battle for free speech. Let us make no mistake about this. While sexuality is perceived as a powerful – and, by some, as a threateningly powerful and uncontrollable – force, there will be strenuous efforts to dictate what may be said about it, and who may say what may be said. A main motivation of the pro-censorship lobby in this country is their urgent desire to control what is said and published about sex, where, when, and by whom, and what is taught about it. Yes, and what is thought about it, too, if only they could! Fortunately 1984 is still three years off, but I'm told they are working on a fantasy-monitoring device (known as the peter-meter) which we shall all be compelled to wear as part of our new-age regulation issue gadgetry.[2]

And this, for me, is the crux: does sound sex education consist of imparting the fullest available factual information which the teacher honestly believes to be accurate, followed by encouragement for the learner to assess and evaluate that information in his or her own way, or does it consist of indoctrination – of telling young people, and adults too, what they *ought* to think and do? Or, more usually, what they *not* to think and do?

Unfortunately, in spite of all the progress made during the 1970s, there again seems to be a growing segment of opinion (even in academic quarters which one would have hoped knew better) that the latter approach is the proper one in sex education if nowhere else in the curriculum; or that it is at least less objectionable in respect of sex education than in relation to most other subjects that are taught.

My friend the late Dorothy Dallas of King's College, London, who was one of the most knowledgeable and experienced trainers of sex educators in Britain, often said that the starting point for an understanding of sexuality must be awareness of human variation; and that there could be no sound sex education which did not take into account an individual's philosophy of life – and also their philosophy of death. She also said that in sex education the first thing you have to do is to clear morals like clearing trumps in bridge.

Another very wise and skilled sex educator, the late Professor Nathaniel N. Wagner, Professor of Psychology and Obstetrics/Gynecology at Washington State University, whom I worked with in the early 1970s, declared[3] that

> Sexuality is an integral part of an individual's total personality. Therefore, sex education has to deal fully and honestly with emotions, thoughts and values as well as with physiology and the know-how of intercourse. People have a right to objective, full information about sexuality. . . . Sexual behaviour which is held to be within an acceptable range will vary from person to person and from group to group. Consensus may not be possible. Divergent views should be respected if they are based on principles of honesty and mutuality. Rather than imparting any individual code of morality, the aim of a comprehensive sex education programme should be to develop problem-solving skills so that young people can make their own decisions about their lives in an informed and rational manner.

This requires that teachers of sex education must be adequately trained and qualified, and prepared to be honest with their pupils about their own standards and values:

> If the purpose of 'sex education' is in fact educational, and not an effort to indoctrinate to a particular view, then academic freedom is as important in sexuality as it is in political science, history, psychology, medicine, or any other body of knowledge. Can it be imagined in a history class or a physics class that a teacher could respond to a legitimate subject-matter question with 'we can't talk about that'? It is unthinkable that students should have concerns and questions about sexuality that are not the subject matter of instruction in sex education. Incest, bestiality and oral sex, regardless of what one may think of them, are as real as venereal disease, love and marriage.

On the still hotly argued question of parents' rights to control the ideas and concepts presented to their children, Wagner pointed out that

> No-one disputes the rights of parents to know what their children are being taught. But whether a minority, or even a majority, of parents has the right to determine the content of an educational programme is another question. . . . This issue of parental rights and responsibilities is one that does not lend itself to a simple resolution. Sex educators must continue to pay maximum attention to see that all parties are treated in a manner which respects their legitimate rights, within the guidelines that people have a right to objective, full information about sexuality.

He had, he said, great faith in the good sense and strength of young people to reject unhealthy attitudes and to question incorrect or misleading information.

Professor Wagner's confidence in the good sense of the young is borne out by a recent newspaper report that a survey by the Scottish Health Education Group had found that 'what teenagers really needed was more openness. They desperately wanted to be able to discuss sex "normally" with teachers, and above all with their parents.'

We cannot split off anyone's sexuality from the rest of their personality, any more than we can split off sex education from education in personal relationships. As Nat Wagner said, people have a right to unbiased, comprehensive information, to personal privacy, and to their own beliefs, thoughts, and feelings. Sex educators must be adequately trained and competent. And pluralism is an essential feature of sexuality in a democracy.

That's quite a tall order! If, just for a start, British ROSE concentrated on finding out how far these objectives are currently being realized in sex education work in Britain, we would have our hands pretty full for the next decade.

We are first and foremost a research organization, and I would not wish British ROSE to get caught up in polemics with those who dispute the Wagner approach to sex education. We must, however, keep well in mind the need to evaluate the conflicting claims which are being made by the various parties to the public debate as to the effects of different types of sex education. Could we construct reliable ways of assessing what effect different methods of sex education have on the recipients' subsequent behaviour, attitudes to sex, and enjoyment of their lives? We must look not only at how best to promote good sex education in the classroom, but also at how best to promote a more meaningful, better informed public debate about sexual issues.

The greater openness of the past decade provides us with an opportunity: the increasingly strident backlash against that openness presents us with a challenge. The contention that much sex education is amoral, immoral, subversive, or all of these, is in reality an anguished cry of protest from those who are incapable of questioning their own values but wish to impose them on others – and especially on the younger generation. It is ironic that some of the loudest and most persistent protesters confess themselves baffled when asked how *they* would do it! Mrs Valerie Riches of The Responsible Society, for instance, is quoted in *NOW!*[4] as saying: 'I tried it myself once, but I found it quite impossible in a classroom to deal with every child's needs. It's all so sensitive. I didn't want to press upon them. . . . I don't want people to talk dirt to my children.'

The trouble is that people like Mrs Riches are apt to construe the most neutral reference to certain aspects of sexual behaviour as 'dirt'. She and her allies in Parliament and the press have been bitter critics of Jane Cousins' best-selling sex education book *Make It Happy*, which Ronald

Butt described in *The Times* as 'quite the filthiest book of its kind I have encountered'. Indeed, it is an open secret that as a result of political pressures generated by The Responsible Society and their like, the Department of Health 'requested' the Family Planning Association (who depend on the Department for a £60,000 annual grant) to drop *Make It Happy* from their bookshop and reading lists because the Secretary of State was being embarrassed by the attacks upon it.

One of the reasons why *Make It Happy* is in such bad odour with the likes of Mrs Riches is because it actually dares to mention bestiality without strong overtones of disapproving disgust. In fact, there are only four sentences about bestiality in the book – all of them statements of fact without any comment. They are:

> Some people feel sexually attracted to animals. It's not against the law to kiss, masturbate or be masturbated by an animal. But it is illegal for a woman or a man to have intercourse or buggery with an animal. It's totally impossible for a woman to get pregnant by having sex with an animal – or for an animal to get pregnant by having sex with a man.

That information of this sort in a book for teenagers can cause a public outcry in this day and age is a measure of the changing social climate for sex education. Clearly it is, and is likely to remain, a high-risk area and one where not just the content of the syllabus, but also whether anything at all should rightly be taught, is at issue.

Personally, I agree with Dr Elphis Christopher that it is time to move away from the traditional emphasis on 'constraint' as the key concept in sex education towards 'comfort' and 'commitment'. But how? As I see it, our task as sex educators, and that of British ROSE as a research body, is to map out the best ways forward through this scary jungle. We have no choice but to do this in the context of the society we find ourselves living in. While some of you may think I have been too negative and gloomy, and that the pressures are not as adverse as I have made out, I shall be very surprised if there is a sex educator here today or anywhere else who does not feel under at least some constraints in their work.

Notes

1. Wardell B. Pomeroy, *Dr. Kinsey and the Institute for Sex Research* (Nelson, 1972).
2. With the advent of electronic tagging, this is no longer so far-fetched – or as amusing – in 1997.
3. *Viewer's Guide* for Telecourse on 'The Psychology of Human Sexual Behavior', produced in consultation with Planned Parenthood Center of Seattle and Washington State Medical Association [*c.* 1973].
4. June 1980.

PART SIX

THE GAY MOVEMENT

It was inevitable that there would be problems in relationships between the Albany Trust and the emerging 'homophile' movement in the post-law-reform years after the 1967 Sexual Offences Act. As will be seen from the preceding pages, the main thrust (apart from counselling and casework) of both the Homosexual Law Reform Society's and Albany Trust's work was aimed at educating Parliament, press and the general public about the unjust treatment of homosexuals by society, and the need to improve it through better legislation and social action.

The Trust was not itself a homophile grouping. While many of those of us actively involved in running it were ourselves gay, none of us was 'out' (except in the discreet sense of not denying our sexuality or pretending it to be otherwise); while there was a strongly paternalistic element among our straight committee members and parliamentary sponsors who viewed emancipation as a gradual, quiet process of social acclimatization and regarded gay self-help – especially of the strident Gay Liberation Front variety – with disapproval and even dismay. Such perspectives led to unavoidable clashes with the new breed of gay activists, and to their dislike of the Trust.

In the 1960s there were only a few homophile groups in Britain, and these were very small. When I visited the United States on a lecture tour soon after the 1967 Act was passed, I encountered many such groups working actively for gay rights, even though homosexual behaviour was still illegal in almost every state of America. Back home, there were then only a handful of tiny lesbian groups and, on the male side, the North-Western Homosexual Law Reform Committee, beginning its process of self-transformation into the Campaign for Homosexual Equality (CHE), and the Scottish Minorities Group (now Outright Scotland) north of the border. It was not until the Gay Liberation Front erupted onto the scene at the end of 1970 that large numbers of lesbians and gays were prepared to become flamboyantly visible.

My own position was private sympathy with, and behind-the-scenes support for, the new generation of self-help activists. But I was inevitably constrained by the alarmed disapproval of some of the Albany Trust's and HLRS's committee members. This contradiction led to misunderstandings, and subsequent prolonged bad relations, between the Trust and CHE over the latter's move to set up social clubs. At the time GLF was born I had left the Trust for what (contrary to my expectation) turned out to be only a 'sabbatical' year – so I was able to go to GLF's early meetings freely as myself, unfettered by any need to pay regard to an Albany Trust 'line'. The first of the pieces which follow ('Minority on the March') was written at this time. In fact, my personal relations with many GLF supporters were, and remained, friendlier than those I had with some of CHE's leading members.

The rapid growth of the gay movement in the early 1970s, and the multiplication of groups, made it all the more important for homophiles to secure a foothold in the national voluntary scene. A conference on social needs held at York in 1970 under the joint sponsorship of the Albany Trust and the Yorkshire Council of Social Service (whose Secretary, Raymond Clarke – later head of the National Organisations Division of the National Council of Social Service – was always a stalwart supporter of the Trust's work) led to the formation in 1971 of the National Federation of Homophile Organisations (NFHO), whose chairman I was surprised to be invited to become. In my view, NFHO had a useful – indeed, essential – function to perform; sadly, the now fast-growing CHE and SMG decided otherwise, and after a couple of years' lukewarm participation pulled out, leaving the remaining 'minnows' without sufficient membership clout to survive. My 'Open Letter to the Homophile Movement' expresses my disappointment and frustration with this short-sighted action, which I still believe cost the movement dearly in terms of 'establishment' leverage.

'Gay Stocktaking' sums up my views of the achievements, and shortcomings, of the movement during its first full decade, the 1970s. 'Not So Gay News' expresses my dismay at the collapse (which could and should have been prevented) of Gay News – the only broadly based community paper we have had so far.The concluding pieces are more recent, and deal with the still very controversial topic of 'outing'.

Minority on the March

NEW STATESMAN, JANUARY 1971[1]

The Gay Liberation Front was started by a couple of people in October 1970, and now draws 250 or more to its weekly meetings. Far-reaching plans are being made, and the media have so far been kind. But in cold fact, the movement is on a far finer knife-edge than some of its young and militant founders seem to realize. Rousing slogans and demonstrations are all very well, but 'coming out' is a far bigger and hazard-fraught step for the middle-of-the-road, middle-class homosexual man or woman in the professions, industry, and commerce than it is for students or for hippies. Yet it is the active involvement of the middle-of-the-road homosexual that any successful large-scale self-help effort will require.

There can be no doubt of the urgent need for such an effort, not only in the interests of homosexuals themselves, but for the sake of our entire society. For there is a huge amount of unnecessary human misery and sheer social waste caused by man's inhumanity to man over sexual behaviour and feelings. Until the whole community begins making a much more conscious and concerted effort to rid itself of its hang-ups, there is little point in talking about a healthier environment for us all to live in. GLF is right in thinking that liberation must come, in the first instance, from inside oneself; and the uptight, 'straight' attitudes of mind which cause the trouble need to be shed by everyone – whether homosexual, heterosexual or bisexual.

Politicians are notoriously reluctant to enter this arena. Yet it lies at the root of social policy making. How many people are going to live where in 1975, 1980 and 1990, and in what sort of community patterns, depends upon decisions which need taking now about the provision as a national service of sex education (which, in its broad and proper sense, means an awareness of human relationships in their emotional and practical aspects as well as of the physical details of intercourse and reproduction), of family planning advice, and of adequate counselling and social help not only for the married but also for minorities such as unmarried mothers and homosexuals.

Any member of the 1966 Parliament who deceives him or herself that they participated in a great social reforming crusade by voting for a few tepid and long-overdue Private Members' Bills on divorce, abortion, and homosexuality is surely a victim of that strange occupational disease afflicting denizens of the Palace of Westminster, too many of whom appear to believe that they are being incredibly courageous leaders of social progress when they brave the wrath of Moral Rearmament and Mary Whitehouse by finally enacting proposals which have been canvassed for ten, thirty, and sometimes fifty, years by single-minded individuals and pressure groups who are frequently far more fully informed and better aware than anybody else (including Government departments) of the salient facts and necessities.

Sex, we are frequently told, is an electoral minefield. It is also a personal and social casualty area without parallel as to the extent of human unhappiness involved and the sheer inadequacy of resources available to help those who are sad, lonely, or disturbed. Anyone who is seriously concerned about the state of the nation should obviously be considering, as a first priority, the reallocation of public and private funds as to prevent and remedy as much as possible of the waste which sexual misery causes.

But no amount of benevolence or 'soup kitchen' social work will remove the prime need for self-help on the part of minorities who face both an internal and an external problem in their attitudes to themselves and to one another and in the attitudes of the majority towards them.

Homosexuals publicly proclaiming their preference and demanding their civil rights may seem shockingly novel in England, even to some of the supporters of the 1967 'consenting adults in private' Sexual Offences Act. It is, in fact, surprising that homosexual militancy has not emerged far sooner here, in view of its existence in the United States and in some European countries (notably Holland) for the past twenty years. While the styles employed have differed, the common denominator, hitherto lacking in Britain, has been the assertion by self-proclaimed homosexual spokesmen of their right to equality of social justice. The most depressing feature of the British law reform campaign was, of course, the paternal way in which it was conducted. Whether this was as politically essential as Lord Arran and Leo Abse thought I have always doubted: I have never understood why it is more discreditable for a homosexual to support a better deal for his own kind than for a shareholder to oppose capital gains tax or for a trade unionist to fight the Industrial Relations Bill.

One unhappy outcome of the over-condescending attitude of those who wished to change the law a little, but had slight insight into the needs, feelings and wishes of homosexuals themselves, was that a too-hasty attempt by a local Manchester support group of the Homosexual Law Reform Society to set up social clubs for homosexual people met with frantic disapproval from the Act's chief sponsors; they had not (they said) reformed the law in order to perpetuate homosexual ghettoes. That such 'ghettoes' exist because of the absence, rather than through the presence, of homosexual organizations devoted to the welfare of their members apparently still escapes the comprehension of a great many 'straight' liberals. Individual counselling and casework such as the Albany Trust's is patently not enough – especially as loneliness and the lack of opportunities to meet other like-minded people in congenial and wholesome surroundings has been the commonest complaint of those coming forward for help. As a charitable social work agency, the Albany

Trust could do little more than inaugurate a series of informal social evenings with the co-operation of sympathetic clergy and social workers. The North-Western group – now the Committee [and, later, the Campaign] for Homosexual Equality – have continued to advocate the establishment of 'Esquire Clubs', though none has as yet started; CHE have, however, a growing number of provincial branches.

In Scotland, the Scottish Minorities Group[2] has encountered even stronger adverse currents in its efforts to promote law reform (Scottish law still[3] formally penalizes even the 'two consenting adults in private' situation), and has recently lost the hospitality of the Church of Scotland's social centre in Edinburgh, apparently because the desirability of permitting homosexuals to foregather for an evening's discussion and coffee drinking is regarded as a doubtful contribution to their moral welfare. Northern Ireland's state is even bleaker – no group whatever exists there, and although a handful of individuals have bravely and doggedly sought to promote public discussion of the issue Ulster has so far shown even less regard for the needs of its homosexual minority than for those of other, more vociferous, sections of the population. A national federation of homophile groups, including those which exist for women, has been discussed but not as yet implemented.

All this is in contrast to the American scene, where for a decade and more homosexual spokesmen have, with growing success, demanded dialogues with the churches and with public representatives, including Congressmen and the Civil Service Commission, in their campaign for civil rights. And this has occurred despite the fact that only two out of the 50 states have as yet adopted 'Wolfenden type' laws. In last summer's 'Gay Pride Week', more than 5000 homosexual men and women marched up Sixth Avenue from Greenwich Village to Central Park; the organizers expect more this year. There are at least fifty college and university campus homophile groups in existence, holding weekly gay dances and also participating in terms of integrated equality in non-gay social events.

Under-21s are, of course, still the main victims of anti-homosexual prejudice and prohibitive laws here. The 1967 Act not only increased the maximum penalties for some behaviour by over-21s with under-21s; it also refrained from taking the homosexual relationships of two youths both aged under 21 out of the criminal category. The unrealism of this state of affairs, obvious enough even in 1967, has since been enhanced by the lowering of the age of majority and the extension of voting rights to 18-year-olds. Any belief that it is individually or socially desirable to treat young homosexuals as potential criminals in this way has been effectively demolished by a report prepared for the Dutch Government by a specialist committee of the Council for Health, which has recommended that discriminatory laws against homosexuals should be abolished, not merely in the best interests of the homosexuals themselves, but for the sake of reducing irrational community prejudices against a group of people who are in fact harmless. Consequently, the legal age for homosexual acts in Holland is likely to be lowered this year from 21 to 16.

Not only freedom of sexual behaviour, but freedom of association and freedom to communicate are essential if homosexuals are to improve their situation. In this respect, peripheral laws about 'conduct likely to cause a breach of the peace' and 'conspiracy to corrupt public morals' are as much in need of amendment as the sexual statutes. The recent conviction of *International Times*, whose 'Males' advertisement column was represented to the court by the prosecution as a squalid conspiracy on the part of the advertisers, is a sample of what Gay Liberation activists may expect if they persist in their intentions to educate schoolchildren about homosexuality and to demonstrate against psychiatrists who practise 'sexist chauvinism'. That they have anticipated the possibility, and intend to go forward, is evidence of a new spirit whose manifestation may well do more to help the timid and isolated 'closet queens' towards greater self-acceptance and self-respect than all the do-goodery in the world. For if 'Gay is Good' – and it can be – we have to make it so.

Notes

1. *New Statesman* © 1971.
2. Later the Scottish Homosexual Rights Group, and now Outright Scotland.
3. Until 1981.

An Open Letter to the Homophile Movement

GAY NEWS, 1973

Dear Fellow-Workers!

I address you, known and unknown, Ms's and Mr's, friends and not-so-friendly, in this fashion because what we are all doing in our various ways is, after all, *work* – even if some of it is enjoyable: and this, I think, is what distinguishes homophile activism from all other forms of gay communication, which have immediate personal pleasure as their primary motivation. Perhaps it is the unaccustomed effort it takes to get along with other gay folk one wouldn't ordinarily wish to go to the cinema with, or eat with, let alone sleep with, that produces the internecine abrasiveness sometimes apparent in homophile utterances which appear short in brotherly (or sisterly) love.

Having been castigated recently rather as if I was Browning's Lost Leader, may I disclaim the parallel, which I think springs from some rather basic misunderstandings.

First, to clear up the niggling point about the Albany Trust not being part of the homophile movement, the fact is that the Trust isn't, as a matter of history and of fact, a homophile organization. Nor was the Homosexual Law Reform Society, whose sponsoring committee was a very broad and diverse collection of people, including a lot of prominent 'straights', who were united only in believing that a law which punished what consenting adults did in private was wrong. They would most probably have fought amongst themselves like a bagful of Kilkenny cats about everything else to do with homosexuality; and we didn't make the tactical error of trying to get them to agree on any other proposition than that the law was unjust. And on that basis it got changed, with all of them supporting us.

The Albany Trust is a charity, set up originally by some executive committee members of the HLRS, with the objective of 'promoting psychological health'. In practice, this means that the Trust tries to help not only gay people, but members of other sexual minorities – transsexuals, transvestites, fetishists, and masochists, for instance, all come to us for advice from time to time – and to educate the public, and more especially professional people, about their needs.

None of this is new: both the HLRS and the Albany Trust were set up in 1958, whereas to my knowledge the homophile movement didn't surface until 1963, when the North-Western Homosexual Law Reform Committee (which ultimately blossomed into the Campaign for Homosexual Equality) and Arena Three were both founded.

But while the Albany Trust predated the homophile movement, and has wider aims in some respects, they are surely complementary in many ways, and one would have thought that there was much room for fruitful co-operation – notably in the development of counselling and befriending for gay people.

This letter, however, is not primarily about the Trust. It is more personal, from me as a person (because I am one – not just an institution!), to you as people.

It was alleged in *Gay News* recently that I disapprove of much that's going on in the gay movement, because it 'rocks the boat'. On the contrary, if it's the Establishment boat that's meant, my criticism would be that the movement doesn't always rock it hard enough or in the most effective ways. What *does* worry me, increasingly, is whether the good ship *Homophile* is the right one for us to be in at all at this stage of our progress; because it seems too small and exclusive for the voyage we are trying to make, and we certainly need a much larger and more varied crew.

For if we want – as I at any rate do, and I hope you do too – not merely to have gayness fully accepted by today's hypocritical, uptight, repressive, and hilariously misnamed 'permissive' society (all of which is surely a contradictory goal, anyway), but to transform society itself, I do not think that the way to get such transformation is by continually harping upon specifically gay – and usually specifically male – grievances which, quite frankly, however real and burdensome they are to some gay people, must by now seem either boring, or trivial, or both, to most straights – even sympathetic ones.

Rather, should we not be carrying the struggle out of the home ground of gayness and onto the truly advantageous battleground of society's ignorant, prudish, guilt-ridden, and largely joyless attitude to *all* sexuality? Here, surely, is the winning pitch; and millions of straights who are eager to be liberated from the fuddy-duddy obscurantism of Mrs Whitehouse and her cohorts are our potential allies who at present lack a spearhead. Surely it is not beyond our wit to provide this.

Let's start making it loud and clear that the battle we fight is *everyone's* battle – not just our own selfish one: that the liberation we want isn't just gay liberation, or the equality just homosexual equality; but that we seek universal human sexual liberation and equality in the right of everyone to love whom and how they wish, and we will settle for nothing less.

At the same time, could we please have less feuding and bitchery amongst ourselves, both personally and organizationally? If I wanted to, I could set down here a long recital of put-downs and devious dealings which I and the Albany Trust have had to put up with from certain individuals and groups in the homophile movement – not least when I was occupying the thorny chair of the National Federation of Homophile Organisations! But to do so would merely reopen old sores which I had hoped were healing by now.

I would, though, like to appeal to those in CHE and SMG[1] who have decided that it is a waste of their time to co-operate with the smaller NFHO groups or the Albany Trust in matters of common interest to reconsider. Even if NFHO was not the best machinery for this purpose, a more flexible framework could have been devised if the will had been there. Rightly or wrongly, the impression was created that the will was not there, and that only those who toed a CHE 'party line' were welcome in the movement so far as the CHE hierarchy were concerned. I think this is a pity, and I believe that most members of CHE would think so too.

Those of us who are active workers for other gay people are (if we are gay ourselves) a minority of a minority of a minority – for most gay people don't belong to any homophile organization, and most members of homophile organizations aren't active workers. We therefore have a very real privilege, and also a responsibility – not least to one another. Personally, I don't harbour grudges, and it is rather sad that there seem to be some people around in the homophile movement who do.

There is so much for all of us to do, in further law reform, in counselling, and – most important of all, really – in educating society out of prejudice and joylessness, that every moment spent on bawling one another out is time ill spent. If this is interpreted as merely pious, bland platitudes by our bilious polemicists, so be it: but I think most *Gay News* readers will know what I mean.

Love and peace.

Note

1. The Campaign for Homosexual Equality and the Scottish Minorities Group [now Outright Scotland].

'I Love Me, I Hate Us!'

1977

The guy in the Rotterdam bar was intently explaining to me how different he was from everyone else there. 'All these people', he said, gesturing contemptuously, 'are immature – they just want sex every day with someone new who is young and pretty. I have worked through my problems, come to terms with my bisexuality, and accept myself.' He added a lot more in the same vein. The bar crowd looked perfectly ordinary to me; just considerably friendlier and more relaxed with one another than their London equivalents. When he paused for breath I asked him 'Well, what are you doing here if you are so different from the others, and find them so distasteful?' He brushed the question aside.

I was still thinking over this encounter when, a few days later in Amsterdam, I met a COC group for foreigners living in Holland. There were four or five Englishmen, two Americans, a Swiss, and a Frenchman, with a Dutch teacher moderating the discussion. He spent some time explaining how he made a point of letting his colleagues and pupils know he was gay, and it was apparent that some of them made him feel on the defensive although the majority accepted it quite matter-of-factly. The discussion turned to the comparative levels of acceptance in England and Holland, and it was not long before the young Englishmen present were decrying the hollowness of the Earl's Court scene, with its surface glitter and inner emptiness. One-night stands, they complained, aren't enough.

Well, it's an old story, and one which is drearily familiar to anyone involved in gay counselling. I have heard it for all of fifteen years, from hundreds of different people. But this busman's holiday in Holland set me off thinking once again about the need for something more positive and dynamic to counter this malaise which undoubtedly afflicts many people who are confronted with the gay 'scene' as their only means of alleviating loneliness and, hopefully, finding someone to love.

GLF, CHE, and other homophile groups, have made brave endeavours to provide a more human and less exploitive atmosphere, and have undoubtedly helped many people. But these are still only a minority; and there are still far too many lonely and isolated gays, even in London.

Nowadays, for most people a sexual encounter is not all that hard to come by – but what about mind-contact, as well as body-contact? It's possible to have sex with a dozen different people every week, without getting to know any of them – or even speaking to them. This can be quite fun, and stimulating for a while, but without good mental contacts as well, an endless round of casual sex eventually becomes profoundly depressing. To live a fulfilled and well-balanced life, everyone needs to have some secure and long-standing friendships and to be able to give and receive love. This is just as true (perhaps more so) of gay people as of the non-gay.

Ability to relate well with others is grounded in a sound relationship with oneself. It is here, I believe, that many gay people miss out. You cannot love others unless you love yourself. By 'loving yourself', I do not mean a smug, sickly, fatuously self-satisfied 'Oh what a lovely person am I' attitude, but a realistic stocktaking of one's own strengths and weaknesses grounded upon the knowledge of your inner integrity and good intentions towards other people and life generally. (If you haven't got such an inner integrity and good intentions, don't bother reading on – it's a waste of your time.)

Of course, no one can be *totally* honest and realistic with his or her self, but we can all at least try. As Canon Douglas Rhymes once remarked, 'there are four selves to every human being: there is the self I know and let you know; there is the self I know and am not going to let you know; there is the self other people know and I don't, because I get angry when I am told about it; and there is the self that neither I know nor they know'. We can at any rate work on the first three of these selves, and let the fourth work beneficially on us.

This effort to know ourselves positively is essential, because without it we shall never relate positively to other people – and especially to other gay people. We shall merely project onto them our unresolved guilt, fear and self-dislike; attributes to which, unfortunately, a great many gay people are still prone. It has often struck me how many of us feel *guilty* because we are gay – whether we recognize the guilt or not, it is all too frequently there. We need not merely to accept our gayness, but to accept it gladly, as a very positive part of us, before we can offer ourselves creatively to other people. I am thankful that at long last this is now increasingly being done by the very caring people who are beginning to provide community services such as *Gay News*, Gay Switchboard, and the various gay counselling and befriending agencies.

These are a good start, but much more is needed. We have to cater for the many gays, young and old, who remain isolated and in that state are experiencing one of the three main gay life crises – those of 'coming out' in the teens or early twenties; of 'now the ball is over what have I worth living for?' in the thirties and forties; and of 'I'm just another lonely old queen nobody wants' in the fifties and sixties. (I know that not everyone experiences all – or any – of these syndromes, but plenty do.)

A big part of the answer, it seems to me, is to stop moaning (like the man in the Rotterdam bar) about the things we dislike about the gay life and other gay people, and to try to see that *we*, at any rate, don't act out any of the attitudes we despise: that *we*, at least, don't make dates and then stand him or her up; that *we* don't cut dead that trick we couldn't wait to get into bed with last week and then wondered why we'd bothered – even if he wasn't the world's most exciting, we can at least smile and say 'Hello' when we see him again.

Maybe manners aren't everything – but they are a start towards civilizing life. And a good many of us would agree that gay life could be more civilized. It's no use demanding to be first-class citizens if we are third-rate individuals.

Obviously, fundamental changes in outlook and behaviour won't happen overnight. They need working on. Surely that's worthwhile doing.

Gay Stocktaking

NEW HUMANIST, 1979

'We are rapidly approaching a situation in which homosexuals are the *only* natural minority who are still regarded, by some, as intrinsically evil, and who are still liable to be mocked or persecuted by people claiming to represent ordinary social opinion, or the Christian church.'

This is perhaps the key sentence in a recently published document, *Towards a Charter of Homosexual Rights* [hereafter referred to as *TC*], signed by the Editor of *New Humanist*, myself, and 172 other sponsors, including many Christians. The document is the first major attempt in the 1970s to rally a significant cross-section of the community as a whole, as distinct from specifically gay activists, behind the cause of homosexual emancipation which, despite several heartening developments during the past decade, seems to have largely run out of effective 'push' since Parliament passed a watered down version of the Wolfenden reforms in 1967.

Yet *TC* has been predictably attacked, in *Gay News* and elsewhere, as tepid UncleTom-ism, likely to do more harm than good because it fails to grasp the real nature and extent of homosexual oppression. The text is indeed less than perfect, and in one respect, at least (its reference to bisexuality), misleading. But its basic statements of position are sound – above all, its branding of homophobic people (whether religious or not) as the real social casualties, and its recognition that, whether they like it or not, gay people will never achieve the total social acceptance they rightly demand solely through their own unaided efforts: they need non-gay allies, as the pre-1967 reform movement did; and *TC* is a modest first step in rallying such allies.

The history of the gay movement in Britain is, indeed, paradoxical in this respect. Before the private homosexual activities of consenting pairs (but not groups) of males aged over 21 were decriminalized in 1967, those of us who were working for the reform were surprised and depressed by the conspicuous absence of overtly gay organizations in Britain. Whereas such bodies existed in some strength in various parts of the United States (all of which then had similarly prohibitive laws to the British), nothing of the sort existed here in the mid-1960s, with the then tiny exceptions of a small lesbian group (Arena Three) and of the North-Western Homosexual Law Reform Committee (which was later to grow into the Campaign for Homosexual Equality).

The Homosexual Law Reform Society, founded in 1958 largely on the initiative of Tony Dyson (who is also the moving spirit behind the Campaign for Reason, which produced *TC*), was deliberately broadly based and had an Honorary Committee so stuffed with Bishops, leading Humanists such as Professor Ayer and Bertrand Russell, and distinguished people from many walks of life, that it was sourly dubbed by a hostile journalist 'the pick of the lilac establishment'. It is hard to realize it now, but twenty years ago the word 'homosexual' was still so unfamiliar, and indeed shocking, that to incorporate it into the title of a society which included at its masthead the Archbishops of Canterbury and York was a major coup. In those days, all that most people knew about homosexuality was gleaned from the sensational Sunday papers' reports about erring men – frequently connected with youth work – accused of what were mysteriously and vaguely described as 'serious offences'.

Given the abysmal lack of public education about sexuality, and the absence of a British civil rights tradition analogous to that fostered by the existence of the American Constitution, the lack of any groups of gay freedom fighters in the 1950s and 1960s is understandable. The gay activists of the 1970s would do well to remember that they are a novel phenomenon; and that if those of us who are gay and were working for the Wolfenden reforms in the 1960s had made such a point of personally 'coming out' as they now do, we would merely have disabled ourselves and damaged the cause. I do not mean by this that I or (to my knowledge) anyone else involved was deliberately hypocritical, or told a lie if asked a blunt question – merely that we argued the case for reform on general principles of legal and social justice, and not *ad hominem*.

And this, I believe, is how further progress will ultimately be made. While it is healthy and good that at least some gay men and women feel able to be more open and honest nowadays about their own sexual orientation, it is not just 'coming out', but the positive convincing of a majority of the community at large that the social and legal treatment of homosexuals is still abominably unjust, and in fact harms the whole of society (as *any* ignorance, prejudice, and discrimination must do), that will bring about further changes. The fatal flaw in the 'Come out, everybody' exhortation as a political tactic is, of course, that by no means everybody *will* come out. As the late Gilbert Harding is supposed to have said, the homosexual 'problem' would be solved overnight if everyone who was homosexual or bisexual turned the appropriate shade of blue – for there would be so many people around ranging from pale violet to deep indigo that the absurdity of society's present pretence that homosexuals don't (or shouldn't) exist would be instantaneously apparent. Unlike coloured people, however, homosexuals and bisexuals can – and do – 'pass': so that the minority who are able and willing to come out merely make themselves in some respects even more isolated and vulnerable.

Even so, I regard Gay Liberation, with its awakening of gay consciousness and gay pride, as one of the best and healthiest things to have happened so far in the ongoing struggle for gay rights. Those were heady and exhilarating days when a thousand pansies bloomed in the basements of the London School of Economics in 1970 and 1971, and I am glad and thankful to have been there. 'Gay Lib' bubbled over with hope, spontaneity and enthusiasm: beside it, the apparatchiks of the Campaign for Homosexual Equality, with their paper-ridden bureaucracy and endless committee meetings, looked drab and uninspiring. But because it rejected organization, Gay Lib was inevitably a shooting star which exploded into many fragments – some still energizing later gay projects.

Besides Gay Lib, three most significant events of the 1970s have been the birth – and, still more, the survival – of *Gay News*, which from an enthusiastically amateur collective has grown into a highly professional and generally admirable paper under Denis Lemon's editorship; the growth of gay self-help services – notably the various Gay Switchboards and FRIEND (originally the counselling arm of CHE), which have channelled the dedication of many volunteers to good purpose; and – on the debit side – the emergence of virulently anti-homosexual, mostly Fundamentalist Christian, pressure groups which make a point of attacking homosexuals and homosexuality whenever they can.

In the 1960s, curiously enough, vocal opposition to law reform, and also the display of uncharitable attitudes towards homosexuals as individuals, were conspicuous by their absence. Such personalized hostility was certainly not considered respectable by most Christian spokesmen, even if they were opposed to law reform. Now, however – perhaps goaded by the openness of gay activists and their fears that 'Christian civilization' is tumbling about their ears – the doctrinally primitive have mobilized themselves, backed by money muscle from undisclosed sources, and indulge in holy queerbashing at every opportunity. Although Mary Whitehouse protested that her blasphemy prosecution was not aimed against *Gay News* but was in order to protect her God, I suspect that she would have thought twice about prosecuting if the offending poem by James Kirkup had been published in *The Times* or even in *New Humanist*.

What of the future? Just as Mary Whitehouse has proved not to be merely a paper tiger, so the gay movement has been, in some respects, a sheep in wolf's clothing. It would be idle to pretend that I have unbounded respect for its collective shrewdness, or for some of its tactics in recent years; and I do not think the sum of its achievements since 1967 compares favourably with the track record of the poor old Homosexual Law Reform Society in the decade between Wolfenden and the passage into law of the Sexual Offences Act. *Gay News* No. 146 asks editorially: 'Can we really be proud of a gay movement angry and divided so that just as much energy is spent on internal wrangles as on presenting a united and confident front?' Though the article proceeds to answer 'yes', we all know that the present state of the quest for a saner sexual society leaves much to be desired. Not merely society's treatment of homosexuals, or of members of other sexual minorities, but its sense of sexual balance and psychic health is now at stake. With the vociferous bigots slinging everything they can lay their hands on at everyone who is working for better sex education, sound counselling, and the spread of charitable understanding of other people's sexuality as well as one's own, and with their pressurizing of Parliament and government departments more relentlessly and effectively than Canute could beat back the waves, the chips really are down.

As Tony Dyson says in reply to the critics of *TC*, 'the battle is bigger than gay rights. It is against prejudice, one of the greatest social evils in the world. . . . Time is running out. There's a real danger of polarization in British politics, leading to semi-populist campaigns in search of scapegoats.' We shall only win if we fight. And unless all of us, whether gay, heterosexual, or bisexual, Christians or Humanists, who are people of goodwill with an urgent concern for the sexual health and happiness of this and future generations stop bickering and stand shoulder to shoulder, we shall fail.

Not So Gay News

NEW HUMANIST, AUTUMN 1984[1]

The collapse of *Gay News* in 1982 after just over a decade of continuous fortnightly publication was the biggest disaster that has befallen the homosexual rights movement in this country to date. This book, by a former editor and staff reporter, makes it crystal-clear that the paper's death was a self-inflicted wound – not the result of attacks from outside enemies, though of course they exulted; and the liberal establishment's deafening silence may have betokened (as *New Society* speculated) private relief that 'yet another of those damned hornets that escaped the Pandora's Box of '68 has been eradicated'.

I read *Title Fight* with deepening sadness and mounting anger. Sadness that it had to be written at all, and that the lively talents of its authors couldn't be deployed to constructive things; anger that the appalling state of affairs at *Gay News* which it reveals as stretching back over several years was allowed to come about. As narrative the book is gripping throughout, at times positively racy, and written with surprising urbanity and detachment considering the authors' personally painful involvement in the events described. As fiction the book would be 'a jolly good read', tossed aside at the end as an enjoyable but implausible whodunit: surely real-life people would never behave like this? But it seems they did.

How factually accurate is it? The main elements of the story – one of go-getting financial wheeler-dealing involving sums of money which the protagonists hadn't got and could only conjure up by milking the paper's tangible assets (its freehold office building) and future profits, and cynical disregard for mutual loyalties too easily and naïvely assumed by some of those who ended up feeling victimized – haven't been denied or controverted by those depicted here as the 'villains'. The former owner–editor, Denis Lemon, has indeed said that *Title Fight* 'only tells 50 per cent of the story' – which leaves one wondering what on earth the other half can possibly be! No one has sued anyone for libel, though the book could well be regarded as highly defamatory of several people. It is clear that the 'victims' played as crucial a role in the paper's downfall as the 'villains', disregarding elementary legal and financial prudence in the earlier stages and then, as disaster loomed, spurning outside offers of financial and other practical assistance because of an ingenuous reliance upon a Greater London Council bailing-out operation which fell through at the last minute (because of hostile political pressure?).

Some of my anger is directed at the present ineffectual state and inept performance of the gay movement in the wake of the disappearance of *Gay News*. Discriminated-against minorities inevitably tend to create their own inner world, to refashion reality more to their own liking, and to live in a private cocoon. Doing so, they invent new myths and stereotypes for themselves, and risk deceiving themselves about the nature of life outside their own charmed circle. To some extent *Gay News* did this, for its readers and for itself. Yet the general level of its reportage and comment remained consistently and surprisingly high throughout its existence, thanks to both Denis Lemon and Andrew Lumsden, its two successive editors. Its function as a community lifeline outweighed in importance everything else which homosexual people have created for themselves, except perhaps for its own happily surviving brainchild, Gay Switchboard.

It's very apparent from *Title Fight* that the team lived from day to day in an introspective, claustrophobic, private world: oddly, some of the most 'out' gays of all were in the stuffiest closet. Perhaps that was inevitable, given the pressures and stresses they were bound to be subjected to, even without financial crises and ownership disputes. But it led to an increasingly distorted sense of proportion over a whole range of matters.

Possibly this, too, is almost inevitable for homosexual people, who are still, twenty-five years after the Wolfenden Report, widely regarded as freakish, abnormal, immoral, dangerous to children, and security threats. As Kinsey's collaborator Dr Wardell Pomeroy has said, 'there is probably more nonsense written about homosexuality, more unwarranted fear of it, and less understanding of it than of any other area of human sexuality'. It's difficult to preserve one's sense of equanimity when one is relegated to the fringes and crevices of society and regarded as a threat by the prejudiced and ignorant.

What is urgently needed, in the currently retrograde atmosphere – and more than ever now in the absence of *Gay News* – is a much bigger effort at widespread public education of a reliable and matter-of-fact nature, not just about homosexuality but in all aspects of human sexual behaviour and desire. Sadly, the adolescently prurient 'shock-horror-snigger' syndrome towards all sexual matters which pervades so much of the media, and the humbugging vogue for 'Victorian values', make any immediate prospect of this happening unlikely. All who value sexual honesty and frankness are diminished by the end of *Gay News*.

Note

1. Review of *Title Fight: The Battle for Gay News*, by Gillian E. Hanscombe and Andrew Lumsden (Brilliance Books, 1983).

'Out, damned spot! Out, I say!'

GAY AND LESBIAN HUMANIST, SPRING 1995

Early in 1995 there was widespread controversy over the tactic of 'outing' closeted homosexuals. OutRage!'s approaches to several Church of England Bishops, inviting them to disclose their sexual orientation, was universally (and more than somewhat hypocritally) condemned in the national press, and caused a fierce argument between gay groups – OutRage! being dubbed moral blackmailers by the Stonewall lobby group. In consequence, I and several other veterans of gay rights campaigning issued a statement pointing

*out that the real target was the closet itself, and its crippling effects in
bolstering prejudice against lesbians and gays and sustaining ignorance of
their numbers and actual roles in society. The following article develops
the theme.*

I now regard the option of the closet as the biggest handicap to the social
emancipation of lesbians and gays. It was not always so. In the 1950s and
1960s, when we were campaigning to decriminalize consenting adult
behaviour, all of us were in the closet, and thankfully so. Honesty would
have been suicidal. I remember Lord Arran asking me why I had wanted
to be Secretary of the Homosexual Law Reform Society. 'Because I am
homosexual myself', I replied. 'I wish you hadn't told me that', he retorted.

Now, things are different. Thanks to nearly three decades of progress
since the law was changed in 1967, many gay people of all ages are out
and proud. But far too many are still in the closet and frightened to come
out. That is the significant issue – not whether 'outing' is right or wrong,
or whether you agree or disagree with OutRage!'s tactics.

My own view is that it is now high time the closet went the way of
the Berlin Wall; and that those who are still cowering inside have a critical
duty, not only to themselves, but – most importantly – to other lesbian,
gay and bisexual people, to examine their consciences scrupulously and
to face up to whatever it is that prevents them from coming out. The
burden of proof that it is still essential for them to wear the mantle of
hypocrisy now rests upon them – not upon those who urge them (as I am
now doing) to come out.

This is especially true of those in public life. I find it indefensible that
people who choose a political, ecclesiastical, judicial, professional or
business career should in 1995 still consider that they are behaving
ethically by being hypocritical about their sexuality. It is not one's
orientation, but how you live your life and whether or not you treat other
people kindly, honourably, and considerately, which determines your
integrity.

And the closetry of public figures does not only affect themselves: it
has adverse consequences for the many thousands of less prominent gay
and bisexual people – and especially the young – who suffer discrimination and prejudice because those who ought to be standing shoulder to
shoulder with them in fighting bigotry and ignorance are not doing so.

The closet also has seriously adverse consequences for the 'gay
community' (begging the question of whether such a fabulous 'Queen's
Beast' exists) and for gay rights. For we are the only large discriminated-
against minority who are deprived of our natural leaders by their ability
to 'pass', and therefore to disown us. If we were a religious minority, or
an ethnic one, or a cultural one, none of our members would have the soft
option of escaping from the prejudice and the hostility by disassociating
themselves from us: they would be visible willy-nilly, and would – if they
had any guts – play the parts in our affairs for which they were best fitted.

We would know who were gay MPs, judges, soldiers, civil servants, doctors, and academics. Some of them would be (and are) people of high distinction whose names would add lustre to the state of being homosexual, and would give the lie to those who vilify us as inferior and inadequate. What would they have to lose? As a friend once said to me, 'It's like the stock exchange. What matters isn't which shares most people *think* will go up, but which ones actually *do*.' My belief is that if the eminent closeted gays came out now, they would be respected by the world at large for their honesty. They would also bring a great access of strength to our cause. . . .

The closet has got to go – the sooner the better. It won't go without some folks feeling hurt – even outraged. But that, I'm afraid, is inevitable. There are still far too many humbugs taking secret advantage of the freedom which I and many others have won for them, while they make homophobic noises to gull their constituents and congregations.

When the 1967 Act reached the Statute Book, Lord Arran pompously admonished those whom he considered himself to have liberated to behave themselves with discretion and dignity, and to shoulder manfully their 'all-time burden' of being 'the odd men out; the ones with the limp' who must inescapably be 'the subject of dislike and derision or at best of pity'. I begged him not to make this absurd speech when he showed it to me beforehand, but he persisted; and it was, after all, his hard-earned day of triumph. But I for one was not prepared to live by those precepts then, and I shall most certainly not do so now. Nor should any other self-respecting lesbian, gay or bisexual individual.

So 'come out, come out, wherever you are'.

Review: *Queer in America* by Michelangelo Signorile[1]

GAY AND LESBIAN HUMANIST, NOVEMBER 1995

If any gay, lesbian, or bisexual people still doubt the evil effects the closet has upon us all, a perusal of this book will surely dispel their illusions. Written by the best-known American exponent of 'outing', it is more than just an 'outer's bible' – outing, indeed, is merely a side-issue in Signorile's devastating indictment of the political, social, and personal corruption spawned by the closet. He documents a degree of self-serving deceit and ruthlessness on the part of numerous privately closeted and often publicly homophobic American politicians, Hollywood moguls, and media personalities which is quite shocking. More sickening still, many of these people (he alleges) use their powerful positions to coerce employees and underlings into providing them with the secret sexual satisfactions they dare not publicly admit to wanting.

If I had not known the closet was evil before I read Signorile, I could have no shred of doubt now. And if I was confused or dubious about the justification for outing in at any rate some instances, I would now be totally convinced by Signorile's arguments that it is sometimes a legitimate weapon, and that no one in a public position has an absolute right to keep their sexual orientation secret, as distinct from protecting the details of their private lives from prurient prying.

As Signorile says, the homophobic media – who are always eager to indulge in a spot of juicy outing when it suits *them* – falsely portray outing as an attack by gay 'terrorist militants' upon their 'respectable' brethren, instead of showing it as what it really is: an attack on the closet – an institution created and enforced by heterosexuals and homophobes in order to give us all the clear message that if we want to 'make it' in straight-dominated society, we'd best pipe down and stay right inside.

Signorile observes that when outing first hit the headlines most of the established US gay groupings (much of whose funding and influence came from wealthy, conservative corners of the gay community) denounced it as an indefensible attack on privacy, but that within a year or so even they admitted that it was sometimes effective. There is an endorsement on the back cover of *Queer in America* from Sir Ian McKellen, who observes: 'No-one should condemn outing until they have read this book.' I don't know whether Stonewall's executive director, Angela Mason, had taken his advice when she asserted on behalf of that organization that 'outing is never justified, even in the cases of people who have been homophobic and hypocritical'.[2] But I do hope Stonewall now has the good sense to abandon such a simplistic po-faced stance.

Notes

1. Abacus, 1995.
2. *Pink Paper*, 31 March 1995.

225

Review: *Virtually Normal* by Andrew Sullivan[1]

NEW HUMANIST, NOVEMBER 1995

Although not 'the most important book about homosexuality ever to be published' (as its publishers unblushingly claim), this is an eloquent statement of a socially and politically conservative homosexual's viewpoint. Sullivan is the English-born editor of the influential right-wing American *New Republic* magazine, so his public declaration merits attention.

In personal terms, *Virtually Normal* is brave and moving, but politically it disappoints. While I welcome Sullivan's adherence to the currently unfashionable civilized standards of public debate, under which one reasons courteously with one's antagonists instead of merely vilifying them for presuming to differ, he does not to my mind provide a sufficiently rigorous analysis of the current state of homosexual politics. His discussion of four main approaches (which he dubs the 'prohibitionist', 'liberationist', 'conservative', and 'liberal'), while rightly critical of the shortcomings of all of them, does not address some of the practical social problems which they create.

While Sullivan welcomes the greater openness which the past half-century's struggle for gay rights has brought, and honourably encourages gay men and women to come out, he doesn't sufficiently recognize the huge personal pain involved in such campaigning. Yet he objects to 'outing' – even of prime humbugs – because of the relatively minor discomfort caused to those who are outed. And though I share his dislike of 'positive discrimination', I still think – though regretfully – that in the present state of society it sometimes has a necessary role.

His own proposals for taking the political heat out of the homosexual issue are disappointingly thin and unconvincing. He spotlights two key issues which he thinks should be conceded by society at large so as to assimilate gay men and women into the wider community and remedy their grievances. These are the right to serve in the armed forces, and legally valid homosexual marriage. The latter – which he says is 'ultimately the only reform that truly matters' and 'not a radical step, [but] a profoundly humanizing, traditionalizing step' – would, he asserts, eliminate 90 per cent of the political work necessary to achieve gay and lesbian equality.

If Andrew Sullivan believes this, he could believe anything. Like so many pundits of the Right ('old' or 'new') who claim to be hardheaded realists, such facile claims expose him as a sentimental Romantic. The very notion of 'gay marriage' makes the 'Family Values' crowd foam at the mouth; and a great many gay people (including myself) think it would create more problems than it solved.

The reality is still that homophobia – the irrational gut-prejudice, fear and hatred which leads its addicts to mistreat homosexuals – is still far too strongly entrenched (especially in the religiously righteous) for superficial 'solutions' such as Sullivan's to be widely acceptable or politically practicable. Homosexuals remain the only significantly large minority in the Western world still widely regarded as a legitimate target for abuse and hatred by self-styled 'respectable' people.

That, of course, poses an uncomfortable dilemma for the many socially conventional homosexuals who, like Sullivan, regard themselves as 'virtually normal' (whatever that question-begging phrase may mean). But until they face up to the inescapable reality that sweet reasonableness won't suffice to face down visceral hatred, they will inevitably (if unfairly) be derided as Uncle Toms by the battle-hardened protagonists of Gay Liberation. All of which is a pity, because 'political correctness' – whether it stems from the Left or the Right – is no ally of those of us who aspire to parity of esteem, whatever our sexual or political orientation may be.

Note

1. Picador, 1995.

PART SEVEN

PAST, PRESENT, AND FUTURE

Past, Present, and Future

As we approach the twenty-first century, there is no room for complacency. Looking back over forty years, we have chalked up some impressive gains. But none of them has been easy to achieve, and much is still depressingly negative. Hostility to gay, lesbian, and bisexual people remains widespread. Gay rights are not nearly as secure in Britain (or anywhere else in the world) as I would wish, and the certainty of their progress cannot be taken for granted.

The need for gay rights campaigners to be active citizens in fighting prejudice, bigotry, and intolerance on a broader front than the single issue of our sexuality is obvious. We need to involve ourselves in campaigns which will ultimately benefit and strengthen our individual and collective rights as gay people, such as constitutional and voting reform and a Bill of Rights, and to give support for others' civil liberties as well as our own. For us even to survive safely, let alone to flourish, there has to be a society which is much more firmly committed to free speech, and welcoming of diversity in all walks of life, than the one we are living in now. Much of what I wrote in past decades attacking prejudice, ignorance, and intolerance remains topical in the late 1990s.

Gay Visibility – Strengths and Weaknesses

The most obvious, and welcome, change since I summoned the courage to write my first anonymous (and lonely) campaigning letter to *The Sunday Times* in 1954 is the visibility which gayness, and gay people, have achieved.

Today's self-accepting lesbians and gay men in their twenties, thirties, and even forties require a strong effort of imagination to comprehend the stifling blanket of silence in which my generation grew up and spent the early part of our lives. When the Homosexual Law Reform Society was founded in 1958, the choice of name was itself a deliberate act of courage. As Lord Wolfenden recalled in his autobiography, *Turning Points*,[1] when he was appointed as chairman of the Government committee on homosexual offences and prostitution in 1954 the great majority of people had never even heard of homosexuality, and most of those who had, regarded it with much disgust and little if any understanding.[2] Even after the committee reported in 1957, homosexuality was still generally considered a particularly nasty form of criminal vice – so the establishment of a campaigning organization setting out to change legal and social attitudes towards this unsavoury topic, and sponsored by some highly respectable and well-known people, was a bold novelty.

The Society's determination not to let the Wolfenden Report gather dust in some Home Office pigeon-hole presented a challenge to the politicians which led to the passage of the 1967 Sexual Offences Act; it also began getting the matter more widely and sensibly discussed by the press and the public. What I called my 'outreach' work during the law reforming years of the 1960s when, besides writing many articles for the press, I addressed hundreds of national and local meetings – political, religious, and professional groups, Rotary Clubs, Mothers' Unions, university and school debating societies, and so forth – was as important as the direct lobbying of Parliament. A consistent and sustained educative 'outreach' to non-gay people is still vitally necessary to dispel the widespread illusion that there is no serious anti-gay prejudice or discrimination any more.

By the time the 1967 Act became law, the issue of homosexuality had been opened up to the extent that some supporters of reform felt it would be better under wraps again. This attitude caused the disapproving outbursts with which the Act's parliamentary pilots, Lord Arran and Leo Abse MP, opposed the move by some members of the North-Western Homosexual Law Reform Committee[3] to sponsor 'respectable' social clubs similar to those existing in Holland. I was acutely aware of the miserable isolation and loneliness suffered by many gay people, especially outside London, and sympathized with the objectives of those who wished to set up such clubs, although I thought their initiative was too hasty. After I was instructed by the HLRS/Albany Trust committee not to lend my name to the venture, and to resign as a Vice-President of the North-Western group, there was inevitable resentment and ongoing friction during the 1970s – a sad waste of time and energy.

The sudden upsurge of the Gay Liberation Front in 1970[4] ensured that gayness would never again be 'the love that dare not speak its name'. One consequence was the emergence of what had been conspicuously absent during the law reform campaign – an organized homophobic backlash. Centring in its early days around the pugnacious figure of Mrs Mary Whitehouse and her traditionalist Christian allies such as the Festival of Light, this targeted permissiveness in general, and homosexuality in particular through the *Gay News* blasphemy prosecution of 1977.

Gay News itself was a beacon of visibility: its successful launch as the flagship of 'out' gay journalism fostered a spirit of self-confidence and levels of community awareness hitherto unknown. *GN* and its still very live offshoot, Gay Switchboard, were lifelines for many thousands of gay men and women who would have lacked essential knowledge and possibilities of contact without them. *GN*'s collapse after a pioneering publishing decade of community service still unmatched by any of its successors was a tragedy which still rankles – all the more so because it could have been avoided.[5]

Since the mid-1980s the barriers of reticence have burst, and today's mainly commercial gay press discusses all aspects of gay sexuality and its performance with total frankness, as well as carrying explicit advertising which contributes a significant proportion of its revenue. This factor, together with the business ownership of 'our' press (in contrast to the collective which launched the old *Gay News*), puts a damper on frank criticisms of some aspects of the gay scene.

I experienced this myself in 1994, when I submitted an article to a leading gay journal in the course of which I said:

> In order to win public and parliamentary sympathy and support, gay people need to pay careful attention to the images of homosexuality which they project outward to the world. We shall always have powerful and vocal enemies – but there is no need to encourage them by shooting ourselves in the foot, as we so often do. Because gay people are now so much more visible than we were in the 1950s and 1960s, we are also more vulnerable to unscrupulous attack. . . .
>
> If we want to coax the successful, influential, and outwardly conventional gays – of whom there are many – out of the closet, and to motivate them to support gay rights with their voices, their votes, and their money, there has to be a gay public image with which they can identify comfortably. This is not the case at present. We are constantly vilified by some sections of the tabloid press as warped, dirty-minded child molesters; while the contents of the gay press too often depict gay people (gay men, anyway) as all being young, irresponsible, and brainless – interested only in round-the-clock lust and the on-demand availability of an endless string of anonymous pick-ups, and happy to equate sex with 'dirt', 'sleaze', and 'filth'. . . .
>
> Is this tawdry rubbish really what most lesbian women and gay men identify with – let alone believe to be in their best interests? Don't concepts such as self-esteem, dignity, and high regard for one's own sexual personality and activities, and for one's partners' humanity and worthwhileness, deserve promoting and presenting to the wider world as important parts of gay living? . . . If gay people believe that 'anything goes', and that, so long as they get what *they* want, it doesn't matter a hoot in hell what becomes of other people, the tabloids will of course delight in serving up succulent 'gay scandals' to the goggling masses. Under such spotlighting, those gay people who indulge in exploitive, sleazy, and sordid behaviour, and who are callous and dishonest in their relationships, inevitably besmirch all the rest of us.

The editor was unwilling to print my article unless I modified the above passages, because he considered them too sweeping in their strictures and wanted me to balance them with references to the selfless devotion of many gay people to AIDS work and other community projects. Of course I admire and applaud such activities; but I did not see why I should be censored when I wished to comment on some of the less edifying aspects of gay behaviour. I would have been quite content for my views to be published as they stood and to have them attacked by other correspondents.

Even more than the gay press, the mainstream press is a cause for continuing concern.[6] In the 1940s and 1950s, homosexuality was scarcely ever mentioned in the newspapers except as a mysteriously vague 'serious offence' in the court reports of the Sunday popular press. The Montagu case, and the subsequent publication of the Wolfenden Report, provided the 'quality' papers and journals – notably the *Sunday Times*, *Observer*, and *Spectator* – with an opportunity to express disquiet at the state of the law, and to throw their weight behind reform. In the mid-1960s, the opening up of the subject by several nationally known 'agony aunts' was a major breakthrough. For the first time, the existence of gay sons and brothers was broached to mothers and sisters – though gay husbands and fathers were still kept under wraps!

In the early 1970s gay liberation (and even GLF itself) received broadly favourable coverage. It was not until the Mary Whitehouse/Festival of Light 'moral backlash' gathered political clout, and Mrs Thatcher's Tory Party began waving its equivocal banner of 'Family Values' in its bid for the 'lace curtain' vote, that the now familiar tabloid menu of homophobic rant interspersed with jocular ridicule came into fashion. Such unscrupulous journalism can do even more damage to individuals than to the collective image of gay people; so it is interesting to observe the way in which the continuing public popularity of out and 'outed' gay personalities such as Sir Ian McKellen, Elton John, and Michael Barrymore seems to have caused a re-think in some editorial offices where populist homophobia has more to do with selling newspapers than with genuine moral outrage.

We are now at a stage where gay visibility is irreversible, because so many people are 'out' in so many different walks of life that it is no longer possible for anyone seriously to pretend that gayness is an abnormal condition confined to a few unfortunate freaks. But we have not yet reached a point where enough of us are out to make proclaiming one's gayness to all and sundry other than hazardous for many if not most lesbians and gay men. We are the only sizeable minority which suffers from the crippling handicap of the closet, in which a great many gay and bisexual men and women in influential positions still hide, helping to perpetuate the old, false myths about us all being unstable, unreliable, irresponsible mediocrities. That is why coming out about one's orientation (though not about the intimate private details of our personal relationships) must now be regarded as a positive duty, and why those who remain in the closet should be left in no doubt that their self-serving hypocrisy is letting every other gay person down. As my reviews of the books by Signorile and Sullivan make clear, I do not accept that 'coming out' can any longer be regarded as each individual's totally personal and private decision, with no wider implications. Those who stay lurking in the closet – especially if they are prominent in public life – should not be surprised when they are publicly confronted with their obligations to other gay people.

The Law

Further progress with law reform since 1967 has been disappointingly slow. The failure of a well publicized campaign to obtain an equal age of consent in 1994, over a quarter of a century after the original limited decriminalization of male homosexual acts, and the continuing legal and social discrimination in other respects (not least the still frequent prosecutions of 'victimless' – i.e. consenting – behaviour), cannot convincingly be hailed as a triumph by gay lobbyists.

I and my colleagues in the Sexual Law Reform Society moved as quickly as we could after the 1967 Act to press for a complete review of all the laws relating to sex. We urged the Criminal Law Revision Committee to recast these in accordance with logical principles which would underpin the law's protective function, whilst getting rid of 'victimless crimes' which are a hangover from the nineteenth century when upholding conventional morality was seen as being the law's proper function.

Although our ideas did not find favour with the CLRC (whose own far more tepid proposals for reform have not yet even been fully discussed, let alone accepted, by Parliament), the SLRS principles set out in earlier sections of this book are in my view a sound, forward-looking agenda for sex law reform, and provide the basis of a campaign strategy capable of uniting all reformers, gay and straight alike. Adequate reform of British law must incorporate positive provisions outlawing discrimination on grounds of sexual orientation, along similar lines to those already approved by the European Parliament.[7]

Politicians and Public Opinion

Homophobia is a mind-set which, like any other, can be modified, if not completely eradicated, by determined and well articulated opposition. Self-respecting gay people should take every opportunity to challenge and refute anti-gay myths and stereotyping. I know, from my own experience as a journalist and as a political lobbyist, that as few as a dozen letters on a particular topic are enough to convince MPs that a groundswell of public opinion is running.

Whether or not they are morally earnest in private, it is the stock-in-trade of politicians to appear so in public. This is tolerable, so long as public figures who are gay but closeted do not support legislation such as Section 28 or express homophobic sentiments damaging to those with whom they are secretly in sympathy. But the hypocritical closetry of publicly homophobic, or non-supportive, politicians when gay rights are on the parliamentary agenda is deeply obnoxious. There have always been plenty of closeted gays in politics – some of them in high office. Fortunately, those who were around during the 1950s and 1960s, when the Wolfenden Committee was sitting and during the subsequent law reform campaign, either kept quiet, or were actively helpful.[8] There was a political risk in supporting homosexual law reform, not just for them, but whatever the sexual orientation of those doing so. I have the utmost respect and gratitude for all those MPs and Peers who served on the HLRS executive committee or sponsored successive reform bills, sometimes in the face of constituency disapproval.

One knew where one was with the homophobic ranters; some of them (as Archbishop Michael Ramsey charitably remarked to Lord Arran) may have had 'a terrible time at their public schools', and others believed homosexuality was an upper-class vice manufactured in those schools. It was the invincibly ignorant supporters of reform who were (and still are) a heavy cross to bear.

One of the hazards of lobbying for a reform is that your parliamentary supporters choose you – but not vice versa. It is a Member of Parliament's right to take up what causes he or she chooses; all the lobbyist can do is to rally round a too-persistent champion, be as supportive as possible, and as a last resort attempt a damage limitation exercise. Luckily for us, all our leading parliamentary sponsors during the 1960s campaign were of high calibre, and performed always doggedly, often deftly, and sometimes brilliantly.

Best of all to work with was the late Sir Kenneth Robinson,[9] who by the time the campaign was at full throttle had become Minister of Health in Harold Wilson's Government, and so could not continue giving us direct help. Kenneth was one of the most straightforward, honourable, and courageous politicians I have known. In the early 1960s he was always to be found in the thick of controversial issues such as the abolition of the crime of suicide, our Bill, and abortion law reform. He told me that this was because he believed the only way to earn his constituents' respect, if not always their agreement, was to be totally open and forthright with them about his conscientious views, and to put these into practice as energetically as he could.

I was very sorry indeed when the late Humphry Berkeley,[10] who obtained the first successful Commons vote in favour of a 'Wolfenden' Bill, lost his seat in the 1966 general election. Humphry, too, was honourable and courageous (although in those days he felt obliged to remain in the closet), and he and I had similar views as to the shape of the Bill we wished to become law. Lord Arran and Leo Abse – to both of whom an immense debt is owed for steering the Bill onto the Statute Book – were not always so easy to work with. While they were sound on the broad campaigning issues, and Abse in particular excelled in procedural manoeuvring, when it came to detailed drafting they were not always willing to give as much weight as I would have liked to points of detail, several of which could have improved the Bill and would have eliminated blemishes which later turned into running sores. My main preoccupation was to ensure, if I could, that the Bill became law with as few future hostages to fortune as possible. But, quite understandably, rather than risk losing what they saw as 'their' Bill, Arran and Abse were prepared to make some concessions which I intensely disliked, so that they opposed amendments (proposed by HLRS supporters) to reduce the age of consent from 21 to 18; accepted the restrictive definition of privacy which the Bill's opponents successfully voted into it; and did not press the Home Office for clauses prohibiting common law conspiracy charges and banning police *agent provocateur* behaviour.

During the debates they, as well as other supporters, said some inaccurate and patronizing things about homosexuality and gay people which caused me to squirm. In order to rally hesitant allies the compassionate card had to be heavily played, and the essentially paternalistic nature of the whole operation was demonstrated by Roy Jenkins in 1960 when he said: 'I am not concerned only with what homosexuals want or even primarily with what they want. I am concerned with what I think is a reasonable law for a civilised country.'

We are still not entirely rid of such patronizing attitudes. While she spoke with admirable courage and common sense when introducing the 1994 age of consent debate, Mrs Edwina Currie had scant knowledge of, and no respect for, those of us who were campaigning for gay rights many years before she took up the cudgels – we had all been (she announced) 'mere headbangers'. She then demonstrated her own mastery of that gentle art by brusquely informing me that I was not her 'cup of tea'[11] and telling Peter Tatchell to 'piss off'.[12] She would have been a still more effective and admired champion if she were a more attentive and understanding listener.

Religion[13]

With the increasingly open presence of gay clergy (especially in the Church of England), homosexuality is nowadays a far more embarrassing topic for the churches than it was in the 1960s. Then, it was possible to discuss the issue with most religious bodies and audiences on a safely distanced 'them' and 'us' basis, in terms of the need for Christian compassion. But nowadays it is a much more *parti pris* battle between opposing homophile and homophobic factions. There is polarization between the evangelical traditionalists who abominate homosexual conduct as the worst of all sins and the Lesbian and Gay Christian Movement which argues for a radical revision of theological tradition to allow for full acceptance of homosexual sexual activity by both clergy and laity within committed relationships.

Theirs is a revolutionary demand, and I do not see much prospect that even liberal denominations of the Christian faith are going to move that far – the Church's entire theology of sex centres upon the unique exclusiveness of heterosexual marriage and condemnation of all other physical sexual expression, whether heterosexual or homosexual.

Having been involved in two earlier Anglican agonizings over the issue, I could only summon a weary smile when the latest effort to produce a statement acceptable to both 'conservatives' and 'liberals' struck the same rocks onto which its predecessors had floundered and sank. While I greatly admire the dogged persistence of gay Christians of various denominations, and am glad that they exist to help and comfort those who are distressed by the antagonism of their faith to their sexuality, their optimism that the Churches are about to abandon age-old principle and practice in their favour strikes me as starry-eyed. For myself, I long ago reached the conviction that self-acceptance and a rational code of responsible personal morality are far more easily achieved by gay people when they do not hanker after religious acceptance.

Young People and Sex

This is, and looks set to remain, the major battleground of sexual emancipation. To say that children are sexual beings, even if they are not yet fully awakened to that aspect of themselves, strikes me as simple common sense: the fact that merely to say it out loud produces such paroxysms of fury from so many otherwise sensible adults tells one far more about the latter's refusal to face facts than about children's needs.

Even though children *are* sexual – and even when they are sexually aware – adult paedophiles who find them emotionally and sexually fascinating have no right to exploit them. But neither should children be punished for their natural sexual curiosity. I agree neither with paedophiles' contention that puberty is of little if any significance, nor with the absurd notion that adolescents who have attained it should continue to be regarded and treated as children, instead of as the young adults which they are.[14] That is why I think there should be an 'age of protection' during the teenage years. I strongly disapprove of relationships between paedophiles and pre-pubertal children which involve genital activity. But I distinguish between those paedophiles who genuinely love children and desire their welfare and the conscienceless adults who are child abusers. I recognize that some paedophiles do have honourable non-sexual emotional and educational friendships with children which can be highly beneficial if they remain non-sexual. Some of the best and most devoted schoolteachers and youth workers are people of this temperament, and it is utterly wrong that they should be demonized and persecuted because ignorant and bigoted people wrongly regard them as bad and dangerous. The wicked and cruel adults who abuse children physically and sexually are not paedophiles in any accurate sense of that much-abused term, but simply hate-filled psychopaths.

As a leading American campaigner for lesbian and gay rights has pointed out[15] (as truly of the UK as of the USA), governments are happy to spend large sums putting paedophiles in jail and keeping the bogeyman of 'kiddy porn' before the public in order to justify inflated law-enforcement budgets and draconian obscenity laws, but the State is not willing to take the radical action required to protect child victims of abusive adults – because

> that would mean challenging parents' ownership of their children. It would mean providing viable alternatives to the family. Minors who are given the power to say 'no' to being sexually used by an abusive parent or relative are also going to assume the right to say 'yes' to other young people and adults whom they desire. You can't liberate children and adolescents without disrupting the entire hierarchy of adult power and coercion and challenging the hegemony of antisex fundamentalist religious values.

There seems little hope of greater objectivity and competence being injected into social work training and practice, or into teaching and youth welfare work, until the key issues of children's rights as well as adults' responsibilities are candidly addressed. Yet venturing to say so is sufficient to stir up the wrathful fulminations of those who have evidently forgotten their own childhoods and who refuse to face uncomfortable truths. Because of the seemingly compulsive need of so many adults to perceive children as 'innocent' (by which they mean sexually ignorant and unaware), and sex itself as 'nasty', this whole debate has become hopelessly enmeshed in coils of unreality and falsehood.

Besides remedying the deficiencies of social work, a drastic improvement in the quality of sex education is required. Here also, public debate suffers from massive distortion and misrepresentation of the actual beliefs and practices of competent sex educators by 'the less we tell them, the better' brigade. Children and adolescents not only want, but are entitled to get, full and factually accurate information about the physical aspects of sexual behaviour, with all their pleasures and dangers, as well as sound emotional and moral guidance. It has repeatedly been shown that when such full information and responsible guidance is competently and conscientiously provided, the incidence not only of teenage pregnancies and abortions, but also of premature sexual experimentation, is lower than amongst the 'innocently' ignorant.

Sadly, frank discussion of sex in terms that youngsters can relate to is still a red rag to bullish prudes. In 1994 Dr Brian Mawhinney, then Minister of Health, denounced as 'smutty' and refused to authorize publication of *Your Pocket Guide to Sex*, a frank booklet for teenagers written in a deliberately unstuffy way at the request of the Government's Health Education Authority. Needless to say, the tabloids leaped into the act, and the author, Nick Fisher, felt himself drowning under 'a wave of moral madness'. Luckily, his book – hailed as effective and long overdue by many sex education professionals – was rescued and published by Penguin: it was, after all, as he pointed out, intended for young adults who wanted to know more about sex – *not* for Government ministers who knew too little themselves and thought young people already knew too much. As I have repeatedly said, the battle for sensible and adequate sex education is one of the most fiercely contested free speech issues, and has still to be won. Professor Nat Wagner's guidelines[16] need to be more widely known, debated, and (I would earnestly hope) accepted by all concerned – including Government Ministers responsible for health education.

The Gay Movement

While gay and lesbian individuals and organizations have achieved a great deal over the last quarter-century, the history of the gay movement has also seen wasted opportunities. Quite a lot of the copious good will and generous cash donations poured in by successive generations of gay people and others[17] since the early 1970s has regrettably been squandered.

A major culprit has been egotism – an unwillingness on the part of many gay activists to get to grips with the nature and complexity of the problems facing them, and to learn from the knowledge and experience of others. Not least because of the closet, gay enterprises too often lack professionalism.

From the 1960s onwards, we at the Albany Trust were regarded almost with contempt by some in the newly emerging movement as outmoded, ineffectual, establishment 'Uncle Toms'. Our ability to talk to the 'powers that be' in Government and other conventional agencies in their own language, and our readiness to make use of the bridges we had pains-takingly built to them over the previous decade,[18] masked the radical nature of what we were saying from those whose main concern was to 'cock a snook' at authority. A lot of time and energy was wasted in the early 1970s in unnecessary squabbling, not only between 'gay militants' and the Trust, but also between different factions within the gay movement – notably GLF and CHE – who sometimes regarded one another with mutual distaste amounting almost to loathing.

This petty fratricidal strife has unfortunately continued into the 1990s, with unedifying squabbles between Stonewall and OutRage! I have had no direct involvement in either organization, but I consider each has a useful and necessary (in fact, a complementary) role to perform, their contrasting 'respectable' and 'radical' styles appealing to and mobilizing different segments of the community. The essential thing is that each should be as efficient and effective as possible in its preferred way. Inevitably, Stonewall's approach will be welcomed as the more 'responsible' (and comfortable to deal with) by politicians and socially conservative gays who dislike OutRage!'s media-grabbing demos and street theatre as too boat-rocking. But 'spectacles' can be a powerful consciousness-raising tool, so long as they are strategically planned and well executed.

The concept of 'gay community' has been around for a quarter of a century now, at some times exerting a potent influence on lesbian and gay campaigners, and at other times being seriously questioned if not dismissed as a myth.[19] While I certainly do not think that it should be taken for granted, or too easily assumed that there is a well-defined and broadly based community with which anyone and everyone who is lesbian, gay, or bisexual can or should identify, I do believe that all same-sex lovers, whatever their social, political, and economic lifestyles, share at least two attributes in common from which a sense of community, and the stimulus for communal action, can grow. First, the sexual and emotional attraction which we all feel towards other members of our own sex; and second, the resulting social oppression and stigmatization.

Both of these attributes, while possessed in common, are also, of course, experienced uniquely by each individual. How agreement is to be reached, and effective joint action undertaken, by those who otherwise may have nothing else in common is the central issue which faces, and always will face, our movement. It is made more complex because of the closet. We can urge the duty of 'coming out' upon our closeted brothers and sisters, and the need to politicize themselves upon those (probably the majority) whose community involvement is primarily pleasure-seeking; but creating and sustaining a high level of cohesion is likely to remain an uphill task.

Unlike many other minorities and causes, we lack a broadly based forum where our concerns can be debated and prioritized. The failure of the National Federation of Homophile Organisations in the early 1970s, and of later attempts at effective networking, leaves us without a representative body – a serious weakness which I believe all sections of the movement need to address in a co-operative rather than a competitive spirit.

The hurdles to social and legal equality for gay, lesbian, and bisexual people are still numerous and entrenched. It will take sustained and long-term effort to break down these barriers. If we are to do so, a much more energetic campaign of public education will have to be undertaken. While irrational and viciously hostile homophobic prejudice is still widespread and dangerous, an even bigger obstacle to progress in the fight for gay rights is the stubborn persistence of sheer ignorance and incomprehension amongst the public at large about the disadvantaged situation of gay people in society as compared with that of the straight majority, many of whom imagine that we already have all the equality we need or ought to want.

I remain convinced that it is vitally important for those of us who are gay, lesbian, and bisexual to look constantly outward, resisting the temptation to waste our energies sniping at one another. We are none of us perfect – but we can each aspire to excellence in what we do, and we have the right to expect others to aim at equally high standards. Loyalty is important in our working and campaigning relationships, as well as in our personal lives. We all encounter abundant spitefulness from our homophobic enemies, and we can do without more of it between ourselves. When we disagree, let us do so about principles and tactics: not in a personalized way. We shall not always avoid heated arguments and mutual criticism, nor can we always get along easily with one another.

At such times, let us be as forbearing as possible, and never lose sight of our common goal – the social and legal advancement of gay, lesbian, and bisexual people to a position of total equality and complete acceptance as worthy citizens of our country and of the world.

Notes

1. The Bodley Head, 1976.
2. Such was the Home Office's anxiety to spare their female typists' blushes that the committee's name was for a time coyly bowdlerized in internal memos to 'Huntley and Palmers'! (R. Davenport-Hines: *Sex, Death and Punishment* [Collins, 1990], p. 314).
3. Later the Campaign for Homosexual Equality.
4. Vividly described by Lisa Power in *No Bath but Plenty of Bubbles* (Cassell, 1995).
5. See pp. 220ff. above.
6. Painstakingly monitored by Terry Sanderson and other media watchers.
7. Which by a resolution adopted in February 1994 by 159 votes to 98 called on the Commission of the European Union to draft a policy outlawing anti-gay discrimination, after previously accepting the Squarcialupi (1984) and Buron (1989) Reports advocating action in this issue (see Peter Tatchell, *Out in Europe* [Channel 4, 1990], pp. 6–9).

    For a discussion of the complexities facing UK citizens in combating discrimination arising from sexual orientation through the machinery of the United Nations' International Covenant on Civil and Political Rights, the European Convention for the Protection of Human Rights and Fundamental Freedoms, and the various institutions of the European Community, see Conor Foley, *Sexuality and the State* (National Council for Civil Liberties, 1994), pp. 9–21.
8. Jeremy Thorpe, who was then Leader of the Liberal Party, was braver in joining our executive committee than I then realized.
9. Who died in 1996, aged 84.
10. A contemporary of mine in age and at Cambridge, who died in 1994.
11. Because after glancing at the publishers' blurb for *Speaking of Sex*, she totally misconstrued my attitude to the two entirely separate questions of children's sexuality and adult paedophilia, and was then *far* too busy to read what I had actually written!
12. Because she was angry with OutRage!'s 'outing' campaign.
13. Although my comments here and earlier are confined to Christianity, and the Church of England in particular, I recognize the increasingly serious implications of anti-gay hostility in Britain amongst adherents of other religions – notably Islam and conservative elements of Judaism.
14. I also strongly believe that much, if not most, of our endemic youth delinquency problems result from this misguided approach to teenagers.
15. Pat Califia, *Public Sex* (Pittsburgh: Cleis Press, 1994), p. 147.
16. See p. 201 above.
17. Not least, the former Greater London Council.
18. I remember Lord Wolfenden wryly observing that he had spent much of his life building bridges, and that bridge-builders must expect to get trampled on.
19. For a perceptive discussion of the role of 'community' in contemporary gay thinking and politics, see Chris Woods, *State of the Queer Nation* (Cassell, 1995).